Praise for *The UnNoticed Entrepreneur*

"Highly recommended for people who need to make their businesses and themselves stand out from the crowd."

-Richard Robinson. Serial Entrepreneur. Bali.

"It is an invigorating and illuminating read that should be of practical use to business leaders all over the world."

-Giles Fraser. Founder of Brands2Life. UK.

"I would urge any budding entrepreneur to study this book and take action."

-Neil Moggan. Founder Future Action. UK.

"I read the book to find out how agile owner-led companies thrive using digitalization so that we can adopt these practices into our large organization. 50 short essays from experts makes this so easy to digest and to apply."

-Karl Stillman. International Sales Director. China.

"Nice book and must read for a Startup."

-Amazon Customer India

"You will learn many new things and get positive reinforcement on much more! So, get this book and get noticed!"

-Alex Greenwood, Host and Producer, the PR After Hours Podcast. USA.

THE UNNOTICED ENTREPRENEUR

ENTREPRENEUR

STEP INTO THE
SPOTLIGHT

JIM JAMES

CAPSTONE
A Wiley Brand

Registered Offices
John Wiley & Sons, Inc., 111 River Street, Hoboken, NJ 07030, USA

John Wiley & Sons Ltd, The Atrium, Southern Gate, Chichester, West Sussex, PO19 8SQ, UK

Editorial Office
The Atrium, Southern Gate, Chichester, West Sussex, PO19 8SQ, UK

For details of our global editorial offices, customer services, and more information about Wiley products visit us at www.wiley.com.

Library of Congress Cataloging-in-Publication Data:

Names: James, Jim (Writer on entrepreneurship) author.
Title: The unnoticed entrepreneur : step into the spotlight / Jim James.
Description: First edition. | Hoboken, NJ : Wiley, 2023. | Includes
   bibliographical references and index.
Identifiers: LCCN 2022059061 (print) | LCCN 2022059062 (ebook) | ISBN
   9780857089571 (paperback) | ISBN 9780857089632 (adobe pdf) | ISBN
   9780857089649 (epub)
Subjects: LCSH: Entrepreneurship. | Branding (Marketing) | Business
   planning. | Success in business.
Classification: LCC HB615 .J36 2023 (print) | LCC HB615 (ebook) | DDC
   338/.04—dc23/eng/20221209
LC record available at https://lccn.loc.gov/2022059061
LC ebook record available at https://lccn.loc.gov/2022059062

Cover Design: Wiley
Cover Image: © Alhovik/Shutterstock

Set in 11.25/13 pt Arno Pro by Straive, Chennai, India

SKY10041397_011723

Contents

Prologue: Fulfilling the Promise of The Entrepreneur.

This book is to help any business owner to fulfil their promise to themselves to build a better solution to a problem which exists. As an entrepreneur myself I know that just because I can build something, there is no guarantee that my idea will become a successful business. As entrepreneurs we introduce new products and services which we believe will help people, but a central barrier to that happening is for these potential clients to know about us and what we do.

One solution is to hire external consultants to help. That can lead to frustration as it can take longer for consultants to understand the business than it takes to explain it to the real customers. Then of course there is the expense of hiring part-time consultants who cost as much as a full-time member of staff. Keeping the growing team aligned is also key, but external consultants aren't part of the team and so this leads to another set of problems.

As the Founder you are the visionary, you define the brand, you engage others with your mission, but in time you actually become a bottleneck. You also reach the limits of your skill sets and your bandwidth, and this limits the growth of the company. To fill the sales funnels, the Founder needs to build a company brand not a personal profile. If you have investors, there will be investor relations and their expectations to meet also. If you are introducing a new technology or way of working, time is of the essence.

A central question facing all entrepreneurs, then, is how to get noticed quickly, effectively, and efficiently so that they can scale the business from startup to a sustainable market leader without the luxury of a big budget. If the ambition isn't market leadership, it is surely to become cash flow positive before the funds in reserve are used up. In some cases, it is to become attractive enough to attract more investment, or to be a target for an acquisition.

The good news is that fellow entrepreneurs are solving this problem already, and this second volume of *The UnNoticed Entrepreneur* is going to show you how. My background is that since 1995 I have started my own companies in Singapore, China, India, and the UK, including an international public relations consultancy. I launched *The UnNoticed Entrepreneur* podcast to interview experts and entrepreneurs and decided that there was so much great knowledge in these 20-minute episodes that I had to curate them into volumes to be read at leisure.

Being an entrepreneur isn't the simplest career choice, but it is the life path we've chosen because we believe we can make a difference on our own terms. In this book, my promise is to share practical, sustainable, and creative ways which can be used to build the value of any brand. If I fulfil my promise, then you will deliver on your potential, and together we will make the world a better place.

Why PR?

"If I was down to my last dollar, I'd spend it on public relations."
-Bill Gates

Why would one of the world's most successful entrepreneurs and richest men choose to invest his money into public relations? The answer is that when done well, getting noticed can be free and extremely effective, and in this book you have a masterclass with 50 fellow entrepreneurs and experts who will share with you how to do it. This is a really-time efficient way to get up to speed with the latest thinking and tools for your business.

The articles are as the conversations, and I've kept the style and idioms because then you will also have a sense of the person behind the piece. In the first volume of *The UnNoticed Entrepreneur,* I introduced the concept of SPEAK|pr [tm] and imposed that structure on the articles. In this volume, I simplified the arrangement to make it easier to navigate.

My goal is to provide you with short and easy-to-read articles which provide strategies, cases, and tools which you can readily apply to your own business. All the contact details of the authors are in the Directory at the back of this book.

The strategy section will lead you to the realisation that every activity has potential value to your publicity campaign.

The tools section includes a selection of martech applications so that you discover just how accessible and powerful technology is now for the business owner.

The cases section illustrates how other entrepreneurs have taken initiative to create publicity for their organisations above and beyond conventional media relations. I am sure that you will find them as inspiring as I have.

PART ONE
STRATEGY

Chapter One
Introduction

One of the most interesting aspects of *The UnNoticed Entrepreneur* project is that everyone has their own take on the subject. There really isn't a right or wrong way to promote a business. Some are more successful than others, and some entrepreneurs are superb at certain aspects of marketing, e.g. speaking at events, and ignore other aspects, e.g. writing contributed articles. What is true is that there comes a time when an entrepreneur needs to establish their own credible brand and then build one for the company too.

This section has 24 articles dedicated to approaching this stage in the building of a business; establishing the credibility of the Founder. I've included interviews with photographers, stylists, and people who discuss the importance of authenticity. The articles address the building blocks of personal branding and also some handy business development practices because in the early days we are always selling to our networks. I go to experts who talk about getting on stage, being on TEDx, writing books and hosting a podcast, or virtual events.

Remember that all the people I interview are entrepreneurs too; these are not sales pitches, rather handy tips for you and your team to use straight away and most of them at little to no cost.

To make it easier to decide which articles are going to be the ones you want to get to first, let me give you a summary of the people who are going to share their insights with you in this section.

Oscar Trimboli in Australia introduces
the four villains of listening.

Mason Harris talks about the importance
and power of Chutzpah.

Marcus Ahmad explains the importance of your eyes in building rapport through photography.

Nick Hems introduces sartorial statements as part of how you engage your audience.

Robert Da Costa, former agency owner turned coach, explains the key considerations for choosing a PR agency.

Alastair McDermott in the UK explains how he found the value of being in a niche.

Adrian Starks makes lessons from stories learnt inside a hospital trauma unit.

Gina Balarin in Australia accuses marketing people of being liars (now that's a story).

Entrepreneur and storyteller **Nir Zavaro** from Israel, on repurposing content more efficiently.

Akshay Jamwal in India explains how a passion project created a lead magnet.

Danny Levinson on the east coast of America explains the importance of anthroponomy.

JB Owen of Canada explains the best way to engage with self-publishing.

Jeff Hahn in Austin, Texas, explains adjacent marketing.

Sam Palazzolo has advice for entrepreneurs raising money.

Andrea Pacini shares how to animate your audience, not your slides.

GJ van Buseck from Holland explains the power of 60-second videos for LinkedIn.

New Hampshire-based **Jarod Spiewak** explains search engine optimisation.

Richard Robinson joins from Bali to explain how to overcome the fear of public speaking.

Elaine Powell in the UK asks, "Do you have what it takes to be a TEDx speaker?"

The Las Vegas-based "Book Broad," **Julie Broad**, explains how to be a #1 best seller on Amazon.

Nick Vivion talks about how he gets PR for blockchain companies from his RV.

Alex Strathdee explains how to get to #1 on Amazon with book promotion.

Sonali Nair explains the three key features to look for on any virtual event platform.

Chapter Two
Which of the Four Villains Are You?

Oscar Trimboli, Author Listener & Speaker of Oscar Trimboli Pty Limited, Greater Sydney Area, Australia.

Oscar Trimboli is on a quest to create 100 million Deep Listeners in the world. He is an author, host of the Apple award-winning podcast–Deep Listening', and a sought-after keynote speaker. He is passionate about using the gift of listening to bring positive change in homes, workplaces, and the world.

Courtesy of Oscar Trimboli

Through his work with chairs, boards of directors and executive teams in local, regional, and global organisations, Oscar has experienced first hand the transformational impact leaders and organisations can have when they listen.

The four villains of listening are the Dramatic, the Interrupting, the Lost, and the Shrewd. When you're dealing with complex collaborative, constrained, or conflict situations, listening is one of the most important superpowers you have as an entrepreneur.

The Importance of Listening

Many of us haven't been taught how to listen. Most people know Mathematics, wines, and cheese. However, there is no language around listening.

Through his listening quiz, Oscar is trying to honour a conversation he had with a vice president, who once took him aside at the end of a meeting. The vice president told him back then, "If you could code the way you listen, you could change the world." At that moment, it did not make sense to him because all he did was cheer knowing that he wasn't fired (he initially thought that he'd get fired).

As a marketing director of Microsoft at the time, he eventually pondered on the question: Is it possible to code how people listen? Because it can be done for Maths, English, or Chemistry.

Afterwards, he set up an assessment tool that features 20 questions as a way of coding how to listen longer term. Now, he'd also love to have automated tools or applications within Zoom, for example, that could tell one's listening ratio. For instance, he imagines a percentage bar at the top of the screen.

Listening is crucial because the more senior you are in the organisation, the more listening you should do during your day. The more sales you do, the more your listening should also be. Unfortunately, this is not the case.

When you're dealing with complex collaborative, constrained, or conflicted situations, listening is one of the most important superpowers that you'll have as an entrepreneur. Without that, you can't bring people along in the journey with you.

The difference between hearing and listening is the action you take. A lot of employees get frustrated with business owners to whom they keep telling the same thing yet get nothing. For business owners, listening is when you act on something you're told about.

The Four Villains of Listening

Oscar and his team have done a lot of work with behavioural scientists, market research companies, computer software professionals, and academicians for two and a half years. The goal was not only to create a quiz but to prove it's valid across English-speaking cultures.

One important thing to know about listening is it's situational, relational, and contextual. You'll listen differently in many different situations. You'll listen differently to a police officer than you will to a school principal, actor, or accountant.

According to their research, there are four villains of listening: the dramatic, the interrupting, the lost, and the shrewd.

The Lost Listener. If you're a lost listener, you would forget everything you're listening to because you're drifting off somewhere else. You might be thinking about something related to what you're told about. The lost listener is completely lost in their devices or something in the conversation that triggers them to think about, for instance, a holiday that they wish they had. Of the 11 000 people who took their quiz so far, 22% belong to this category.

The Dramatic Listener. Dramatic listeners love listening to your story. They engage with you really well and often do too much of connecting with you. If you say to them that you're struggling with a staff member, they'd say that you have to wait and listen to their problem about their staff member. Simply put, they love the spotlight being back on them. Though they love having a connection, they don't understand the difference between empathy and sympathy.

The Interrupting Listener. The interrupting listening villain is the most overt listening villain. They're the quiz show contestant who presses the buzzer, anticipates the question and the answer, but gets it wrong. They value time, and productivity matters to them. They have a mindset that they've already heard something before, so they tend to jump in and get to it quicker. While their intention isn't wrong, they're still considered impatient.

The Shrewd Listener. The shrewd listeners are problem-solving machines. Although they give you a great face and you feel like they're really engaged in listening, in reality, this is what could be on their mind: I studied this long. I'm such an expert in this field and you've got such a basic problem. I'm going to think about three to six problems that you haven't even thought about. However, speakers can sense this. They can see the cogs going on in these listeners' wheels, turning over and going through the issues. Their mindset then is to stop these listeners from trying to fix those and get them to listen to what they've got to say.

The shrewd listener could also be thinking that they're that kind of listener at work, but they're a lost listener at home. When you take Oscar's quiz, you'll get a primary type of listening and a secondary one. The former is who you are at work; the latter, at home.

He always points out that labels are good on food jars and pharmaceutical products, but not on people. That's why during the episode, he reiterated that they're not labelling you but your behaviour.

On Self-Awareness

When it comes to listening, many people think that they're above average. Oscar mentioned that around 74.9% consider themselves as well above average or a long way above average. And this shows an issue with self-awareness.

There are five levels of listening. The first level is knowing what your barriers are.

Most people aren't even aware of what gets in their way because when listening, they're taught that the focus should be on the speaker. However, he's not saying that you shouldn't listen to the speaker; rather, you shouldn't start there. You need to start by listening to yourself.

Until you know your villains, you can't introduce yourself to your superheroes. And for each listening villain, there's an alternate superhero. If you take his quiz and sign up for the 90-day challenge (which can be found at the bottom of their five-page report), you'll start to discover which one of those superheroes can emerge from you as you explore the world of listening.

A Little Neuroscience Hack

Oscar mentioned three numbers you need to know: 125, 400, and 900. On average, a person speaks at 125 words a minute (If you're an auctioneer or a horse race caller, you can probably speak at 200 words per minute). Moreover, an individual can listen to up to 400 words a minute. These show that there's a disconnect between the speed at which people listen and the speed at which they talk.

Genetically and neurologically, you'll get distracted. However, Oscar isn't talking about mindfulness; he won't teach you how not to get distracted. Because, ironically, if you'll get distracted, it will help you reset your attention much quicker. Keep in mind that you can only listen continuously for 12 seconds.

The number 900, on the other hand, refers to the number of words you can think of per minute. If you're an entrepreneur talking to a customer, investor, or supplier, the other party is thinking of at least 900 words per minute. If you speak at 125 words per minute, it means that your listener is only listening to 11% of what you're thinking about.

The Three Questions You Need to Ask

You can get a fair advantage and get the next 125 words out if you learn three simple questions. And these will be significant in knowing your customer's problems. As an entrepreneur, you can get a customer for life if you know your customer's problems.

The first question is: Tell me more. The second is: And what else? The latter, especially when saying 'and', should be done in a respectful way.

If you notice that your listener takes a breath in, their spine gets erect and their shoulders go back–that's when you can use, 'actually' or 'so'. This will help you talk about your proposition better (e.g. 'Actually, now that I think about it a little longer, I think it's more important that we talk about this'.)

The third question is the shortest yet the most powerful: silence. If done poorly, however, it can intimidate.

In Mandarin, 'ting' means 'to listen'. If it's not pronounced correctly, it can mean 'to stop'. When it comes to China, listening is six-dimensional. It's about seeing, sensing, feeling, respecting, being present, and being focused. This is what 'ting' means.

One of the critical skills that the East teaches us is silence. If you can practice that, you can hear things that other people will never get told about. And it's because you took the time to listen to something that's not said. With it, you can uncover things much more than the next person – who merely engages in a dialogue – can.

In the West, there's this thing called pregnant pause, or the awkward, deafening silence. In the East, this is viewed as a sign of wisdom, respect, seniority, and authority. It's not uncommon for there to be long pauses.

Silence needs to be skilfully used because it can be intimidating. It needs to be skillfully done especially when you're in some kind of a relationship and trust is being developed.

Most of Oscar's clients, particularly those who are entrepreneurs, often say that they don't have the time for all the listening stuff. However, he counters it by saying that it also takes up time if you launch the wrong product, or if you lose a great staff member. All these are unprofitable ways to spend the day and make use of your time and money.

Although listening takes a bit longer, especially during the beginning, what you can do is to start to listen to what speakers are thinking and what they mean, rather than merely listening to what they say. If you're an entrepreneur and you listen to what your customer, investor, supplier, or employee says and what they mean, you'll have them for life.

On Being an Entrepreneur Himself

When asked about the entrepreneurial aspects of business, Oscar discussed his failures first.

For example, when he was attending an industry conference about seven and a half years ago, sitting next to him was someone named Dermot who was originally from Ireland (He eventually became his good friend).

During a workshop, they were asked to share a problem that they're working on. Back then, he had been blogging for two and a half years straight on the topic of listening and nobody was engaging with what he was doing. What Dermot said is, "If you're talking about listening, you do a podcast. You don't blog."

He realised that if people are interested in listening, then they'd probably want to listen to it.

He then started one, which was another 'spectacular failure' – until he discovered a wonderful book called *Selfish, Scared, and Stupid* by Dan Gregory and Kieran Flanagan. They hypothesised that you can do all the ambitious, inspirational, and aspirational work you want. But take note that most people relate to their weaknesses more rather than their strengths. Thus, his creation of the villains of listening.

Initially, he thought about talking about aspirational listening superheroes. But nobody could relate to them because they're artificial gods of listening. On the contrary, he hasn't met yet a single person who can't relate to his four villains of listening.

Oscar also considers publishing as a thing he does well. However, it doesn't simply mean publishing a book. It also encompasses sharing ideas with somebody else.

In this aspect, publishing can mean doing webinars. In his practice, he also runs a community where people in his newsletter lists can attend webinars once a month for free. He also uses this as a way to test ideas and get feedback.

Additionally, these people also share with him contemporary problems that they're dealing with in their workplaces. If he'd listen carefully, he'd be given a lot of great opportunities to think about.

One of the things that emerged from that is the deep listening playing cards. When people asked, "Why don't you put all those tips you talk about into a set of playing cards?" He did as such. When the idea of making a jigsaw puzzle was brought up, he and his team also made a jigsaw puzzle. The same with the assessment quiz and his book.

Another thing that he'd done well is the podcast. A few years ago, it won an award from Apple for the category that it's in. The podcast offers a different take on the communication topic. It talks about listening and features interviews with expert listeners to deconstruct what good listening is and how to make that commercial. Now, a lot of his clients came from those interviews that he'd done two to four years ago. These are people who heard and continued to follow him.

Publishing, for him, is also about going through that process of speaking to people out loud. It's important because someone can eventually connect with what you're saying.

In the old days, Oscar used to speak at public events. Now, even up until midnight to 2 o'clock in the East Coast in the US, he has sessions. He also has evening sessions in Hamburg, Munich, London, and even Copenhagen. Amidst the pandemic, so many opportunities have come about, extending his work around the world.

While he made a lot of mistakes, Oscar stressed out that it's through them that he got ideas and feedback. For him, the key to his success is persistence and some kind of plan.

Online Tool for Listening Scoring

Oscar and his team work with a third-party software organisation called Evaluation Solutions, which does assessment tools for people around the world. The tool was integrated into their CRM system (in their case, it's Infusionsoft).

Through the quiz, they get rich information about people who take the quiz. Then they connect them to a 90-day challenge.

About a third of the initial quiz responders opt-in for the challenge, and 20% of those people complete all 13 weeks. And from these 13 weeks, they get to notice behavioural patterns (e.g. Which newsletter copy do people connect with and not?), which they then apply. This is why the challenge that they offer is different now than how it was a few years ago.

Chapter Three
What is the Attitude You Can Lead With?

Mason Harris, Motivational Speaker, Listener, and Author of *The Chutzpah Guy*, Gaithersburg, Maryland, USA.

Encompassing self-confidence, audacity, purpose, and even humility, a 'chutzpah' approach leads to business and life success. Mason Harris, author of *The Chutzpah 'What is Chutzpah?'*, on what it takes to survive in the world. Are you born with it, or is it learned? Is it good or bad to be thought of as someone with chutzpah?

Courtesy of Mason Harris   I don't know you, my curious reader, but I know this. You aspire to go bigger, be bolder, and do better. And perhaps you're already an entrepreneur. You face many obstacles but have chosen to move forward despite the objections, rejections, and setbacks that happen to people like us.

However, as with many tools and skill sets, sometimes we overlook our assets, existing positive traits and characteristics, while struggling to find a magic key. In this case, we're all trying to unlock the secret to leaving our unnoticed status behind.

So, let's explore the keys in our possession and solve this problem.

Which of these apply to you? Are you self-confident, audacious, purposeful, persevering, brash at times, or humble? These descriptions and about another 40 were provided to me during my research for *The Chutzpah Advantage*.

Why do I have a lifelong interest in chutzpah? I have seen that a 'chutzpah' approach leads to business and life success.

What is Chutzpah

Most people are familiar with chutzpah though they can't define it. Chutzpah describes someone with ambition, a desire to go bigger, be bolder, and do better. I associate the term with the courage and the grit to stretch personal and business boundaries.

However, it's not all positive as the same chutzpah skill set can be used for self-serving reasons instead of the win-win approach most of us bring to our lives and businesses. When someone says, "I can't believe the chutzpah of that guy," it could mean that the guy is being rude and dishonest. Let's contrast that with this observation, "I can't even imagine all of the obstacles she had to overcome to build that company! That's chutzpah." In one sentence, we're describing arrogance; in the other, we're expressing admiration.

I've referred to chutzpah as a skill set, a blend of personality traits, and learned skills that combine to provide exceptional results. A skill set is a tool, and the user chooses to use it for constructive or destructive purposes.

For example, you and I may earn degrees in software development. We're both pretty good students and adept at creating programmes. However, while you develop software to assist in healthcare or create business efficiencies, I write ransomware and blackmail companies to pay me or lose their data.

It's the same skill set – software development, but different people use it with radically different ethics and results.

The Chutzpah Advantage

PT Barnum, an American circus owner, is credited with this quote: "There's no such thing as bad publicity."

I'm not sure this applies to political scandals, monumental failures, or bad reviews on a dating site, but I personally have never operated a circus. Regardless, for the unnoticed entrepreneur, generating awareness through differentiation and a culture of chutzpah can be of great value.

So, what is this model, and are the characteristics relevant to your situation?

In my book, 'chutzpah' is an acronym for the eight behaviours and characteristics.

'C' is for *Carpe Diem*, a Foundation of Your Future

Carpe diem is a Latin term for 'seize the day'. It's about both implementing plans and moving quickly on moments of opportunity.

In essence, people with carpe diem have an objective and move forward to make it a reality. For instance, let's say you have an idea for a book. You imagine it in your mind, and you see the pages coming to life. Unfortunately, you can't find the time to start, write, stop editing, or complete the book. Why? It's easier to procrastinate; our 'To Do' lists are already full after all.

We're all guilty of procrastination, a constant destructive voice in our head that keeps repeating, "It's okay, you can do this when you have more time." Your forward momentum is interrupted as your life and business wait on the sidelines. Without embracing *carpe diem* and seizing the moment, you're unlikely to find the time.

'H' is for Handling Objections

We're creative people, and we constantly generate new ideas. Some are good, others, not so much.

However, there is one constant, whether you're in sales and providing a needed solution to a prospect, introducing new procedures to your team, or trying to get your teenager to help you with something. Objections abound.

If we're working with subordinates in an organisation, they may be less willing to object. After all, they know that you'll be doing their formal evaluation. More often, we're communicating with colleagues, family members, investors, and bureaucrats who gain immense satisfaction from disagreeing with you.

Regardless of whether you propose a good idea or a bad idea, it will spark an objection from someone. Effective persuasion, a key characteristic of chutzpah, requires that you anticipate and overcome objections. If the objection is unique and can make your idea even more likely to succeed, a good series of questions and thoughtful solutions will create more opportunities for success.

'U' is for Uncovering Need, Pain, and Opportunity

Clients all have needs, and often we have a better solution. Sounds simple, right? We should be on a fast track to success. Unfortunately, even people who believe there are better solutions to address their needs won't act on your superior offering.

Why is that? Psychologically, many needs wait on the sidelines because they are not perceived as urgent. Pain, however, requires immediate attention. Personal pain leads to emergency room visits. Business pain leads to employee layoffs or a 'going out of business' sale.

When we're successful in helping clients understand the pain of an existing situation instead of hoping they're smart enough to be proactive, we're creating sufficient value for a change. This is our opportunity.

Let's look at dental care as an example. Some people go for regular cleaning and checkups with their dentist. Others wait until they wake up in agony from tooth pain. The former group addresses a need for preventative dental care; the latter acts only when pain is evident. The dental practice's opportunity? Create the patient relationship to avoid the inevitable pain that results from neglect, and focus on a healthier, non-emergency lifestyle.

'T' is for Trailblazing

No one wants to fail. It's embarrassing, costly, potentially devastating, and doesn't look good on a resume.

Chutzpah requires a willingness to fail, learn from our mistakes, and do better the next time. We can trailblaze with a truly unique service, solution, or problem-solving approach and accept that failure has a higher probability than 0%.

Elon Musk's SpaceX is an example. Reusable rockets and cost-efficient space travel for governments resupplying space stations, along with the average person who has both a sense of adventure and way too much money, are objectives of this ambitious company.

Uber was a trailblazer. There were many existing options for transportation, and yet Uber changed behaviour around the globe with its business plan.

Trailblazers know that not every decision they make and not everything they implement will work as planned. Despite the risk, they're still willing to take a couple of losses because they know they can recover from them. They're going to get back up and try something different.

'Z' is for Zigzag

Some obstacles seem to be insurmountable. It's more than simply overcoming an objection or two; instead, it's never-ending roadblocks and disappointments.

Perhaps you've exhausted all possible funding sources for your business. Or you haven't been able to get past the second interview despite applying for 100+ jobs. And yet, if not for the chutzpah of people who could have easily given up multiple times, we would be without lifesaving medications, remarkable technology, and even books that bring joy and wonderment to our worlds. Learning to zigzag around, under, or through obstacles is about persistence, grit, and determination.

There is a UK-based author, close to poverty, whose work was rejected by 12 publishers. Most people would have given up after two rejections. For someone who was very persistent? Maybe seven rejections would have ended the search for a publisher. In this case, the 13th publisher (12 rejections!) said they don't typically do books like this one, but they gave her a chance. The publisher's young daughter read it, and frankly, most authors would not choose a 12-year-old literary critic to evaluate their life's work. Fortunately, this young reader loved the magical story of a boy, his friends, and their adventures at a school for fellow wizards. (It makes you wonder about the other publishers, right?) And that's how the brilliant author, J. K. Rowling, who wrote *The Harry Potter* series and more, zigzagged to success.

'P' is for Purpose

Procrastination, objections, risking failure, perseverance – good stuff, right? But these items are under our control.

Now let's add the inevitable bad luck that strikes everyone, regardless of their kindness or selfishness, race, education, or upbringing. The urge to give up, feel sorry for oneself, and identify as a victim of other people and circumstances can be hard to resist. Despite our best efforts, planning, and optimism, bad things happen and get in our way.

The COVID pandemic, for instance, has caused the deaths of millions across the world and bankrupted millions of businesses. Many people, including some of us, have been living off savings because industries and sectors of our economies have been decimated. And I haven't even mentioned the emotional issues, both short and long term.

So how do we get through the bad stuff, the setbacks, the inevitable 'kick you when you're down' parts of life. Which chutzpah characteristic helps in this situation? It's our 'purpose'. Oh, and I don't mean a goal like 'I want to lose 15 pounds this year'. Purpose can change over time, but it needs to be meaningful. It's the purpose mindset that gets you through trauma and an urge to simply give up. It focuses on the long term, a more foundational objective and reason to persevere.

I recommended Viktor Frankl's *Man Search for Meaning* as a resource for those who want to understand purpose and how it can get people through the deepest and most challenging moments in their lives.

'A' is for Ambiguity Minimisation

As you can tell, success in life, both personal and occupational, can be enhanced by these elements of chutzpah.

For example, if you need to choose between multiple job offers, *carpe diem* is about evaluation and selection. As we can't know with certainty that our decision will be correct, we have the option of letting the fear of a mistake freeze our action. Sooner or later, the decision becomes evident because job offers are withdrawn, leaving us with one choice.

Therefore, not making a decision becomes the decision, and it's a pretty sad way to go through life. Reducing the ambiguity that holds us back or leads to consistently bad choices is paramount.

There are many models of decision-making that can help us be more efficient and correct. Equally important, most of the decisions we make are subject to a 'do-over' if they don't work out.

'H' is for Humility

Including this characteristic in my chutzpah model sometimes puzzles people, especially those who see chutzpah as rude, selfish, or purely self-serving. Yet research and analysis of successful leaders demonstrates that humility is typical among the respected and successful CEOs and Presidents.

Those with constructive chutzpah know how to share our successes with those whose help and teamwork created a positive and winning culture for all. There's an adage, Success has a thousand fathers while failure is an orphan.

A humble person acknowledges and credits colleagues and team members throughout the organisation for their roles. The leaders who believe that their efforts alone create success, while failure is the result of mediocrity from others, have very active recruitment needs for personnel replacements instead of growth.

Chapter Four
Should You Invest in Corporate Headshots?

Marcus Ahmad, Personal & Corporate of Branding Photography, Greater Bristol Area, UK.

Personal branding in photography is a relatively new concept, but it's one photographer Marcus Ahmad has already mastered. According to Marcus, everyone can have their own personal brand as long as it is authentic and has a personality. How Marcus brings personal branding and photography together is through fashion, which is about making people look good, and advertising photography, which is all about selling a product through an image and focusing on that with his business clients.

Courtesy of Marcus Ahmad

His background in photography began when he worked as an advertising assistant. Eventually, he got into commercial photography, in particular, fashion photography. His studio was in London, but he would often fly to New York, Los Angeles, Paris, and other places around the world for work. Later on, he became a senior lecturer in fashion and advertising photography at the University of South Wales.

One word that Marcus finds has a lot of value to it is 'authentic' because these days, it's all about being real and showing people who you are. There's a saying that people buy from people, and no would be enticed to buy from a website that has no personality, and so Marcus helps his clients use their personality to attract more customers. One's authentic self and the company brand are the same, because any business owner would want the company values to match their personality, and it's about getting across who you are and what you do in a photograph.

How to Take a Great Photo

Even without a professional photographer, it's possible to get a great shot by simply using a camera phone. To do that, Marcus' first tip is to make sure the background doesn't distract people from the subject of the image (aka you). A plain wall or a wall that has the same brand colours as you works brilliantly. Your head should fill about three quarters of the frame size, so it's not too far, not too close up, or not too far back. Then, make a few different expressions: smiling, serious, laughing, etc. Marcus suggests trying different things out and taking a lot of shots, so there are many options to choose from. To summarise, the important points are background, frame, expressions, many shots. Also, don't forget to have a tripod or mechanism to hold the camera.

Another important aspect in any photograph is light. The kind of light that works really well, believe it or not, is not a sunny day. Nice, diffused light is the best. Window light inside or outside when it's a cloudy day works best. Not too many shadows or highlights is really good for photography as well. Being a fashion photographer, Marcus deals with light all the time. To keep it succinct, if it's coming three quarters to you and it creates some shadow down one side and it's a bit brighter, that will give what is called good modelling, or basically shadows or highlights. If you take your shots when there are light clouds, you don't need to worry too much about the light, as it is good coming from any and all directions.

Focus on the Eyes

When it comes to posture and whether to lean in or lean back or tilt your head, Marcus said it depends what the shot is intended for. On social media, display pictures are often really small, so you have to maximise that space and it's all about eye contact. What Marcus does with the people he photographs is he gets them to lean into the camera, because he finds that it gives you an immediacy and a presence to your portraits, headshots, or profiles. This also exaggerates the eyes and brings out the eye contact, making it a subtle yet powerful style that Marcus prefers. It sounds cliche that the eyes are the window to the soul, but Marcus believes it really is all about the eyes. In fact, in Marcus' studio, if a client he's shooting has blue eyes, he'll put a blue background behind them for a monotone look to accentuate the person's eyes.

Clothing is very important, but it depends on what you're trying to portray. Undoubtedly, it's got to match. For women, Marcus suggests avoiding a scoop-neck top, especially if you're doing a close-up shot, because it can sometimes be a little bit too revealing or it doesn't give you a border or an edge to the photograph. For guys, Marcus has noticed that if that person doesn't normally wear a suit but puts one on for a photograph, it never looks right, so it definitely is about the clothes you wear and what you feel comfortable in. Don't try and be something you're not, even with what you're wearing. In terms of colours, neutral colours like black, grey, navy blue for guys is great, and then for women, Marcus advises not wearing too many patterns. What you wear in the three photographs doesn't need to be the same. In fact, in some ways, there might be more value in wearing different outfits, because then it shows that it might have been shot on different days and you've gone to the trouble and expense of getting a photographer on different times. Also, the colour that is key is your branding colour.

The Three Important Shots for Your Brand

If you're taking a picture of yourself, the best time to take it would be when there is natural light. Midday is not a good time for natural light portraits, as the sun is overhead. When shooting, Marcus always uses a flash, so he can shoot any time of the day, and it always looks the same. However, it's more than just the profile photograph and the headshot. Marcus' strategy involves three photographs that really define one's brand. The first is the headshot, which is a great way to start. Next is the image on the website, as the first image people see on the website is a real crucial part as far as photography goes. In that image, you want to get across a great portrait of you, with hands included, possibly making some gesture or using a prop that suggests what kind of business you're in. Simply put, that picture on the first page of your website should show you doing something and engaging with your audience. The third picture is the services photograph, and this should show somebody using the product or service. If you offer a service, it's a bit more challenging, but it could be a photograph of you having a one-to-one interaction with somebody. So, those are the three important photographs every business owner needs: the profile shot, the shot that shows what you do with your company, and the shot of your providing products or services. Those three are crucial elements to defining one's personal brand.

When it comes to post-processing images, again, it's about being authentic, so try to put it out there without much editing. It's about truthfulness and honesty. A bit of touching up is fine, as long as you stick to the person's authentic self. Adding in photos on your website of your family or even with your pet help, as it builds trust, because before you even make that sales call or make that connection, people feel they know you already, and that is the great power of photography. Why a photograph is so much more powerful, in Marcus' opinion, than a video or moving image, is because a photograph will tell you information in a second or less. From that, you can make a judgement and you can get something from that photograph. Aside from that, a photograph is open to bringing in your own personality, meaning, and story to it, so you can interpret in lots of different ways. Whereas with video, the story is already there. You don't need to bring anything to it. It's got a beginning and an end, and you're immersed in it still, but with a photograph, so much can be understood without even actually speaking or hearing anything.

That's a great way to synthesise personal branding and photography. In the end, it's all about authenticity. If you're getting photography done, do consider getting a professional. It can really make a difference. But in the meantime, use some of the tools and tips that Marcus has suggested, because those will make even the best start for you.

Chapter Five
Why is What You Wear Important?

Nick Hems, Men's Personal Stylist of Nick Hems Style, Bath, England, UK.

Courtesy of Nick Hems

Nick Hems is a UK-based style consultant and a great one at that. When it comes to looking confident as a business owner, Nick says you first must find inner confidence and authenticity for the way that you appear. It begins with one's clothing and body language, because looking like a leader helps secure the buy-in from people, and there needs to be some authenticity there. You need to feel like a leader and believe that you are. You need to find the right reflection in the way that you dress, so that it is still you.

Clothing and grooming have a big impact on one's confidence, leading Nick to talk about style personality, which is not something everyone understands. It's not a sense of wanting to look 'good'. because what does that mean, really? Nick could never dress two people in exactly the same way, because it just doesn't work. To look good, you've got to feel good, and that is individual to everyone. Everyone has a personality and a way that they are. Finding that fit of clothing that you wear is really important. That way, people see through what you're wearing, that reflection in your personality, and it's the strongest way you can bring yourself about authentically and reflect who you are.

Clothing and Accessories for the Confident Business Owner

To determine what you would look best in, first make sure that whatever you've got fits, because that's where the majority of people already fail. If it doesn't fit, have it altered. It's not just about how you dress and the clothes you wear. It's people's perception of you, and when you're wearing something that looks terrible, even if it's expensive or branded, you may come across as sloppy, possibly translating into the way you work. Once you're sure your clothes are the perfect fit, figure out how to accessorise the look without spending too much money and also giving you variety from day to day. For men, accessories could be pocket handkerchiefs, and for ladies, necklaces, bracelets, and broaches could do. If you've got a suit, Nick says to think of it like this, "How can I change the look of this suit throughout the week?" With accessories, it makes you look as if you care, and people pick up on that even if they don't necessarily know it straight away.

For most men, watches may be the only accessory they have. Watches are a really powerful, strong accessory. However, not everyone has the budget to go out and buy an expensive watch, and you don't need to. A timepiece is a really nice accessory for a man, and it's all about finding that timepiece that's going to go with what you're wearing. You can play around with the watches you've got, the different kinds of straps you may have, whether it's leather, metal, or mesh, as long as it goes with what you're wearing. It may even be good to buy two lower cost watches, one casual and one formal. You can even buy exceptional-looking watches on a budget. You just need to do your research.

When it comes to shoes, they set off the entire look. You can have a really well-fitted suit, but if you're wearing the wrong shoes, they completely take away from the entire look. Getting shoes right is really important, and so is making sure that you care for them as well in the right way, and that's imperative. With shoes, you can come at it from a cost-per-wear basis. Sometimes, you can go out and buy a cheap pair of shoes, which might get worn out fast, or invest in shoes that will maybe last you longer. Shoes are an essential item which can last years, certainly, if you take good care of them.

You and Your Staff Dressing for the Occasion

Dress for the occasion and also dress for the environment you're in. For instance, you may be looking for a new job and going in for an interview, so do your research. Have a look at what other people wear, where you're going, and dress for that environment. If it's an occasion where you're making a formal statement to a group of people, keep in mind your clothing. You don't want to come in with your really expensive suit and Rolex watch and tell your staff, "I'm really sorry. We can't afford to keep you on. We're going to have to let some of you go." This paints a bad picture.

Clothes are important too, not as a uniform, but as a dress code. Every company has a brand, whether they know it or not. It's the way they want to be perceived. When staff are seeing clients, they should be given guidance as to what to wear, so that they reflect the brand. Also, it's worth noting that if you have the name of the company on an item of clothing, you can offset that against tax. If you were to give your staff shirts or jackets with the company name or logo, that's a tax-deductible item, so that's also worth thinking about.

Appearance Matters, Even (or More So) in Virtual Meetings

With many companies transitioning to a work from home setup, Nick says that to create a good impression online, again, it's about dressing for the environment, not necessarily the home environment, but the environment you're transporting into. Truly, you wouldn't want to dress too dissimilarly from how you would be dressing if you were going into a meeting in an actual office. Remember, you set the tone with what you wear. There are many factors to consider, even for a virtual meeting, and the way you dress is one very important factor. Lighting and sound then become just as important, because people can't see all of your body language, they can't see you, they can't see everything that you've got to offer as if you were in an office, so you need to project yourself in the right way, and lighting and sound help you do that.

In terms of colours, for those looking for a basic assortment of clothes, the world's favourite colour is blue, and it's a calming colour. It's reasonably neutral, and it's available everywhere. If you're looking at ties or squares, blue would be great. If you're looking at the actual suit, for Nick personally, he'd stay away from black. He prefers a navy blue or grey suit, because it's more generic. You can wear that to many different places, whereas a black suit is sometimes a bit too dull. It's not something that you'd want to be wearing to a business meeting.

If people are looking for sources of inspiration, depending on where you are in the process of style, where you want to be, there is inspiration everywhere online. There are people on YouTube that give advice on style and dressing, and they're not hard to come across. If it's more inspiration about what to wear, have a look on Instagram. Find people that are around the same age as you, that represent a look that you like, follow them, and look at their photos. If you are lost at where to go completely, have a conversation with someone like Nick. He has a website, and he's on Facebook, Instagram, and LinkedIn as well. Hopefully, you have learned about dressing appropriately, even if it's for a Zoom meeting, how to accessorise an outfit, what shoes to wear, and how to project yourself as a business owner worthy of recognition.

Chapter Six
The Key Considerations for Choosing a PR Agency

Robert Da Costa, Business Owner of DA COSTA COACHING LIMITED, Worthing, England, UK.

Courtesy of Robert Da Costa

Robert Da Costa is an agency owner and a coach helping clients get the most out of agencies. Before business owners can get the most value out of an agency, Rob says they must first take a step back and ask themselves, "Why am I hiring an agency in the first place?" Businesses think they can outsource their problems to an agency, and they think once they've got the agency on board, that's the end of the problem and they can move on to the next thing. However, those relationships fail, because the agency will fail to live up to their expectations, and the business owner will get frustrated and ultimately decide this isn't working.

If you're thinking about hiring an agency, you need to think about what you're trying to achieve by hiring that agency and how you're going to measure success of the engagement with the agency. Rob always tells agency owners that the business needs to make sure they can tie back the work that the agency is doing to the bigger business goals. Without a way of measuring that, then they are heading towards an unhappy or failed relationship. For some businesses, that looks like lurching from one agency to another without actually looking at themselves and realising that they're not managing the agency very well. They don't realise that they need to change the way they're behaving, managing the agency, and how they're communicating with them. When hiring an agency or any kind of external partner, you need to build a good partner–partner relationship, not an imbalanced customer–supplier relationship, because it won't work out in the end.

The Kind of Agency You Want

In terms of picking the right agency, Rob suggests finding an agency that's a specialist in the sector, so they not only are able to do the discipline of whatever the agency is, whether it's PR, web design, SEO, or whatever it is, but they also have a really good understanding of the sector. Then, find someone that you're going to get on well with, an agency that you feel you can build good empathy with, an agency that understands your values at the cultural level as well as at the commercial level, and an agency that is a good listener. It's amazing how sometimes agencies don't ask questions and don't listen to their customer. They just tell them how great they are and what they're going to do, but there's no opportunity for them to build any empathy, because they're not listening. So first, find an agency that is in a niche you work in and one that you feel you're going to have a good working relationship with.

Next, find an agency that can demonstrate their ROI. Find one that's going to ask you the questions about what your business goals are and then work with you to put a set of metrics and KPIs in place that can tie back the work they're doing into the results that you're trying to achieve for your business. Another fundamental factor is communication. You are going to work with closely this agency, so you need to be communicating informally with them very regularly, but formally sitting down with them monthly and quarterly and reviewing your plans and reviewing their strategy to deliver your goals and working with them to change things. If there's one thing the coronavirus situation has taught people, it's the need to be nimble as business owners. Instead of setting plans in concrete and trying to deliver them by hook or by crook, be willing to pivot and change based on what's going on in the world.

Many times, the agency puts together a proposal with remarkably little information about the client, which can be a source of miscommunication at the very beginning, so Rob advises against doing this. If the agency can't get the necessary information they need from the client, then walk away. If you're a web development agency and you're going to do a pitch, if part of that pitch is providing the client with mockups, it would be unwise to agree to that, because you will have a process which gets under the skin of the client and understands what they need before you start doing that. Again, the business needs to be willing to work in partnership for the client to realise that they actually have to dedicate time and resources and give access to information in order for the agency to come up with a solution that's really going to deliver the results the client wants for the business.

Always Ask Questions

One of the selection criteria Rob advises a business on is understanding what that brings in processes. This involves asking questions around, "How did you learn about our business? What's your process that you will take us through, so that you can get a look under the bonnet and really understand the inner workings to make the best recommendations that are going to help us deliver the results that we want to achieve?" This sounds as though there's a fundamental change in mindset required by companies that are procuring or engaging agencies. It is usually a procurement function, but it sounds that to be effective, clients really need to look at the agency as a strategic partner. It might be a pyramid function from the recruitment department, but the people that are going to be managing that agency on a day-to-day basis absolutely have to see them as a strategic partner and recognise that the business has to make an investment of time to work with and manage the agency, and to give access to information.

There have been instances where you are taken on to do media relations for a client, and in the pitching and breeding process, you've talked about some of the things that you're going to need, and some of the access to people that you're going to need in order to create the stores and hoping to achieve, and then they're just too busy. They don't give you the case studies, they don't give you the customers, they don't make their senior staff available to you as spokespeople, and then they get upset, because you're not delivering results to the point where you're trying to justify why you're not delivering results, which is because of that lack of access. It just sounds like excuses, so this stresses the importance of developing clear communication and trust in the early stages of that relationship, that the agency is very clear about their process, and the business gives them access to that. Ask an agency about their briefing, their fact-finding, their immersion process. If an agency can give you a very clear, methodical approach to that, then they're going to be a solid agency who has experience onboarding businesses like yours.

An agency is a purchase of trust as much as anything else. Due diligence could be asking three, four, or five agencies to pitch, but it also involves obvious things like asking for samples of work or previous campaigns. Another suggestion of Rob's is to talk to the business' customers. When clients are taking Rob on board, they normally ask him for two or three clients to talk to. They want to pick up the phone and have a chat with these people, because they don't just want to get the canned, written response testimonial. Rob believes that if an agency isn't willing to give you that, then that could be a warning sign. Have a look at their website, their LinkedIn profiles, and the past work they've done before. You want to see the process the agency took the clients through to deliver these end results and also speak with some of their customers, not just one customer but maybe two or three, to get that honest approach.

Another issue for clients is often about the cost. When a client says, "Can you write a proposal?," and the agency says, "Can you give me a budget?," and they say, "No," the agency then is completely stabbing in the dark. If they haven't got a line item on their P&L and they haven't allocated a budget towards whatever this is for, then it may be better to just walk away, because there's a good chance that the client isn't serious enough. The first thing is that the company has to have set a budget, which can either be based on previous experience, or they can go and get some advice on what the costs are. When it comes to picking an agency, clients need to base it on all these other considerations already before they base it purely on price. If you just pick the cheapest agency, you may not necessarily get the best results. If you understand what the bigger business results will be from this intervention, then you're going to be more willing to spend money on it. Whereas if you're thinking about a very tactical thing like, "I need to get five pieces of coverage in the media every month," then, well, how do you measure that? If you're measuring it in terms of outcomes for the business, then you're going to be able to apply a bigger budget to it. It is a bit tricky to get the budgeting right, because obviously, the company doesn't always know what they should be spending. But in that case, if you really don't know, every business has got a peer network, and every business has got people that they are connected with that they can go and ask these questions to get a sense of what their budget should be. They also need to listen to the agency and be willing to hear from them what they think the cost should be.

There are companies like R3 in Singapore and America that help businesses select agencies. In terms of agency facilitator companies, Rob doesn't know of anybody that's gone through that process before, so he doesn't know whether that is a totally objective service or whether you pay to be part of their business, and therefore they put you forward. Once a company has made a decision about which agency to use, to make the most out of that, the key thing is regular communication, the right reporting, and tying back the work to the business goals. A lot of agencies report to a marketing manager, and that person might have certain goals in mind, like a number of new leads generated or the amount of coverage they've gotten. But then other people that they report to, the managing director or the finance director, might have different goals. So, it's really important that the agency has these honest conversations early on with the client about how to measure the success of the campaign, and that they keep using those metrics and revising those metrics regularly with a client, so that the marketing manager can report back to their colleagues about how the campaign is going.

As an agency, make sure that you constantly review the strategy put into place at least on a quarterly basis to reflect the changing environment for the business. If things change for the business, like with the coronavirus, not only is there a plan, but the team is prepared to execute it as well. That involves sitting down with the client and saying, "Let's look at where you're at a business. Let's look at your priorities over the next quarter. Let's make sure the campaign we're delivering is driving towards those business goals."

The last piece of advice Rob had is to make sure that if you have a really good partner relationship with the business and the agency, then you can also have an honest relationship. An honest relationship means that the agency can hold their hands up and admit if their strategy is not working and suggest changes on both ends to make their strategy work. With an honest relationship, there's a much better chance that the agency and the business are going to stay aligned and be happy with the work.

Moving onto legal matters, whether companies should have a retainer, a project, or a hybrid model with an agency, the retainer model is changing a lot. Most people don't like that word anymore, because it sounds like clients are paying you a fixed amount of money every month, but you're not entirely sure what you're getting for it. So in a way, the word 'retainer' doesn't help much. Nowadays, people are focusing more on the hybrid model. It's where they put, say, a six-month campaign in place. And then in the fifth or sixth month, you discuss whether or not to proceed with the next six-month campaign. In effect, it is a retainer, but the outcomes and the focus are much clearer. Obviously, from an agency's perspective, having a retainer is a desired thing, because it means you can do your budgeting. You know how much revenue you've got coming in each month. On the flip side of that, a project-based campaign means that they can be much clearer about what's included in that project and what isn't included, because agencies may sometimes get asked to do more work.

When Rob started his agency back in 1992, they were using Excel spreadsheets for time recording internally, they were using Word documents to produce reports, they were sending faxes to their clients, and all that. Since then, the world has changed a lot in terms of technological advancements and how they use it for work. There are a lot of great collaboration tools Rob uses like Google Drive, so his clients have got access to the shared documents together, they can see plans that they're working on, they can update it themselves, and they can see when Rob's updated them. There are also great project management tools on Monday, Dropbox, Asana, etc., that you can use both internally in the agency, but also collaboratively with a client. When selecting an agency, understand the tools being used to create the collaboration, because without them, again, that's a bit of an amber warning light. Whereas if they have a really clear engagement process with the client that not only talks about how they're going to communicate physically with each other, but how they're going to communicate virtually, then that will give you more confidence in that agency.

If you're a business owner looking to hire an agency, hopefully this has given you some clarity on how to pick the right agency for you and what you would then need to do on your end to make sure that you have a meaningful relationship with that agency.

Chapter Seven
How to Be Seen as an Authority in Your Industry?

Alastair McDermott, Podcast Host, Digital Marketing & Business Strategist of The Recognized Authority, Ireland.

You can remain an 'invisible expert', unknown to all but your referral network, and have a successful business. But apparently the riches are in the niches, or the cash is in the pigeonholes, according to Alastair McDermott.

Removing Your Invisibility Cloak

Courtesy of Alastair McDermott

He realised that he had this problem of wanting to build his authority and be more well-known yet he felt like he's wearing an invisibility cloak, like the thing from Harry Potter. And he needed to remove that cloak.

He then heard this piece of advice: Put yourself out there. However, this is not easy; there's a process that you have to go through. He started figuring that out and what he found was that the really important part of the phrase 'recognised authority in your field' is the last part – 'in your field'. You have to niche down, you have to specialise.

Talking to smart consultants, experts, and generalists, he realised that this is the really difficult part. These people are good at doing lots of different types of problem-solving. But they find it hard to actually niche down.

Picking Your Field

As the old issue goes, the riches are in the niches. However, the anxiety is that you're leaving money on the table – and that it's not possible to get enough money if you're from an individual niche.

According to Alastair, you can be an authority in one field and sustain your business if you pick a field that's big enough. There has to be enough business in that niche. You can niche down too much. Basically, you're a big fish in a small pond.

He pointed out that this is how the world works today. With Google search and things like that, only the top people in a particular field are going to come up at the top of the search results. These top people are going to get the most recommendations. There's certainly an advantage in being at the top of the pile. If you're not on top, then go find a smaller pile and be at the top of that.

And this is not just about Google search. It applies to the whole concept of being recognised as an authority, of becoming known as the go-to person for that one problem for that one area.

On Being Pigeonholed in One Area

Alastair mentioned that 'pigeonhole' is one of those trigger words for him. People use it in such a negative way. When he was listening to Blair Enns talking to David C. Baker, his co-host on the 2Bobs podcast, he was saying that pigeonholes are stuffed with cash. So why are people always coming out of pigeonholes?

For Alastair, pigeonhole is not a negative term or concept.

While people who are multi-talented and smart don't like the idea of being constrained in some way, the reality is that if you niche down, it will actually open up a lot of opportunities for you. The problem area is much deeper than what you'll initially realise. There's a lot more there that will fascinate you than you think there will be if you only have a surface visit to the problem area. When you go deep into any kind of specialisation, you'll realise that it's actually fascinating and there's a lot more there for you.

Factors Affecting Niching Down

Niching down applies to both companies and individuals. It ultimately depends on the size, the scale, and a few different factors.

For instance, Alastair mentioned that when you're right at the very start of your career, you can't niche down immediately because you need to first build a certain breadth of experience. This will help you make a good specialisation decision later on. You need broad experience to be able to say, "I do like this and I don't like that. I like this kind of people and I don't like working with those."

On the other end of the spectrum, take, for example, Seth Godin or Mark Schaefer. These are industry experts who have become very broad and big to the point that they were able to build such a massive audience that they don't need to be niched down. The same applies to companies: When they reach a certain size, they don't need to niche down.

But for a lot of people, particularly solo consultants, small businesses and firms, specialising can offer a tremendous advantage. When you're competing with somebody who has general experience, having specialist experience is advantageous. It doesn't warrant a comparison even, just like when you're comparing apples to oranges. It's not the same, and it just makes you stand out.

Letting People Know You're in a Particular Pigeonhole

Alastair reiterated that you need to get some broad experience first so that you can actually end up in a position where you'll have enough expertise to be an expert. Because you have to be an expert to become an authority.

At that point, you have to choose a journey of authority – you have to pick a field. It's not possible to be an authority without having a specific area to be an authority in.

There are people who seem to be generalists, but in reality they're not generalists but specialists in some particular areas. For example, Gary Vaynerchuk answers questions in a very authoritative manner on a wide range of topics. But when you dig into it, he does have huge and deep expertise in wine, video production, and social media.

Going back to developing expertise in certain areas, he then pointed out that after having a broad experience and developing some expertise, you have to get to a point where you want to have more impact, command higher fees, work with better and bigger clients, and help more people.

For some people, the route forward can be different ways. Other people build out their referral network and do a lot of networking. When Alastair did some research and surveyed over a thousand consultants, he found that referrals were the number one source of business for about 95–99% of consulting businesses and business-to-business firms. This is not just true for small consulting firms.

However, at a certain point, networking won't scale anymore. Today, in particular, when it's hard to run and attend networking events, you want to have something else. This is when he talked about another route forward, which he prefers because he's more of an introvert: content creation. He likes to write, record YouTube videos and podcasts, and do other related things.

This kind of route to authority gives you the ability to do inbound marketing. Inbound marketing is content marketing, authority marketing, or education marketing – because you're educating your clients about their problem and your solution to that problem; you're building your authority with that.

Not an Easy Task

Sounding and looking like an authority is not an easy task.

Alastair shared that when he looks back on his older videos on YouTube (he has about 15 years of YouTube video history), he finds some of them cringe-worthy. It's so bad that he doesn't actually recognise himself (Check out his video called "Why Start Before You Are Ready?").

For him, it's really about getting some experience. You don't learn how to swim by reading books about swimming – you actually have to get to the pool.

Also, part of that route to authority is demonstrating your expertise. This means publishing, talking, speaking, and writing in public. You have to expose your ideas and your thoughts to the public. And you have to do it through different modes and methods. There's podcasting, like what he and I are doing. He also starting to get more into YouTube and video. Some people prefer to write blog posts. Seth Godin, for example, has been writing a blog post every day for decades.

There are lots of different ways but you do have to start. If you look back on anybody's beginning, you'll find many things that don't look great. However, they still kept doing it. If you look at some of Gary Vaynerchuck's old videos from his first two years making *Wine Library TV*, they were amateur-looking. Today, he's worth $200 million.

It's not easy but it's simple. You have to start somewhere – pick a niche and just start.

What Alastair suggested is for you to do some deep research into a niche or specialisation, dig more into the problem, talk to clients in that area, start to look for patterns, and start to learn more about that problem than anybody else. Because this is the thing that the specialisation will give you: It will give you a deeper understanding than other people have.

2Bobs podcast co-host David C. Baker wrote a book called *The Business of Expertise*. Part of the concept that he's talking about is a test called 'Drop and Give Me 20'. It means that if he's sitting beside somebody on a plane and they're true experts in their niche, they should be able to tell him 20 things that would surprise him about his niche that he wouldn't have known by being outside that field.

Alastair admitted that he's nowhere near 20. However, it can be used as a good way of benchmarking your progress about the things that you're learning about your specialisation – things that other people who are generalists might not know about.

How will You Sound Authoritative?

One of Alastair's LinkedIn posts talked about sounding good. In the past, I've also had voice coach Jimmy Cannon on the show and he talked about voice, projection, and proper breathing. The question is, how will you really make yourself sound authoritative?

Alastair recalled hearing about Prof. Norbert Schwartz from the University of Southern California. He came across a study that the professor had done with some colleagues from Australia.

In the research, they took some high-quality audio of scientists and researchers speaking and downgraded the original files to several levels. Then, they asked people to rate the quality of the researchers' work – how likable they are, how intelligent they are. What they found was that you're more likable, more intelligent-sounding, and your work sounds more important if you have a higher audio quality. They did the same test with video and they got the same results.

Therefore, if you want to come across as an authority, you shouldn't sound like you're dialling in from a bathtub or something. You don't want to have a terrible audio quality. When you're working remotely, it's also important to look the same as when you're walking into a real room where you're wearing a nice suit. Through it, you'll earn a certain level of respect and you'll be seen in a certain way.

Alastair also thinks that there's something cognitive about the levels of difficulty in trying to hear what people are saying. For example, if two people are wearing headphones, it will give them better audio quality on Zoom. It's a minute advantage that they have over those that don't wear headphones.

There are other things that you can do to make your audio and video better. You can spend more money on equipment. You can improve your lighting. It can also be as simple as sitting facing the window rather than having the window behind you. You can also buy a $20- or a $30-dollar LED light to light you up. It can create a difference without having to spend money on an expensive camera. You can also spend $200 on a good microphone, which can really make a massive difference.

While this applies well to solopreneurs, it also extends to those businesses with staff of around 10–30. If you have staff who are making video sales calls, they should also have good video and audio.

Investing in how you look and sound is indeed important. It can even apply to people who are in jobs where they're doing remote calls with their team. Their boss can rank them as a better employee or interviewer if they've got a better setup.

On Getting Himself Noticed

Alastair started a podcast about eight months ago and he's now at his 40th episode. The show called *The Recognized Authority* releases episodes weekly and it's about helping people on their journey to authority.

Apart from the podcast, he's also finishing up a training course on YouTube offered by Video Creators. It's interesting because one aspect of creating videos for YouTube is the actual recording of the video and the editing. But it's also important to know what YouTube is – what do they want? You have to incorporate things like story and intention into your videos.

He shared that he's also been blogging for the longest time. But it wasn't effective until he niched down. It was actually the problem that led him to this whole area of specialising. He's been writing lots of blog posts and creating a podcast since 2014, and it took him six years to get it right. This is why he hopes to help people accelerate on that and do it within six months instead.

Chapter Eight
How You Could be Speaking Out?

Adrian Starks, Founder of Champion Up®, Seattle, Washington, USA.

When you think of the word 'champion', you might immediately think of it as a term that relates to an athlete or a winning contestant. But going back to the English dictionary, it's also a word that means an advocate, a warrior, or a defender of a cause. Championing change means being able to go through the challenges that come with something as inevitable as change.

Courtesy of Adrian Starks

Consistency is Key

Before Adrian became the authority figure that he is today, he has been consistent with his message and with what he is doing, even when no one is around. One big mistake that people do is to jump from one thing to another without specialising in that particular thing.

In order for you to become an authoritative figure in a certain subject, you also need to be where people can see you. Today, this is something that you can do on social media. You need to show up on podcasts, put out materials, write a book, and reach out to people. To let people see you as an expert in your field, you don't have to be the smartest person – you only have to back up and practice what you're saying and you're championing.

However, you have to be strategic about it. For instance, as Adrian talks about change (and change can be applied to different things – from business to health and wellbeing to personal life), he makes sure that his message goes into multiple social media channels. He uses amplification tools such as Buffer, where he can load up his social media content and schedule them on different platforms at certain times of the day.

To make your message more effective, you also have to provide your audience with action steps; not just tell them to change and be optimistic. It's also important to show the challenges you encounter. Showing vulnerability is one way of establishing yourself as a leading figure of a particular advocacy.

Establishing a Routine

To help you consistently be present on social media, establishing a routine is essential. For Adrian, he allocates his Mondays, 11 a.m. until 2 p.m. in particular, to do his social media tasks. Calling it his sweet spot, it's a time when his creativity is at its peak. It's a time when he is most efficient in finding content and planning his content schedule – including identifying which platform suits a particular content better and which is the best day to interact with his audience.

No matter when your sweet spot is, you have to choose a social media day that works best for you. This way, you can spend the rest of your week being fully focused on other things that require your attention such as recording and editing content.

Using the right tools can also help you keep your routine going. For instance, for his podcasting efforts, Adrian uses Zencaster. It's a platform that allows users to record content remotely and buffer out background noises at home. For audio editing, he uses Audacity.

Speaking and Reaching Out

During the pandemic Adrian put to practice his method of creating changes within challenges by moving his speaking business to online.

For him, speaking is the most impactful medium when building a personal brand and being a champion of change. Even today, virtual presentations have become vital in engaging and sending his message across to people.

Speaking professionally is a skill Adrian developed for four arduous years. To break into the competitive speaking industry, you have to be different from other speakers. Learn what works for you and have your own style.

When he first started out, he tried to be like everyone and wore a suit-and-tie. His efforts, however, only became effective when he got rid of the suit and the tie and traded them for a polo shirt and jeans. He simply became him. Along the process, he became more aware of what he wanted to do and who he wanted to reach out to.

For speakers, researching is significant. You have to find out who your audience is and what their needs are. You have to research who are other speakers speaking about the topic you want to talk about. You have to know the trend. Giving free talks works as well.

It's also essential to reach out to people to get speaking stints. Social media channels such as LinkedIn and Facebook have become instrumental in connecting speakers and those who provide speaking opportunities. When you join a LinkedIn or Facebook group about speaking, communicate with the members, comment on posts, and share insights to let them know that you exist. This will help others be enticed to check you out and see your profile.

For you to become an effective speaker, you also don't need to always be in a room full of people. Now, you can create a virtual platform by doing a podcast or being on YouTube.

Going Live

Doing live videos is also one of the most effective mediums that work right now. Going live allows people to be with you and interact with you in real-time. This strikes more differently compared to simply uploading a clean, recorded video.

To further improve your speaking game, Adrian advises you to work on presentations. Presentations are crucial because your audience doesn't want to just see your face – they want to see something else as they can be easily distracted by their computer screens. Unlike traditional speaking engagements wherein you can walk around and move, today's virtual speaking opportunities demand good presentations to keep your audience engaged.

While the world is still battling the pandemic, now is the time to sharpen your speaking skills and maximise going online.

There are different platforms that allow people to speak live online – such as Facebook Live, Instagram Live, and LinkedIn Live (For LinkedIn, you need to apply to go live first). Whichever platform you choose, it's vital to let people know that you are going live. If you've got a message that you want to share with your audience, inform them when you're going to go live and what will your topic be. On Facebook, for instance, you can create an event and notify users that you're going live on a particular date.

When choosing a topic, it's also important to hit a pain point. Right now, the people's pain point is about them being frustrated. Taking that into mind, you have to touch on frustration, share some of yours, and give them an action step that they can do. Be creative and find something that interests people.

Monetising Speaking

Many speakers are concerned about the right timing when it comes to charging their clients. According to Adrian, it comes down to you – when you're ready.

When Adrian was only starting out, he immediately wanted to be paid. On the contrary to what he expected, he didn't get paid. And it's because he wasn't doing enough speaking engagements yet for people to say that he is indeed worth paying. Before asking for fees, you have to prove your worth first: Do some talks, speak in major events, put up a website, and show that you're active and going strong.

With proof, you can back up your negotiation about your fees. In some instances, it can even come naturally. For example, Adrian had a client who asked him upfront about his speaking fees and his availability. If people are already asking about your speaking fees, it means that they have already done their research and saw your previous works.

However, it doesn't mean that you have to charge all the time. You can also give talks for free. For instance, you can apply to a Rotary Club in your area and enquire if you can go in as a free speaker. While you may not make money from speaking per se, what you can do is to sell your material (like a book) after your talk.

When building a brand, be consistent and be present in different channels; always show up until you prove that you're worthy to be paid for your service. To learn more tips, visit www.adrianstarks.net and follow him on his social media channels.

Chapter Nine
Who is Your Secret Army?

Gina Balarin, Founder, Director & Content Queen of Verballistics, Brisbane, Queensland, Australia.

Gina Balarin accuses marketing people of having been liars in the past, and of still misleading themselves: today. She asks, "Why does disillusionment with marketing still exist?" And answers: it's because there is one fundamental problem with the way organisations work; people don't communicate meaningfully.

Courtesy of Gina Balarin

Gina Balarin is an inspirational TEDx and keynote speaker, storyteller, author of *The Secret Army: Leadership Marketing and the Power of People,* and a B2B marketing leader. Gina's goal is to inspire meaningful communication as part of a larger BHAG – to eliminate human suffering at work!

Understanding What the Audience Wants

According to Gina, the challenge with marketing is that there's a bit of a bad smell hovering around its very name. However, it shouldn't be like that. And it doesn't have to be like that.

In her TEDx talk entitled, "Confessions of a liar – Marketing in the era of authenticity" Gina explains why marketing today is different from marketing decades ago. When marketing first started, it was about selling everything one could possibly sell to whoever would buy a product or a service. The problem lay in the available distribution methods at the time: people put advertisements on television and simply yelled at everyone.

The thing is, people live in a completely different world now. It's now possible to listen to your customers at scale. You don't just have to pick up a phone and call them or do a survey. You can use the internet to ask them almost any – and every single – question. This means that marketers today can't afford to lie. They just need to understand what their audience wants.

When marketers do this correctly from the beginning, they're able to start with the fundamental problem they're solving for people. And when they're trying to solve a problem, it means that the product or service that they're providing is great and that their customers are happy with it.

By the time they need to collect information about whether they've done things right, it becomes easy for them to get customer stories, testimonials, quotes, and references saying that they love the product or service. In fact, it's a no-brainer; it becomes a circular world of goodness.

When you start with an expectation and you meet that expectation, it builds back into the circle of creating a new product, service, or any other thing right at the beginning of that wheel again. As an entrepreneur this makes absolutely great sense: you start something, get feedback, then refine the product, put it back out there, and it gets better and better.

But Why is This Not Happening?
An Issue of Confidence and Certainty

Gina hypothesises that many entrepreneurs might struggle to tell happy customers' stories, partly because they have a lack of confidence in their ability to serve their audience.

When entrepreneurs first start, a lot of them aren't super clear on the value that they have to add. They learn by trial and error. And most people don't have the confidence nor the capacity to do the necessary audience research before they begin.

If you look at an entrepreneur who has designed an intentional product or service, or someone who's just fallen out of a traditional workplace and into working for themselves, you'll see a different attitude and different approach to their work and their audience.

Often, entrepreneurs are investing in product design for the first time in their lives. If they're doing it intentionally, they're looking at audiences, at whether the product has a market or not, or whether there's a desire for it or not, they're more likely to succeed. But, often, starting a business means making a lot of mistakes.

Getting Feedback at Scale

Most companies fail because they run out of money. The second most common reason they fail is because they provide a product or service that people don't want. So how can businesses get feedback at scale?

Gina said that it really depends on where your audience is hanging out. There are many tools – including free ones such as SurveyMonkey (which is actually quite advanced and sophisticated these days) – and paid-for tools to help get feedback.

She knows product marketers who use Facebook to test a hypothesis. It's even possible to use the little polls on LinkedIn. However, she reminds us to bear in mind that a lot of the answers that you'll get will depend on who you're asking.

One of the great things about using a targeted methodology such as paid Facebook advertising is that you can be very specific about who you want to ask your questions to. You can do the same thing to a certain extent with LinkedIn. When you use paid-for tools, they're specifically looking for audiences that meet your criteria – in other words, the people who are your target audience.

But she reminds us that you're an entrepreneur doing this on a budget, and you want to target or pull the audience that you already have access to. You will to get a biased sample. For instance, your friends on Facebook are likely to tell you what you want to hear because they are your friends. This is why it's important to get a less biased perspective on things – which may require spending money to reach the right audience.

Comparing Models of Communication

During the episode, Gina discussed models of communication. She explained that original communication models included a sender, a receiver, and noise in the middle. The idea was to model how a message is sent one-way.

She reminds us that, when you think about the original marketing and advertising media of communication, they were all 'shouty' media. With broadcast television and radio, you didn't have the opportunity for feedback.

If you look at the next evolution of a communications model, it included a sender, a receiver, noise, and then feedback, which also has its own noise. Looking at communication using this model, it's clear that listening to people started to become more important. Marketing evolved to start listening to customers and getting feedback.

Today, social media has fundamentally changed the nature of marketing communication so that it is no longer possible or advisable for organisations to only have one-way communication.

However, she reminds us, often, marketers behave as if they're using the previous distribution method. They think about how they want to get their message out there and they don't necessarily pay as much attention to the information that comes back, which can almost be more important than the message that they're sending.

Today, there are much better ways of listening to an audience. One of which is simply testing your marketing campaigns. Doing an A/B test, wherein you test one version against another version, for example, lets you see which one will perform better. Ironically, you're actually listening to your audience when you share those messages in the first place: by getting feedback.

How to Do an A/B Test

For entrepreneurs unfamiliar with an A/B test, it may sound like doing twice the amount of work. It's still worth it but, from a practical perspective, Gina suggests this approach be used with caution. She says that, more often than not, entrepreneurs don't have enormously large databases. This means that you can't necessarily get a meaningful, reasonable sample size.

For instance, you could split your database and send message (i) to 10% and message (ii) to 10%, then send the remainder of your audience (80%) the message that performed the best. Unfortunately, you won't get meaningful results if your current database is not large enough.

What you can do, however, is test over time.

Here's how she explains it. For example, think about a newsletter… You can try out a certain format, initially. Next time, you could try sending it with images instead of without them. When you find out that more people respond to the version with an image, you can try changing the headline format or structure next time. A lot of this comes down to iterative refinement, as they say in software terminology. Basically, it means: step by step, get better and better.

In reality, this is what most people do: as we learn, we learn what to do, and what not to do.

On the Fear of Failure

Gina stated that one of the things that drives a lot of entrepreneurs is their fear of failure. This fear can drive entrepreneurs to make their product perfect the first time or prevent them from actually doing things in the first place.

One of the most important lessons that she can share with anyone who's trying to communicate effectively with their audience is to try something – anything!

If you get it wrong the first time, that's great because you can learn from it. If you get it wrong the second time, that's even better because it means that you can test and see what you did differently between the first and second time, and improve accordingly.

Communicating Meaningfully

If people presumably keep failing repeatedly, they can end up upsetting their audience. So how do you communicate meaningfully?

Gina quoted an old phrase, saying, "We have two ears and one mouth so that we might listen twice as often as we might speak." People forget this, and part of the reason why is that when we're communicating, we're often communicating to be heard – not to listen.

She admitted that she's been guilty in the past of waiting for a gap in the conversation so she can get her point in, rather than trying to hear and understand what the other person is saying. The big problem with this is that we assume people hear things in the same way that we're communicating them.

Earlier, she spoke about the problem with noise and communication. Noise can refer to the background noise on a podcast, or it can be the stuff that's going on between people's ears, which you can't predict or interpret. When you're not face-to-face with someone, it's much harder. And when you can't see them, you're relying on an even more limited set of cues. This is why emails are often misunderstood.

Misunderstandings also happen when people have different intentions when they communicate. To illustrate this point, Gina brought up the DISC profile. It's an old tool, but a helpful way of categorising people into four quadrants. Traditionally, D's are thought of as the Dominant group; I's, the Influencers; S's, the Steady-relators; C's, the Compliant ones.

If you look at these categories, the Dominant group tends to be the CEOs of the world. On the opposite end of the spectrum are people who are steady, stable, supportive, and sincere. When they communicate with each other, the D's who are direct and decisive are in opposition with the S's who are slow and sensitive.

It means that no matter how well they communicate with each other; the chances are they're looking to get something different out of that interaction. The D's might feel that they've communicated really effectively, for instance, after they've made a decision. The S's, on the other hand, might feel really disconcerted by that conversation because they don't feel like they've been supported. They don't feel like they've been able to have that steady and consistent interaction – that they've been heard.

The result is fundamental miscommunication: people don't understand that what they're saying is not necessarily being understood by the person who's listening to them.

What Gina's Company Does

Gina has a company called Verballistics. They help people understand who they're talking to and what an authentic message would be, which is absolutely fundamental to making communication happen effectively.

Verballistics is a content marketing agency. They help make sure that people hear the right words and that the words are in the right context. But the future of the company lies in helping people understand what meaning is for them, individually.

She explains that whether Verballistics helps people talk on a TEDx stage or in an interview, or turns people's words into a case study, creates website pages, emails, or blog posts – it doesn't really matter.

At the end of the day, any marketing is only good when people are able to reach their audience in a way that touches hearts and minds. And that can only happen when you listen to what people are not saying, and when you ask them what they think.

The problem with a lot of marketing is that people don't actually want to listen. We're too busy trying to get messages out that we think are going to influence people. The lesson here is that you don't just have to listen – you have to listen with your heart.

There's a very big difference between wanting to solve a problem and actually understanding why people need that problem to be solved – or whether they even have that problem in the first place. Great marketing is about discovering that need, and using words in a way that helps people solve real problems, so everyone benefits.

With Verballistics, Gina and her company try to help people communicate more meaningfully – whether they're looking at actual content production for their organisation, or trying to speak better, listen better, or build communication skills in your team.

This is what Verballistics stands for: genuinely meaningful communication.

Honesty with Your Brand

When communicating with your audience, the kind of language and tone of voice that they're familiar with and they're willing to listen to is important.

If you're an entrepreneur bringing a marketing agency onboard as your business grows, the first thing that you have to do is to define who you're talking to and how you want to communicate with them. You might have a tone of voice that's very vibrant and vivacious, or something that's very formal and a little bit process-oriented. The important thing is to think of your brand as a reflection of who you are and who you want to appear to be. This really comes down to defining how you want to talk to people.

Gina personally finds ghost-writing for the CEOs of organisations enjoyable because there's nothing that makes them prouder than seeing their own voice in writing. When clients compliment her writing, she says that kind of writing is possible only because of the CEOs themselves. All she does is to listen; her output is really a reflection of the client – their personality, what they believe in, and who they are.

Going back to the question of honesty, Gina noted that the great entrepreneurs are those who are honest enough about their brand and what it stands for right at the beginning. And that honesty shines through in their marketing. It allows them to touch the hearts and minds of their audience. As a result, if they ask people what they think about their product or service, they'd get that honesty reflected back at them – in a way that allows them to attract new audiences in exchange.

How She Gets Herself Noticed

A lot of entrepreneurs in the Software as a Service (SaaS) space or in the B2B world end up working in organisations where they're part of an extended team or an extended marketing team.

Gina considers herself fortunate in the sense that she has clients across the world. When these clients get delighted, they tell other people about her. For her, word of mouth is a very important way of reaching new audiences. So are things like newsletters. She also uses LinkedIn extensively.

Her book, titled *The Secret Army: Leadership, Marketing and the Power of People,* is also a great way of introducing the thoughts that she tries to put in front of people. People, in fact, often call her book a thick business card. Gina also regularly writes blog posts for relevant publications, including the Content Marketing Institute, where she has a quarterly column called The Content Therapist. She also uses podcasts to reach out to people.

For her, it's a delight to be able to share the knowledge that one accumulates over time; to be able to help others feel less afraid of sharing their own voice.

If there's one thing that she wishes she could teach entrepreneurs, it is to be brave and to realise who they are and what drives them, because it's what will also drive their organisations to success. She also believes that the world needs to hear more about their stories – what makes people happy or angry, why entrepreneurs are running their businesses, and why they created their brand-new initiatives, businesses or products in the first place.

Chapter Ten
What is 'Repurposing Content?'

Nir Zavaro, Founder and CEO of Streetwise, Tel Aviv-Yafo, Tel Aviv, Israel.

Nir Zavaro is based in Israel and is a marketer at heart. His company, Streetwise, helps companies with the story, brand, marketing, and sales. He has written two novels and is about to publish *Fuck the slides how to help you raise from seed to A and above.*

Courtesy of Nir Zavaro

Efficient Content Creation

Every person on the planet wants to talk and be listened to. If someone asks you, "Hi, how are you? What do you do?" You can ramble on and on for days and you won't shut up about it. Now, if you'll be asked to turn that into amazing content, Nir said that there could be two possibilities: You could say "I'd love to, but I don't know what to do" or "I don't know what to say."

It shows how all of a sudden, people clam up and get stuck.

What Nir and his team do is to help you understand that you can ramble on and on. You just need to find the right ways to record it and create content.

For instance, he'd jump on a call with me and ask me a simple question, "Could you give me three tips about podcasting?" Having done about 430 episodes, he assumed that if he'd ask me to tell him in 60 seconds what

I do with my podcast and what are the three tips that I could teach him if he wants to start his podcast, I could probably give at least a dozen good tips.

But for Nir, three tips are enough. If I summarise that and record it, I will have about four or five minutes of video content. This is what they call a pillar piece of content, which they will then start dividing so that every tip that I mentioned would be a video. They'll take on one quote and create video content out of that.

In sum, Nir and company can create about 30 pieces of content on every social platform using a five-minute video.

It's About Value

When asked about which question can prompt a conversation, Nir said that it's about what you can teach.

No one wants to hear about your problems. People don't care. But if you give them some value, it becomes something because everyone talks about value.

For example, you wrote a book. People might say that they've read these 30 000 or 40 000 words and they remember one tip. They could have spent eight hours listening to an audiobook or reading, but in the end, they only get one or two takeaways from your book.

At the end of the day, it really comes down to the essence of what you've learned.

If you do tips, it's easy because you can create many on a weekly basis. If he asked me about tips for the podcast and I'd give him a dozen, we already have four videos.

You can go on platforms like Descript wherein you can put in the notes. The moment you do that, you already have subtitles. Then you can divide that, take one picture, add that to the video, and have a thumbnail. Then you can publish that on Twitter, for example.

It's a transformative tool for content creation and repurposing.

You can take a five-minute video (which has about a thousand words) and do a transcript, which becomes your blog post. You can take those blog posts, copy their URL to Medium, and now, you have two articles.

You also have the main video that can go on YouTube. Every tip will also have a separate video, so that's three more videos on YouTube. You can also upload them on Facebook, Instagram, LinkedIn, Twitter, or wherever you want. So that's another 16 videos.

The important thing is that you don't upload them all at once. What you need to do is to create a content calendar. For example, if you have four five-minute videos, you can have the main one go in the first week. Then, the second video will go in the third or fourth week, and so on. This will give you about a hundred pieces of content for the next quarter.

Nir shared that he was recently in London to write his new book called *Fuck the Slides*. For 30 days, he didn't have the time to upload almost anything in terms of video. But his team was still able to keep uploading short videos on social media through the said strategy.

Managing Schedules of Content

Scheduling is another part of the programme. Once you've done production and post-production, you'll have to manage promotion and schedules.

Nir shared that internally, they use everything – from Monday to Trello – as there are many different platforms available today. But when it comes to social platforms, he said that it depends on the clients. His agency, Streetwise, offers outsourced marketing services. So they take a big content calendar and break it down because they work with companies with different platforms.

For him, the simplest way that you won't get confused is by opening a spreadsheet. You record your five-minute video and say that is your main pillar. Then create three more videos for each of the tips that you can put out on Facebook, Twitter, or LinkedIn. Then add all those details on the spreadsheet.

Remember, however, that you can't handle or do all platforms.

For example, he himself has been enjoying more of Twitter and a little bit of LinkedIn for the last couple of months. It means that the usual content that they upload will go to all platforms, but they dedicate less time now, for example, in uploading to or communicating via Facebook. While he's still on the platform (he posts about two to three times a week), he doesn't spend all his attention on Facebook.

The idea of focusing on one platform is helpful. While you can schedule the posts, it's the follow-up to get the engagement that really takes the time.

Engaging in Social Media

Talking about Twitter and LinkedIn, Nir mentioned that all he's interested in are the hashtags that might be relevant for his business or hashtags that he knows he could be of help to someone.

What he does is to go on tweets and follow the thread, then look at the replies. For example, there's a good thread about social marketing. He might see a guy who posted five or six tweets and the filter of the photo is really good, he'll give his two cents, then everybody will see them.

He'll also go to the hundreds of comments, start liking and replying to things so that he can give value. This goes back to him wanting to be heard.

It's also about wanting to serve others because you can answer other people's problems as opposed to necessarily just posting your own views.

Nir also talked about being a member of the EO or Entrepreneurs' Organisation when servant leadership was mentioned during the episode.

As a member, he doesn't just pay money to be a member. He also volunteers his time to help other entrepreneurs in the organisation. Though some of them are even more successful than he is in terms of money or size, he still volunteers his time to help improve the organisation so their members can get better, succeed, grow, and hire more people.

The EO Media House

Nir has been in charge of marketing for the last couple of years within EO. And during the last six months, he mainly focused on building a media house for entrepreneurs in Europe. This means that they become the creators of the content.

They have a website for EO Europe that they're now populating with good stories by entrepreneurs. It's not about EO itself but interesting success stories – stories about love, failure, money, and anything that you can think about, such as scaling. EO currently has 23 chapters and around 1800 members are giving them stories.

He's also doing a podcast where he interviews EO members. Again, this is about trying to give value to young entrepreneurs throughout the continent of Europe.

Now, they're also creating an interesting concept wherein they reach out to people from the same industry in different countries. Then, Nir is going to facilitate an event starting in January.

If you have a public relations agency, this will give you the chance to talk to people from different nations about the same topics and, in the process, get value and understand that EO is the place to be. Or if you want to open a PR agency or you're at the beginning phases, you can attend and find value in listening.

If the media house becomes strong enough, the next phase would be to launch an entrepreneur's newsletter. The newsletter will curate content from all the things that they do. Then, the next step is to create more content in terms of videos and articles from their partners. Recently, EO signed with Fiverr as a partner. Nir shared that they want them to start giving them content.

All these show that there's a lot of variations as to how you can start creating content.

Reframing How Slides Should Be

Nir's new book seems to not be a fan of slides.

However, he clarified that he and his team still use slides. The problem is this: He's been doing mentorship in accelerators, hubs, and startup companies for years. But when he goes to a demo day and there'll be 10 companies, for instance, he can't distinguish them and he can't understand what they do. He doesn't even get what's so interesting about them or what are the differences among them. They all look the same. The structure that people are used to doing is opening PowerPoint and populating it.

When he asks a startup or a manager whether their presentation is ready, they'd respond yes. But though their slides are ready, their presentation is not.

This means that there's a need to rethink the way we create the process. It's still about the slides because that's the way the world works. You can't talk to an investor and not have slides. There's a common way of doing things but you can start with a story, with what are you going to say.

Nir then related it to watching a movie. When you go to see movies, there'll be a trailer for a new film which can compel you to watch it when it comes out.

For years, people have called it the elevator pitch. It doesn't have many slides. During demo day, Nir recommended having this, which he renamed as the trailer pitch.

In three minutes, you need a trailer pitch enough for an investor to want to get more. You're not actually selling them everything. You're selling an idea.

According to him, the three-minute pitch has a structure and a hook. Once you understand what's in it, you build the slides. For example, you can start with a good case study for about 30 seconds. Then the next slide could be about the competition. It's not necessarily a problem–solution format.

If you look at entrepreneurs' or companies' presentations and run through the slides, you may feel that they're not connected or they're not interesting. But if you tell an amazing story about something that happened to someone – and how it also happens to a hundred million people more and how you can solve it for them — you might actually make a bit of money. You can ask your investors to give you a hundred thousand dollars and help you change the world.

On the *Fuck the Slides* Book

Nir's new book is mainly focused on the structure of how slides should be; how to create everything – from thinking about the hook to making sure that you have all you need. There's also a chapter about the things that you'll need at a later stage in terms of content creation.

When people tell you before a meeting about sending them the deck, it has been mistaken over the years that it's about sending the same presentation. Nir said that it can't be the same presentation.

Why? Because when you have the trailer pitch, you are the presentation. This means that your audience shouldn't read. If they read, they won't be able to listen because this is how humans are structured biologically.

But if you'll be asked to send the slides before your meeting and you send the same presentation, you won't be able to be there – you won't be present. That kind of presentation is what he renamed as the toilet deck because people will read it in their own free time; most of them do it while in the toilet.

If you have a trailer pitch, however, the next step is to understand the structure in terms of design. How are you going to speak? In this aspect, sometimes, a good pause is a good thing because it also says something.

Nir's book also has the do's and don'ts of a presentation. Some of them talk about intonation, why he loves standup comedians, and why, sometimes, you need to understand that for the sake of that presentation, you can say and do whatever you want.

'F**k the Slides' is his third book and it's planned to be published in the first week of April 2023.

Getting Noticed While Locked Down

On his website, www.nirzavaro.com, there's a part in his vision where he wrote that he wants to meet all the people on the planet or as many people as he can and he wants to do as much good. He also understands that most probably, he won't meet all the people on the planet and he won't always do good.

So part of that is to understand that he does want to actively meet people, learn from them, and grow. Just the idea of being in a company.

In March 2020, Israel was already locked down before the whole world did so. Nir lost about 80% of his business in less than 10 days. When his business was down and he didn't know what he could do, the best solution that he came up with was to start calling people on his phone.

Every day, he'd call 10 people and ask about how they're holding up and how he can help them. He lost 80% of his business and he had some free time, and if they need something, he can help. One person said yes. And that's how he got a client.

Then, he also reached out to someone who does something similar but in a different industry. That became his second client. He kind of started rebuilding through that: Every day, when he leaves the office, he goes on his motorbike; he has a speaker, and he'll call someone that he hasn't spoken to in a long time.

At the end of the day, it's about continuing to provide service.

Chapter Eleven
When to Use Your Passion to Promote Yourself?

Akshay Jamwal, Lead Photographer of Akshay Jamwal Photography, Mumbai, Maharashtra, India.

Akshay Jamwal is one of India's leading portrait photographers. Fighting back from a bout of depression, he embarked on a 365-day marathon of self-portraits. His passion project became his calling card, and means of separating himself from others.

Courtesy of Akshay Jamwal

It started in 2013 when he was coming out of a dark place – a place that he got stuck in when a long relationship of his had ended. He also has a photography business, and his passion project (wherein he took a unique self-portrait every single day for 365 days) was a way for him to get his creative juices flowing again. Akshay considered the project as something that is fun to do, but as weeks and months progressed, more people started to notice it. It reached a point wherein advertising agencies began reaching out to use his photographs.

Doing Something that You're Passionate About

Akshay used to share his photos on his Facebook page. Although his page only has a small following, his content became a testament that as long as you produce something good, it will eventually get noticed. Now, he has been doing self-portraits for 17 years already, and is one of the very few headshot specialists in India for nine years. A lot of creative professionals and entrepreneurs tend to think that personal work is unimportant. However, for Akshay, it is these passion projects that will differentiate you from everyone else. And these are what clients typically notice.

One thing that hinders many from being their authentic selves is showing something that may throw off other people in the process. A lot of people are afraid of others judging them. For instance, 90% of people on LinkedIn are considered lurkers (they simply scroll past the feed and don't leave any comment). Akshay thinks that there shouldn't be a limitation of any sort because it is a baseless kind of fear. Though some people might judge you, the world, at large, will want to see what you have to say as an individual. The fact that his photos – whose moods range from humorous to ostentatious – got traction, proves that people are interested in diversity.

Being Visible and Consistent

When it comes to content creation, many entities are torn between using static and moving pictures. Akshay recommends using a mix.

The percentage of your content that uses photos and videos will come down to individual strengths. If you ask photographers, they are going to tell you to share more photos. If you're speaking to videographers, they will probably say that video is the best way to get your message across. If you're talking to writers, they will say that text is best. Personally, Akshay finds that a mix of these will be helpful in attracting people's attention.

The key, however, lies in your visibility. If you consistently show up on social media and update your website, you will get noticed.

Though people have the tendency to keep some content to themselves, Akshay recommends putting them out online. Even if you think that your output won't pique the interest of your corporate clients, it can get attention from others. For example, when he uploaded his Pollinator Project on his website, someone who was writing for *The Ecologist* contacted him and asked permission to use one of his photos. Now, many of his photos from that project have become included in a magazine.

On Corporate Shots

Akshay says that there is no one-size-fits-all answer for concerns about featuring corporate shots on a website. It all depends on the company and the design of their website.

Some companies don't have the need to do as such. But for entrepreneurs and businesses that are just starting out, he advises adding professionally taken photographs. However, the images that should be used need to look natural – they have to look authentic.

Photography in India

When asked about his insights about the Indian market, Akshay shares that India is a bit of a strange country. It's a dichotomy in so many ways. While there are certain markets that are hyper-developed, there are also those that don't have any kind of visibility.

In his country, most people think of photography as mainly fashion and commercial photography (though wedding photography has also boomed over the past 15 years). If you search up headshot photographers in India on Google, you'll mostly find photographers who also do other things such as commercial and wedding photography. If you're specialising only in one field in photography, you'll less likely to be more searchable and notice.

When Akshay was only starting out, Indians would often ask him what a headshot is. Advertising himself as a headshot photographer, he would also encounter people who don't even know what kind of photography it is that he does. It's only today that clients in his country are finally realising the importance of headshots.

The internet has played a critical role in making this possible. As people are now in an interconnected digital space, an Indian can now see how a professional-looking American or British person would look like. This prompted a surge in demand for headshots that can be uploaded on LinkedIn and other platforms.

Another challenge that Akshay faces when taking headshots is Indians being conscious about themselves. As many of his clients are people who haven't done headshots before, he had to really work hard to achieve a great output. However, he considers it a wonderful process to see a person transform from a nervous wreck into someone that's conducive to a profile photograph.

Over the next years, Akshay expects photography and videography to take more part in marketing as more people are now realising these mediums' power.

However, one of the things that people need to remember about India is that it's a price-conscious market. Price, in general, rules over quality. Many companies make the mistake of allocating tight budgets for photography or videography. But as companies begin to understand the value of these services, this trend is now being changed.

For instance, when a client reached out to Akshay for his service and found out that they didn't have enough budget, he shared that the client returned after about four months; they realised that not paying for his service was not fair at all. It's proof of how companies in India are now valuing photographers and videographers more professionally.

Chapter Twelve
Are You Losing 31% of Sales?

Danny Levinson, Chief Technology Officer of Transformania, Washington, District of Columbia, USA.

Danny Levinson is the President, International and SVP Sales of Transformania, a US-marketing tech company that focuses on cleaning CRM databases, formatting data and enriching names in those databases; or what scientists might refer to as an anthroponymy type of business. Anthroponymy is the study of names. Transformania enables companies to abide by GDPR while creating personalised data-led marketing campaigns that are supercharged because they use well-formatted data and names that Transformania provides through its data hygiene and data cleaning platform.

Courtesy of Danny Levinson

With a database of contacts which people add data to manually, from an API, from a web form, or by scanning business cards, that name data goes into a company's database in all sorts of ways, sometimes first name then last name or last name then first name. Sometimes, there are typos or a maiden/pre-married name gets thrown in the mix. It could be difficult to understand if it's a maiden name or nickname, but Transformania handles all that. They'll parse it, format it, and send it back, so one can easily identify who's in their database.

CRM-based marketers, such as folks that are using Salesforce, HubSpot, Zoho marketing, and the like are the people they are targeting. Basically, anybody with a list of contacts would be using their system. The result is both an API which can be plugged into a back end and also a do-it-yourself app. One would simply need to go on their website (which is easy to use); select and connect their CRM; and then Transformania will provide you with the corrected, formatted, and enriched data in a few minutes. Their main competitors are companies like IBM, which has a service like theirs that costs millions and millions of dollars, but while IBM targets financial crimes and national security, Transformania are more focused on professionals who will need to parse and format name data for marketing purposes.

Personalisation at Scale with Transformania

Transformania helps with personalisation at scale by plugging it directly into a CRM wherein Salesforce will send them unformatted data and then they send back the formatted data. Another way they help with personalisation at scale is after the CSV or Excel document has been formatted, it can be re-uploaded, and they have these trademarked new columns of data called the 'DearMe' fields. They have FormalDear and CasualDear fields. For someone named 'Mr. Jonathan James', they'd still correctly place, for instance, 'Jonathan' in the first name column and 'James' in the last name column, but based on other data they enrich, either they go out on the internet to find data or they find data from the file itself, they will know that Jonathan's nickname and correct 'DearMe' for the CasualDear field is Jon. If someone wrote in an email, 'Hey, Jonathan', they probably don't know that person, but if it's, 'Hey, Jon', that's personalisation at scale that can lead to higher ROI.

In terms of how exactly they go about that process of enriching date and how they're able to comply with GDPR, Danny says they're coming out with a North America version first with the European and Asian versions released after that. They do keep in mind that regardless of where they are in the world, they need to comply with GDPR, because they can have clients from anywhere, so as far as GDPR goes, folks who are interested in data governance will be using them as well, because according to some of the data governance rules, both at the legal side and corporate side, one can only maintain and keep data for a certain period of time if it's not useful anymore. And if it's going to be kept for a certain period of time, the value of that should be maximised, and one of the ways to do that is by getting the most bang for your buck from what's in there. When it comes to going out and finding other third-party data, Danny says they do have some constraints on that in places like Europe, rightfully so, but they can also mine what's in the file itself. Often, what clients give them, they can find lots of gems from what's already there. They can estimate someone's gender, age, and other novelty things that help supercharge their client's marketing campaign.

Insights Reports and Transparency

A key part of any CRM and personalisation at scale are the analytics and reports to which they provide an insights report. This includes features that show, for example, what are the largest group of nicknames; what are the largest number of formal names; and the largest number of casual names. You get the idea. They'll tell you if you have a lot of Hernandezes and Smiths and Joneses on your list, or a lot of Mike's, Sally's, Jane's, and things like that. For them over at Transformania, what's actionable is understanding the sender reputation, and this revolves around the domain name and how other ESPs or email service providers look at the domain name, whether it is good or bad. They don't provide data on the 'goodness' or 'badness' of it, but they look at the type of domains your contacts have, for example, if it's Gmail-heavy, if it's Hotmail-heavy, if there are lots of individual domains in there, and they highlight processing messages and codes on things that you might need to pay attention to. The other thing they do is they break apart every single record and give full transparency on it. If a file has, say, a million records in there, for every single row in there, they will give multiple codes on what they did with each record in that file.

For instance, once they format and enrich 'Jonathan James', they'd give a code that says that they first split the name and they added a nickname because 'Jonathan James' doesn't have a nickname built in but they found one and they added one. They also remove the extraneous text and give a processing code on that. They have lots and lots of data to give back, but they also don't want to confuse people. They want to make it easy for users to grab the data, put it in, and use it. That's what the CSV is for. But for folks who really want to drill down, that's what the insights report is for.

Data Segmentation and Mixed Language Campaigns

Regarding campaigns involving geotargeting, Danny says they don't have the ability to send the message, but they do give the data that you can then segment based upon and send via your own email marketing system. He says they are not the CRM, but they make the client's CRM better. If there's data in there based on geography or people's addresses, they separate it, if you're in the US, based on states and cities. They also can give congressional districts in the US and other ways to parse and format that data. Outside the US, they're still looking at different ways to do that, and this is why they're coming out with the North American version first. Having spent over 20 years in Asia, Danny says he knows Asia better than Europe. Nevertheless, they provide the tools for people to figure out how to segment the data.

When it comes to mixed language campaigns and data, by doing North America first which is a melting pot of culture, they actually get to tackle pretty much every name and every ethnicity around the world. For instance, Koreans have about 60 key surnames, but that for Transformania is pretty easy. Their surnames are, by and large, one syllable, followed by their given names, which are usually two and three syllables. For China, that deals with many different dialects. There's Hokkien, Hainanese, Shanghainese, and you have folks in Singapore and Taiwan who have Chinese names and different ways of writing that and maybe even concatenating their English name to that. There might be someone from mainland China whose name is Xie, but elsewhere, especially from Cantonese languages, it might be spelled as Hsieh. Xie can also be a given name, so it's a surname and a given name. You may be wondering then how to tell these names apart, but not to worry, Transformania has done all the hard work and figured that out.

Transformania is at the forefront of technology, commerce, and communications, and in the SPEAK|PR program, which is Storify, Personalise, Engage, Amplify, and Know, under personalisation, the challenge with personalisation at scale is that it requires a data management tool like Transformania that can take large amounts of disparate and ill-formatted content and then standardise the format so that when the mail merge is done within the fields of the database and campaign software, each individual person is getting personalised content, but also the address line, the 'DearMe' as they call it at Transformania, is appropriate.

Especially because countries often have different naming formats, the ability of a product or a service like Transformania to take large volumes of data, sort them, and give them back in subsets that can be used without anxiety sending emails to the wrong people or emails addressed improperly is going to be a great relief. Don't forget that personalisation at scale for media relations, for staff, or for partners, and for customers is an essential part of public relations. Transformania is currently in their beta period, where they're actively working with small and large customers to make sure that they're sending out, on day one, a fantastic product. You can find more information on their website, and there, you can register for the platform and get 50 free credits and full access to the main features.

Chapter Thirteen
What is The Power of Authenticity?

JB Owen, Founder & CEO of Ignite You, Red Deer, Alberta, Canada.

A world–class speaker, 17-time bestselling author, and powerful business owner and founder for Ignite Publishing, JB Owen has been helping people get published and says, "as you're creating something that's authentic, there isn't a right or wrong..."

Courtesy of JB Owen

Sharing Authentic Stories

JB considers herself privileged to work with a multitude of incredible authors, entrepreneurs, business owners, and experts. Her passion is to help people tell their authentic stories – the genuine, heartfelt story of their Ignite Moment, as well as the journey, the process, and the steps that they took to get to where they are. And she feels blessed to teach people how their story matters in their business.

According to her, business has changed so much.

Now, people are prioritising working with people who share the same values, beliefs, and vibration as them. Today, so many businesses and people are blessed to be able to work with others from all over the world, and a geocentric mindset has become essential.

Helping Authors Get Published

Like any great entrepreneur, she saw a problem and figured out how she could make it better.

For many years, she was publishing solo authors. What she found was that, despite an amazing story to tell, they just weren't making it to the finish line. How does one single person know how to write a book – and edit, manufacture, typeset, print, produce, ship, sell, and market it? It's a lot of stress on authors. This is why many authors weren't making it to the success that they wanted.

This prompted her to look at her skill set and the things she excels at. She found that it's about being incremental. She loves those micro wins, those little moves along the way that get people there. So she broke the publication process down into incremental steps that made authors feel like they could accomplish it all, step by step.

Then, she also looked at the second part: loneliness. A lot of authors get really lonely. It can be an isolating process – you will be so introspective; you won't have people to bounce ideas off if you're not sure if you're going in the right direction. JB decided she needed a new way of creating books that involved more connection and kinship.

At Ignite, she and her team created this community where you could work with authors and have them as partners in accountability and masterminding. They also fostered an environment of support, uplifting, and empowerment for every author. JB and her team make things fun, then do the heavy lifting for you.

They will do the editing, the producing, the marketing, and more. They will help you become a best-seller in just four months. They will load up everything and create the files you need, from social media graphics to emails you can send to your local library. All that you have to do is to show up with an idea, a vision, a message. Then, they will help you take that and go to the stratosphere with your exciting idea.

It's a real win-win situation because they will let you be great at what you're great at and they will be great at what they're great at. It saves time, money, and effort while making the process really fun. For JB, if she doesn't enjoy something, if it isn't fulfilling, she won't be doing it.

Currently, Ignite has over 700 authors on its roster. They've also published 17 internationally best-selling books in the last two years, including solo-authored *White Glove* books and their famous compilation books. JB has also published her own best-selling book with Ignite. It goes to show how they've mastered the strategy.

JB believes that having a successful business and a great book is about tools, strategies, and systems. Success comes from them. Learning with every milestone, Ignite has proven that they know how to put book publishing through a system that works for clients.

For her, the great thing about being a coach, publisher, trainer, and mentor for authors is that once she shows them the system, they're off to the races. They gain lifelong knowledge and community through just four months of the Ignite publishing process that they can continue to use in their life and their business. They come back and repeat the system because it works.

In fact, they have authors who are writing two or three books. Their top author has written six books. As they've shown them the system, they can quantify again their message and delivery, and produce a fantastic book.

Writing for Your Readers

One of the things that JB wants to do is to teach you how to fish – not just give you the fish.

She's the kind of person who wants to share her knowledge with others so they can also do it themselves too. She does this because she wants you to succeed so that your business, your message, and your book can empower someone else – it's going to move the needle in their life.

This is why JB always teaches her authors the importance of knowing who their readers are and understanding who their customers are: Who wants the book? Who needs the impactful story within? Who's going to walk into the bookstore and say, "I'm looking for a book about this topic"?

If you're writing a book that only satisfies your needs, understand that it's a passion project. It's something that you're doing for yourself. And that's still fantastic. At Ignite, they have authors who have written stories about difficult subject matter and niche topics. One of their authors wrote a story about her husband who died and how he helped 800 people through organ donation. While it's a phenomenal book, it's not for the masses. It's a book for her.

JB emphasises that you have to know the difference between writing a book for you and writing a book for your customer. If you want to have the next best-selling business, tech, or self-help book, you have to think about your customer: What's your customer's problem? What does your customer need? What can you answer for them? Then, you have to make it interesting; that what's in it is important for them.

It's not about you. It's not like a bad date where the other person goes on talking about himself or herself over and over again. Many authors make this mistake. They write books that are all about them. And the reader asks, "Where am I in this process?"

When you're writing a book, JB pointed out two key things: Think about the process and imagine your reader. Because when you do so, you're writing a story that transforms the readers in the same way your Ignite Moment transformed you.

Keeping the Momentum

I published a book, and it's a curation of 50 interviews that I've done. One of the challenges is about keeping momentum. People often start with gusto and they're excited about the launch. Then, there's that middle part where they drift.

When asked about how she helps people get over that, JB shared a personal story.

Last summer, she turned 50, and she decided to do something monumental for her birthday. She cycled on her tandem bike with her husband 5000 km across Canada. She did it for a couple of reasons.

She wanted to show that it's possible; that you can have an idea, get off the couch, and do it. She wanted to show that everything and anything was possible. You just had to embrace the possibilities around you. She wasn't an athlete, she'd never cycled that distance before, and she wasn't even athletic her whole life. She wanted to be a role model and show others that they could do it.

Talking about momentum, she shared that if all she focused on was getting to the 5000-km mark, she would have never made it to the 200, 500, or 1000-km mark. Focusing on the small wins, the next milestone is what helped her stay motivated. The big picture can be overwhelming, so she breaks it down into smaller, attainable goals.

Here's the interesting part about the whole process: She needed to cycle 5000 km in 56 days. This meant she had to cycle 150 km a day. Since she's in Canada and they have snow up until May, she couldn't practice. What she did instead was to visualise herself cycling. She saw herself pedalling and getting there. She saw the mountains, the vistas, the horizon. She saw her legs moving.

When she visualised the process and got on the bike on the very first day, she was able to cycle 98 km, then 100, then 150. She and her husband even got up to 200 km a day.

It's all about momentum. You do a little bit each day, which gives you the courage and the knowingness to do more the next day, which then gives you the power and the strength to do it the next day.

How do you apply that to your book? JB recommends that you map out your book launch over a period of time. For example, you can map out that your book is going to come out in e-book, on Kindle. Then two months later, it's coming out on hard copy or on a softcover copy. Then three months later, it's going to come out as an audiobook. Three months later, you're coming out with a supplementary course.

What you want to do is to add more valuable things to your book and go for the long haul. A lot of people only go for the short game, the short reward, the instant gratification. But it should be about the long game: How can I keep engaged with my clients? Because with that, you'll always make somebody happy.

The Making of a Best-selling Book

Recently, Forbes magazine picked up JB and talked about her being a heart-centred publisher. Being heart-centred in publishing means being authentic and vulnerable in your sharing.

JB shared that a lot of people are asking her about ghostwriting. What she says is that you can't have anyone swing the bat for you. You can't have anyone kiss your first love for you. You can't have anyone birth your baby for you. This is why you shouldn't really be having somebody write your story for you – because when you go through the process, do the work, climb over the broken glass, dig deep to find the answers, then you'll be so proud and empowered to do whatever it takes to make your book work.

You'd want to stand up on stage and share it. You'd want to do podcasts. You'd want to attend summits because it's your work. You authentically and knowingly believe in your story and your powerful message because you've done the work.

The common denominator among the 17 best-sellers in their roster is that the authors have done the work. They've gone through the process. They've learned what they needed to learn. They've studied. They've had the highs and lows of writing: I hate this. I don't want to do this. This is so hard. Why did I sign up for this? Then they've known the exhilaration of being a writer: I can do this. My grade three school teacher told me I wouldn't amount to anything, she was wrong. It's all possible for me.

All these things can lift the lid. All entrepreneurs know that they need to have their lids lifted – on their limiting beliefs, on the ceiling of whatever they thought was impossible that needs to be shattered. This happens when you do the work.

JB shared that Ignite is known to its authors as the leader in empowerment publishing. They empower their writers and their readers. And that's what makes them different. Empowering and energising is important because to say that you can do something is great, but you've got to keep going through those long miles of the journey and maintaining that energy and excitement is key.

Overcoming Challenges

Ignite has many authors for whom English is not their first language or are dyslexic. They even have an author who is visually impaired.

Despite these challenges, these are voices that deserve to be heard and JB shared that there are great tools out there that can help the writing process. For example, she recommends authors use an AI transcribing programme. It's a great tool that you can speak into and have it recorded and transcribed at the same time. You can also write on Microsoft Word and in Google Docs and have these apps read it back to you. This is helpful because it helps you catch those little mistakes that you didn't realise you made.

There are also companies like Upwork where you can find editors or proofreaders who can assist you and help you move along.

JB revealed that she herself is not great at spelling. She has hearing imparity and never learned to spell phonetically; she learned through memory. For example, if there's a word like 'infatuation' and she hasn't written it for a while, she's got to remember how it's spelled. As a person with spelling issues and hearing imparity, her school teachers always told her that she'd never amount to anything. She was that kid who got her paper back with a hundred red scratches, marks, and corrections.

But here's the thing: spelling and grammar are the least of your worries. For people who are obsessed with their spelling or grammar, you can hire somebody for that. What you want to do is think of a concept, theory, theology, philosophy, message, or impact. This is the unique work only you can do. This is where you want to head to – don't get caught up in the spelling and grammar.

Tips from Her Experience

JB's favourite tool to tell everyone is to get up 30 minutes early each and every day and write. Write before you look at your phone and before you talk to anyone. For instance, JB gets up at 4 in the morning, before the phone starts ringing and her kids wake up; it's her writing and sacred time.

As a great tip, she also advised turning off the WiFi on your laptop. When she writes, she doesn't want to spell-check and see those words underlined with red lines. She'll just write in Google Docs to her heart's content and do the editing later.

She assigns concept writing time, then research writing time, and editing time. Depending on how you're feeling, decide if today is going to be writing, researching, or editing day.

Before you sit down to write in those 30 or 60 minutes before you start your day, just sit with yourself for a few minutes and ask: What's best going to serve me today? If you're feeling creative, write. If you're feeling like you want to catch up, edit. If you're feeling like you want to be inspired, do research.

You are the master of your writing. There are no guidelines. You don't have to write hundreds or thousands of words every single day. Trust yourself and where you're at. So it really is about you creating a habit and cadence and working the muscle of writing. This is what's going to get your book done.

If you did a paragraph a day, you'd be done. If you did a page a day, you'd be done. Many people often say that they want to go to a cabin, block off six days, and write every day. Yet it never happens. The book never gets done.

So do a little bit each day and you'll make it to the end.

As long as you're creating something authentic, there isn't a right or wrong way. Many people suffer from the anxiety of thinking that what they're doing won't be good enough. If you can share something authentic, it won't just be good, it will be great. You can worry about the polishing, the editing, and the promotion later.

And if you think about who your ideal client is, you can imagine yourself talking to them and sharing something with them. For instance, JB wrote a beautiful book called *Enjoying Parenting* and it became a best-seller in eight countries. She had taken her kids out of school and 'unschooled' and 'world-schooled' them. She had done the gamut of all the different unique schooling and parenting things.

She then started writing a book about enjoying parenting and, at first, she was writing to all those conscious parents like her. Then she realised that they already know about conscious parenting. So she needed to shift her book and write it for parents who don't know but want to understand what conscious parenting is. She focused on who her writing would help, who it would transform.

When she sat down to write and was thinking about who her reader was, she gave her a name and a persona. She knew exactly what her needs, wants, and problems were. When she actually wrote, she was writing to her; to that persona. This helped all of the writing flow, because she knew who her customer was and who needed the book.

One mistake that many authors make is that they write for themselves or for the intellectuals or for the masses. They want every single person to like their books. However, not everyone is going to like your book.

When you write with a very specific person in mind, it will be like a magnet that will draw in the right people and help you hone your book.

Get Noticed by Being You

When asked about how she gets herself noticed as an entrepreneur, JB said that it goes right back to authenticity.

People want to do business with people that they like and they get to know. They want to work with genuine people who believe in and stick with their core values. When you tell your authentic story, you'll be vulnerable and you'll be you. So be exactly who you are, because when you're you, it's so much more relaxing and enjoyable. You get to live your wisdom and truth and attract amazing, like-minded people who believe in what you stand for.

Don't try to be somebody you're not. Don't try to compete with anyone. Don't try to follow someone else's journey. It's your journey, your process, your experience, your fingerprint, your snowflake – it's unique to you.

The way you get noticed is to be you. You can be fun, quirky, silly, or intellectual – whatever it is, you have to be that wholeheartedly and authentically. These are the kind of people that other entrepreneurs want to work with.

You're going to be loved or hated; going to be enjoyed or not. But when you are yourself, people who resonate with you will want to work with you.

In JB's case, she vibrates her own way, and she lets herself be silly, quirky, fun, and full of life. She wants to get things done. She's hard-nosed. She wants to get increments and make things happen. She wants to ignite and inspire the world. And as for people who don't like that, she considers it a gift, because it's pointless to waste her time and theirs when their different values and purposes don't align. She leads with her authentic purpose, which attracts the right customers to her who belong with the positive culture her company has created.

Many people say that their customers are not fitting in. Or that they don't like their customers. This happens because your customers aren't authentically understanding you – and it's because you're not authentically delivering you.

So how do you get noticed? Be yourself on every level, JB advised. Find your quirks and your strengths and use them to your advantage. Be that wholeheartedly, because that strength and talent were given to you for a reason. The universe, God, or any higher power wants you to use that strength.

This is how you can pull people in and make them be drawn to you. You want to work with people who like and enjoy you, who accept and admire you for being you. These are the kinds of clients that you want to have.

Chapter Fourteen
What is Adjacent Marketing?

Jeff Hahn, Principal of Hahn, Austin, Texas, USA.

Jeff Hahn is the author of the crisis communication book *Breaking Bad News* and owner of a family of integrated public relations (PR) agency brands in Austin, Texas. Focusing on the foodservice and energy sectors, these agency brands include Apron Food & Beverage Communications, Hahn Public Communications, the Predictive Media Network, and White Lion Interactive.

Courtesy of Jeff Hahn

Getting Noticed through Adjacent Marketing

Reflecting on his time in his agency, Jeff noted that connecting to and joining unaffiliated organisations is one thing that he's continued to do successfully.

For instance, he's in a group of 120 regional civic leaders in central Texas. These leaders have nothing to do with his PR business. However, by staying connected with them and being an active member of the affiliation, he's gotten more referrals in ways that he would have never imagined.

The clients he gets are typically not someone from the group itself, but someone that a group member knows. Jeff calls this indirect or adjacent marketing. He considers being part of something else that's not connected with what you do as investing in something bigger than you.

Adjacent marketing was something that he did naturally and unwittingly in the early days of his PR business. But looking back on the last 15 years, he can say that it's been a really powerful generator of new business for him.

This is why he also encourages his team members to find their own organisation that's associated with their part of the practice (his agency has two big practice areas: energy and food). He'd implore the heads of these practice areas to find an adjacent or orient-affiliated kind of network where they can contribute – and make that part of their natural networking.

In the end, he believes that the investment that you make in building a better world will come back to you.

Jeff's firm started small, and the businesses they worked with were all local. For him, connecting to local people was a natural play. Now, he's thankful that none of their clients are local or even regional. This shows that their company is scaling. They now have enough mojo in their brand, systems, and business processes to become more of a mega-regional, if not national level, PR firm.

Coping with the COVID-19 Pandemic

COVID-19 has made it tougher to go out and play a part in different community organisations. But what Jeff has found effective is being the convener or the person that sets up Zoom meetings and creates the agenda. If you make that effort, people will come. Because there's a real hunger for social networking and socialisation in this era of COVID and Zoom.

Shifting one's talent and energy from going to community meetings into convening and facilitating online meetings has proven to be a powerful way of keeping the conversations flowing.

This has even led Jeff to the discovery of a second, natural ability that he had: Now, he's also getting invited to facilitate the meetings of other organisations, which he can do for pay. Currently, he's facilitating workshops and finding himself inside of other fascinating conversations, even though it's on Zoom. Recently, he did a workshop for 60 people in San Antonio on an issue that he even had no experience in.

This skill that he learned over the years has turned into something that generates more references, as his name and business card are being passed around by other people.

How Content Writing Helps

There are business owners and entrepreneurs who are not naturally gregarious or socialisers.

To a certain extent, Jeff considers his personality to be leaning towards being an introvert. When he facilitates, he gets exhausted afterwards because the activity takes all the energy out of him, rather than putting some energy into him.

In writing thought leadership and posting content online, he found a place where he can recharge. He has recently published a book on crisis communication called *Breaking Bad News*, which he spent seven years completing. But that careful introspection and that long time have allowed him to communicate a whole new point of view into the marketplace, which is still in support of his agency's business practices.

For him, research and writing are tremendous introverted outlets that have kept him balanced.

In the process, Jeff learned that he has an affinity for long-form and good research. But while he thought that people would appreciate that, in reality, they don't. And it's simply because they can't.

The biggest lesson for him is to find a single place (it could be LinkedIn or Medium) and try not to overcook the grits, as people in Texas would say. Try not to write too long because people just don't have the time and the bandwidth to read anything that's more than three to four minutes long. Instead, he advised writing fewer words with more impact (which is the hardest thing to do). As the old saying goes, "I would have written less if I had more time."

So write a good headline, fill the content of the body with three good paragraphs, and you're done. Publish it and you're good to go onto the next content.

Focusing on Writing

Jeff regards writing as the one thing that he wants to stay focused on. As Warren Buffett once advised to entrepreneurs: "Learn how to say No more than you say Yes".

He's decided not to venture into other formats such as video, audio, and infographics. If he's going to write content, he'd do it really well. And what he found, later on, was that he's getting noticed; he's getting inbound conversations. But what's most important is that he's happy with the product that he's putting out. His output is focused, and he's even actually interested in reading it and consuming his own content.

As it has been effective for him, he was also able to get clients to follow the same approach and get the same kind of results. This is especially true in the energy business where there's this enormous shift happening: Around the world, there'll be a change from a molecule-based to a mineral-based energy ecosystem in the future, around 30–40 years away. If a business wants to be relevant, they have to have a point of view today and start talking about that future.

Jeff has written content for clients who are interested in establishing relevance and helping shape that future. The content is being paired up with digital marketing that his team does to help promote it. This one-two punch has proven to be very effective.

Working with Traditional Media Reporters

In terms of working with people in the traditional media, Jeff shared that the reporters they're working with are eager to know that they're speaking to someone who has a genuine point of view – to someone interesting enough to interview.

In their agency, they pitch something that can perfectly fit the article that a reporter is writing or thinking about. They do so by browsing through their library of content and searching for an interesting thing that one of their clients is working on.

Apart from that, Jeff also went the extra mile by producing a podcast for one of his clients. In the podcast, they're inviting reporters as guests, which is a sort of a reverse pitch. The client hosts the podcasts and they get to ask the reporter questions and, in the process, slip an idea or put in a little quote.

Just like any other human, guesting on a podcast is an honour and a privilege for reporters. It's something that strikes the ego and something that they love: They take the time to do it so they can also get into an interesting conversation.

The Challenge of Keeping in Touch with Employees in the Lockdown Era

When talking about communication, it's not just about the external. It's also about the internal or your allies.

To keep in touch with his people during this time and get them aligned, Jeff made significant adjustments. Even as a small company of 48 people, the first adjustment that he made was to hire a Chief People Officer (CPO).

At first, he was completely resistant to the idea until he discovered, especially in the lockdown era, that people have a serious need to connect and have safe conversations. The CPO that he hired talks to their employees, helps them understand what's happening in the company, and becomes a communicator on his behalf when he's not connecting to his people individually. It's an investment he made and it's starting to show real benefits.

Right now, the war isn't necessarily against the pandemic itself; it's a war for talent. Trying to find talented people at a competitive price is difficult. So they're now focusing on retention and not necessarily on recruiting and hiring.

He has also made adjustments in the frequency of his own communication with the entire staff. Before, their all-hands meeting used to be only once a month. Now, they hold it every Thursday.

In lieu of social hours, he also facilitates Zoom gatherings and invites other guests. A few weeks ago, he had a magician join them on Zoom. They sent out decks of cards to everybody and had themselves a social hour with the magician and enjoyed the experience together. They're inventing and investing in different ways to keep their employees aligned.

However, Jeff pointed out that he's quite concerned for the younger generation of workers. As they don't have the experience of growing up inside the office, going to and from work every day, being social, and learning cues – they are missing a lot of things. This is especially concerning with fresh-out-of-school people who also did schooling on Zoom. Now that they're starting their career on Zoom, he's worried that they'd miss the intangible and soft skills of the career that only come through social interactions.

Before, when having early meetings with clients and going to their office, there's a sort of elaborate protocol that simply isn't existing in online meetings. So it's going to be also interesting how today's generation is going to engage with clients.

Connecting with Partners

Entrepreneurs are dealing with three different audiences. Apart from clients and employees, they also have partners to deal with.

To keep his network of partners spinning, Jeff uses storification (borrowing the term in my SPEAK|PR program).

One of the things that he's doing is spending more time with them on Zoom – both individually and collectively – and trading stories with them. For him, it's about finding one of the most important gifts that he can contribute to the continuation of his relationship with his partners.

He pointed out that it's important to tell stories about what's going on in your world. How are you feeling? What are the characters and the setting? What's the conflict and the conflict resolution? This is real storytelling. What he learned from convening these sessions is, the more that he can storify what's happening in their business, the better people feel and the tighter the connections are.

When you simply talk about the particular client you have – the revenue and the work you've done – it's not considered a story. It's merely a list. When storifying, you have to tell the story about your client's struggle. What hurdles did they face? What are the changes that are happening in their business? It's about tapping back into the archetypal stories of overcoming a monster or Goliath. It's about starting from the emotive side, rather than from the business, task-list side.

Jeff employs this kind of approach when connecting with partners and he's found that it's more time-insensitive and stickier.

Chapter Fifteen
How to Talk Money With Investors?

Sam Palazzolo, Managing Director of Tip of the Spear Ventures, USA.

Entrepreneurs miss the target because they focus on their own story and not on what the investors need to hear, and they also pitch to the wrong investors too often. Entrepreneur, Venture Capitalist, Author, Leadership Professor, and Nonprofit Philanthropist, Sam Palazzolo brings a variety of value creation topics to entrepreneurs and business leaders. His ideas and actionable takeaways are captured in his five books, the most recent being *Leading at the 'Tip of the Spear Ventures'.*

Courtesy of Sam Palazzolo

Los Angeles-based Sam Palazzolo helps companies raise money, communicate effectively when they're raising money – and get noticed in the process.

Approaching Clients

Sam's business transformation consultancy uses the same type of methodology that he and his team implemented at the tech company. If you think about consulting, it's traditionally a handshake-type of deal with people who are within your network. They wanted to figure out how to expand that circle. They weren't just interested in buck-shooting – they're keen on specificity.

When they approach a specific organisation, client, or prospect, they want to outreach, connect, and see if they can develop some type of a relationship first. From that, the relationship can ultimately lead to a business conversation, wherein they tell clients how it is that their firm knows how to help them.

Sam said that they're a value creation firm. They believe that each one of the organisations that they work with has a value that they provide to their end client. And how they convey that value can make all the difference.

What Investors are Looking At

Tip of the Spear is currently working with an engineer-led organisation.

Engineers come up with the most innovative ideas and they're considered to lead the best organisations (or potentially the best). However, the problem is that as they're engineers, they want to talk about engineering. If you have a financial background, you might want to know what the engineering specifics are but it's not the only thing that you want to talk about. Engineers can lose those clients.

Now, the engineer that they're working with is looking at putting a presentation before a financial community. The presentation is deep in the weeds; it's so rich with engineering details that a financial investor doesn't really understand.

Financial folks look at numbers all day. But it's one of those things where they're more interested in knowing something about what the business does. If they're from an investor community, they particularly want to know:

What is that you're doing?

What type of traction have you been able to achieve with what you're doing?

If we invest in you, what are you going to do with the money?

What are we going to get in return for that money over what timeline?

There are the nuts and bolts – the essentials – of what an investment community wants to hear.

Additionally, they have a relatively short attention span. This is why you have to be able to encapsulate those parameters within around two minutes. Nonetheless, it doesn't mean that you can't circle back and do deeper dives on each one. What you need is to devise a high-level architecture so you can convince investors that it makes sense for them to have a deeper conversation with you.

Essentially, this is what an executive summary is all about. If an executive reads it and they want to go deeper, they can; if they don't, it means that they know enough to consider something dangerous or risky.

This is what Sam and company use an approach to help organisations share that value that they create and provide to the market.

Reaching Out to the Right Investors

Not all investors are looking for the same kind of investment. And that's why for Sam, it's important to research – what do they like to invest in? This information can give you some of the most productive types of conversations. He also pointed out that the things that don't work are the generic, non-customised types of outreaches.

Specific outreaches and approaches also work in the sense that if the person you're outreaching to can't help you, they can still know somebody within their network who can.

Sam loves this about what they do: The financial and venture space is a community of sharers. If an opportunity is not right for them, they'll share that information with somebody else and vice versa.

When asked if a business should specify who it is that they're reaching out to, Sam stressed out the absolute need for it.

On Being Resourceful

Sam talked about an entrepreneur who approached his firm a few years ago.

The entrepreneur stated his idea and what it comprises. While it's brilliant, the problem was that he was loosely trying to approach investors for about three years. His reason for not making headway with the investment community was that he wasn't born with a platinum or titanium spoon in his mouth – he just didn't have the network.

Sam told the entrepreneur that his company might not be his best resource in that instant if he would give up that easily. He emphasised that most entrepreneurs aren't born with a platinum or titanium spoon yet they are entrepreneurs. Sam himself was born in Detroit, Michigan, in the shadow of Ford manufacturing plants and they had plastic spoons. However, he noted that it's one of those circumstances wherein you have to figure out a way to get through.

This is especially relevant now that there's a pandemic. It's never been easier to get ahold of whoever it is that you want to get ahold of. You can outreach and connect with them and hold a Zoom meeting with them. They never have to leave the confines of their home offices or their kitchen table.

To find people to connect with, there are published listings of some venture capital, private equity, and even family offices. While plenty of such resources are available, Sam also pointed out the need to be a little more organic.

You can set up Google Alerts to see who is investing in a particular space. If you set that up, you can get up to 10 alerts each day. You can click a link to know more and you'll be given a list of some articles that are published on the topic. If it's a business article, somebody has published it, and that author has interviewed somebody. So it's a great opportunity to organically find people and specify who it is that you're reaching out to.

Another thing that works well but nobody takes advantage of is LinkedIn. Sam said that he's convinced that they're in the top 3% of companies that leverage the platform. LinkedIn is a great tool because it will give you geographic specificity as well as information on an industry, organisation, and leader.

Google Alerts and LinkedIn are two things that will allow you to organically search and pinpoint who your prospects are.

How to Make Your Company Different

Over the past years, Sam has encountered all kinds of crazy stuff from people doing outreaches. Some are worth looking at but the majority are not. And he and his company don't recommend that type of hokey, gimmicky type of outreach. The entrepreneurs that they work with drive value and they want to be at the top 3% of their industry or space. If they're value creators, then they have a unique value to offer.

Part of that is the presentation for what it is that they're offering. An entrepreneur can have a unique perspective of their industry that can elevate them to be a valuable authority in their space – and set them apart from someone who's got an organisation that's only looking for some money or looking to connect with the investment community.

To be a valuable authority, it's also about the financial opportunities within their space. And through the solution that Sam and his team are offering, entrepreneurs can bridge those opportunities. The solution entails conducting an executive briefing, which is a 15-minute overview that establishes them not just an entrepreneur but an authority in the space.

If you're looking from an investor's perspective, if an entrepreneur doesn't have a unique viewpoint to bring to the table during that executive briefing, then that entrepreneur is going to miss out.

On Building Tip of the Spear Ventures

For his firm Tip of the Spear Ventures, Sam also did the same thing as mentioned above. They did the same type of organic outreach where they set up Google Alerts for their industry or for specific keywords. They develop their list of prospects monthly. They go hunt, reach out, and connect with people who are also outside of their network.

They also use an email-second-type of outreach approach.

Most people simply want to gather a listing, form a database, put it into a customer relations management (CRM) tool, and begin an outbound campaign where they'll blast emails. At Tip of the Spear, they customise those emails. However, it's only secondary. They're a phone-first organisation: They place outbound calls, and it's what differentiates them from others who reach out to entrepreneurs.

It also serves as the differentiator for the businesses that they work with. It forces the other party to actively pick up the phone. Making a phone call doesn't necessarily mean conducting an executive briefing. It simply provides an introduction and establishes an appointment for a future date to conduct a proper executive briefing.

The outbound approach they're using is value creation-driven, phone-first, and email-second. With this, they can outreach to an individual who doesn't know that they existed two seconds ago. Then, they can introduce themselves, drive value creation, and set up a 15-minute appointment for an executive briefing.

For inbound, they encourage entrepreneurs that they work with to follow HubSpot's methodology (He said that he's been a pre-IPO HubSpot fan since 2014). He has also written books and almost 300 articles on their website, which business owners can use as a resource. They also have a series of white papers.

Sam wants to establish his firm by doing an inbound and outbound approach to prospective customers, managing the sales funnel on a monthly basis, and challenging himself to outreach and connect with 50 different prospects a month. He does this because he doesn't want his team to solely do that. He's not willing to assign anything that he's not willing to roll up his sleeves for. This made team meetings with their outbound people much more productive because they know that he himself is doing it.

Chapter Sixteen
How to Animate Your Audience, Not Your Slides?

Andrea Pacini, Founder and UK Presentation Director of Ideas on Stage, London, England, UK.

Courtesy of Andrea Pacini

Andrea Pacini, Founder and UK Presentation Director of Ideas on Stage, helps entrepreneurs get noticed through presentations. According to him, you need to look at three key areas if you want to have a successful presentation.

First is your ability to develop a compelling and captivating message for your audience.

Second, creating slides is another skill you need to consider. It's not necessary to use slides, but if you need one and it's especially about business presentations, you have to avoid the typical death by PowerPoint (i.e. using a lot of texts and bullet points).

The third one is your delivery skills. Note that having a great message is not enough. You also have to deliver your message in a comfortable and convincing way.

When he works with entrepreneurs and business owners, Andrea and his company look at these three key areas to help their clients improve their ability to pitch, present, and communicate their ideas.

Knowing and Profiling Your Audience

Before having a message, you have to start with your audience. Many people make the mistake of starting with PowerPoint and putting together some slides first. However, Andrea pointed out that when you're giving a presentation, you have to consider it as your audience's presentation – not yours.

Think of a presentation as a present. If you want to give someone a present, it would be that person's present and not yours. Therefore, you have to make sure that you know your recipient to be able to buy something that they like. Similar to that, when giving presentations, you have to think of your audience first – their needs and the context. Before you start thinking about your message, before you open up PowerPoint, start first with your audience.

When profiling your audience, Andrea shared the ABC of presentation. It stands for your audience, their burning needs, and the context.

Audience. Take the time to ask yourself questions about your audience: Who are they?

Burning Needs. Identify what their burning needs are: What do they expect from your presentation? What challenges do they have? How do these challenges relate to your activities or to your topic?

Context. In terms of context: At what time of the day will you be presenting? In what kind of room will it take place? If you want to show some visuals, is there a screen or a projector to help you do that? If it's an online presentation, what tool are you going to use? How are you going to use it? How and when are you planning to interact with your audience?

While you can create a great presentation without this ABC, Andrea noted that you'll have the risk of delivering a fantastic presentation before the wrong audience.

What Separates a Great Presentation from a Bad One?

From a visual perspective, Andrea always encourages their clients to follow a simple visual approach.

If you think about slides, you have to think about them as something to reinforce your message. They are not the main thing. Whatever you show on the screen, it doesn't have to replicate what you're saying because people can't read and listen at the same time.

From a message perspective, one of the key success factors that you need to consider is your ability to simplify your message. Many entrepreneurs – people who know so much about and are close to a particular subject – tend to think that everything is important; that they need to communicate everything. However, if you put yourself in the audience's shoes, if everything is important, then nothing really is important. This is why it's essential to simplify the message.

You also have to develop a clear storyline or structure when presenting. Think about how you can capture your audience at the beginning; how you can develop your key messages; how you can end your presentation with a clear conclusion and call-to-action so that they're prompted to do something after your presentation. Structuring is key to making it easier for your audience to follow you and remember what you say.

Creating a Logical and Compelling Narrative

As Andrea has emphasised, the process of creating a logical and compelling narrative always starts with the audience. But when they work with their clients, they also make sure to have a clear objective. And the objective is not just about sharing some information, which is a common mistake that presenters make. If that will be your sole objective, then there really is no need to give a presentation. The objective has to go beyond just that.

After knowing your audience and objective, you and your people need to brainstorm. Use simple but powerful creativity techniques to identify interesting ideas that can be included in the content of your presentation.

After that, take all your ideas and create a clear structure. One of the simplest but most powerful principles in communication is the so-called 'Rule of Three'. This states that the human mind likes groups of three. It will be hard for people to remember or process things if there are more than three pieces of information. If you have 10 or 20 important things to say, it won't matter. You have to group your ideas into three key messages.

In sum, if you want to create an effective presentation structure, you have to have an introduction that captures your audience. Then, communicate your three key messages. If your presentation is a short one, summarise; if it's long, there's no need for summarisation. Afterwards, have a powerful conclusion by making things clear to your audience: What was your point and why should they care about it?

While there is no magic number in terms of how long an optimal presentation should be, Andrea recommended around 20 minutes. Since 2010, their company has been working with more than 500 TEDx speakers. If you're a TEDx speaker, no matter who you are, you will be given no more than 18 minutes to present. This is because of the difficulty to keep the audience's attention high for more than that amount of time.

If you have an hour, for instance, for a business meeting, it doesn't necessarily mean that you have to consume the full hour. You can allot 10 minutes for warm up, 20 minutes for presentation, and the remaining 30 minutes for discussion.

What About Presenting Without PowerPoint?

There are instances when people just won't have the infrastructure or technology to present with PowerPoint slides or any other presentation tool.

Andrea emphasised that you don't really have to use slides. The ability to create and deliver a powerful presentation has nothing to do with your presentation tool. But it can help in amplifying your message. From that perspective, presentation tools can be useful.

However, you don't have them all the time. If you have a compelling and simple message that is clear, interesting, and enjoyable for your audience, your presentation can still be memorable. If you know how to deliver that message in a way that's comfortable and convincing – whether it's a face-to-face presentation or an online one – then PowerPoint doesn't really matter.

Once you've also developed your message, you should always ask yourself: Would it help to amplify my message if we use some slides? If the answer is yes, then it makes sense to start thinking about how you can illustrate your message in the most effective way. If you think about TED Talks, some of the best ones do not actually use slides at all. And that shows how it's definitely possible to deliver fantastic presentations with no technology and no slides.

Finding and Conveying a Topic for Your Audience

Andrea always says that you need to animate your audience and not your slides. And in terms of communicating a compelling message for them, especially in business, it has to be original and enjoyable.

One of the things that works really well is sharing stories, anecdotes, and examples. Every time you have an important message to communicate, ask yourself if there's a story that you can tell to illustrate a particular point. People remember stories much more than just facts and figures. It doesn't have to be a once-upon-a-time story. It could be a personal story or something that happened to you that made you interested in a particular project. It could be anecdotes of other people. It could also be a story of a brand's success or of an organisation that's effectively doing the thing or strategy that you're talking about. If you think about it, there's always a story to tell.

Another powerful method in communication is doing an analogy, which is a comparison between two things. When you compare something that your audience is not yet familiar with (e.g. your message, or idea of a product or service) to something that they already understand and know, then you can make a connection. That's when learning happens.

For example, when Steve Jobs launched the first personal computer in the 1980s, he used the analogy stating that the personal computer is like a bicycle for our mind. If humans have a bicycle, we can become very fast even though we're not the fastest animal. That's what the computer is for Steve: It can make you become faster and more productive. If he used technical details, nobody would have remembered and understood those details.

Andrea further pointed out that in presentations, especially business ones, people have the need to communicate data. However, many mistakenly assume that data and numbers are intrinsically meaningful. That's not how the brain works. If you want to communicate data, you also need to put it into perspective. When Apple launched the first iPod, they didn't say that it has a capacity of five gigabytes. They said that the five gigabytes are the equivalent of a thousand songs in your pocket. And a thousand songs in your pocket is universal – it's the same thing to everybody.

As some of his go-to inspirations in storytelling and presenting, Andrea mentioned Garr Reynolds, author of *Presentation Zen*, Microsoft's Chief Product Officer Panos Panay, and Ideas on Stage's Chief Inspiration Officer Phil Waknell.

Chapter Seventeen
LinkedIn Video Tips

GJ Van Buseck, Owner of GJ Talks, Haarlem, North Holland, Netherlands.

Hailing from Holland, GJ van Buseck, is a thought leader and influencer in video creation. He has discovered the power of video content creation on a budget, doubling the engagement he has on LinkedIn and doubling the number of connections he has within only 12 months. He now has over 13% engagement on his videos compared to the industry benchmark of 5%.

Courtesy of GJ Van Buseck

From Sales Manager to Content Creator

GJ was a sales manager for an energy company until 2018. He decided to make a complete change of career, studied how to become a documentary maker, and finished a filmmaking course.

But as COVID-19 caught the world by surprise, he had to stay home, hindering him from doing the things he had in mind. He had to reconsider his future – What should he do sitting at home, being quarantined, and not being able to go anywhere? That was when he decided to be more active on LinkedIn, a platform that he hardly used before. When he met LinkedIn content marketing consultant Alex B Sheridan, he was inspired by how he busied himself making content. It prompted him to start making content as well to help other people get ahead.

In September 2020, he recorded his first 60-second video. He simply used a mobile phone to record himself as he put out a message that he thought would be interesting for others. When he posted it on LinkedIn, he expected the worst reactions and responses. However, nobody gave him the criticism he expected. In fact, some people were actually surprised about him making video content.

From there, GJ started building his content. He established a routine of putting out short videos (ranging from 60 to 90 seconds). Then, his network grew from 700 to around 1800 as of writing. He shared that his connections don't only include people that he invited but also those that followed him because of the content that he makes.

Today, he can now be regarded as an expert in using video as LinkedIn content. And this is what exactly is stated in his profile: to get in the picture and make yourself known out there. And for him, the best way to do that is through video.

Making Content and Overcoming Excuses

When he was starting, GJ had nobody in mind as his audience. If his content is interesting for anybody, then anybody could listen to and watch it.

At that time, he was only giving short messages about his view on LinkedIn – how it used to be a platform for recruiters and job-seekers; how it became an avenue for content creators to share their knowledge and help others improve themselves.

Later on, he realised that he had to focus on the subject of video creation itself. From there, he started making videos to show people that it wasn't that difficult to make one. If you have a phone with a camera, you won't need any other expensive equipment such as green screens, lamps, and lights. All you have to do is to switch on your camera, record yourself, and share whatever it is that you know with the world.

There are always excuses when it comes to accomplishing things. You can say that you can't be able to do video content because you don't have the equipment or you don't know about video.

In reality, GJ said that you don't need to know all that much. If you have a smartphone, you can stick it to your window with duct tape or tie it with a little piece of rope through a window. Take advantage of the beautiful daylight falling over you, then just press the record button. He noted that daylight is the most beautiful light that you can use for short video content (Remember: you're not making a three-hour movie). One- to two-minute videos are enough to share an interesting message. They just have to have that something that can entice others to keep listening to them.

Finding Your Own Rhythm

In terms of the frequency of publishing your content, GJ shared that it's about finding your own rhythm.

When he started in September last year, he was enthusiastic about making short movies. He began posting several times a week. But what he realised was, you can overdo things with that. This is why you have to give people the time to digest your content.

Also, keep in mind that if you're going to make a movie every day, it will take a lot of time. You have to record it; if the first take is not good enough, you have to re-record it. You also have to do some editing. However, for GJ, editing is something that you can improve on over time. In the beginning, it's not that necessary because your focus should be on the message that you'll give.

If you're just starting out, you can simply use your phone and use it to make a video of you sharing your knowledge with the world. Keep in mind that everybody has something that is interesting for somebody else. And whether your video has 10 or 10 000 views, what makes it worth doing is having one person finding value in it.

To make his content more accessible, GJ posts videos on his LinkedIn feed. He emphasised that groups are limited in terms of the number of people who can view your content. However, you can still put it on such avenues if you belong to one (in his case, he has a group comprising people who attended the same video-filming course he attended).

Tools for Editing

There are free mobile applications that you can use for editing.

InShot, for example, allows you to add stickers to your video, edit it, and upload it anywhere you want to. These platforms include YouTube, LinkedIn, and Instagram.

However, GJ said that he prefers using professional editing software on a computer because working on a tiny phone can be challenging. His software is Final Cut Pro, which is similar to iMovie but is more expensive and professional.

The Adobe Cloud editing software, another professional tool that you can use, is available via subscription at $8 a month.

On Backgrounds, Content Subjects, Language Used

Currently, there are two schools of thought on video backgrounds. One is having a green screen; the other is using an authentic backdrop. For GJ, your choice of background should depend on the type of video that you're making.

For his weekly video column (which he started in January), he uses a green screen and edits a theatre background into his video.

If you want to record in a natural set-up like a park, you can do so. However, he pointed out that you have to be careful with the sound. In a park, the birds and winds can affect your video's audio quality.

Whichever your choice is, it all boils down to the message that you have and the story that you want to tell. If you need to rely on a background to make your story more interesting, you have to reconsider your story.

For the content of his video column, GJ does a look-back on the news and events that happened in the past week. He performs stand-up comedy as well. Now, he's also doing a 'vide-od-cast' (a combination of video and podcast) where he places himself on a resort-like background. The topic of his content is how you can make videos.

All of the subjects that he uses are those that he thinks are fit for the series that he makes. If his audience will be interested in new subjects, then he'll make a new scenery in a specific format for that.

The audience of his content is Dutch, so he does his videos in Dutch. He only has one video in English to honour his foreign connections.

In terms of response, he uses the Shield App to measure engagement on LinkedIn. The benchmark on the platform is 5% and GJ averages 6.6% across all his content (including slides, articles, and videos). His engagement rate for videos alone is significantly higher – which is 11.3%. His latest video series racks up an average of 14%.

While you have to put in a lot of time in making videos, the feedback and engagement will still be higher compared to written content. For him, filming is the best way to get in the picture and earn high engagement. Again, you just have to find your rhythm, know what it is that you're going to talk about, and make several clips out of that. In his case, he's been fixed at recording everything every week.

If you want to get noticed, try to make a video and get in the picture. Muster the courage, use your phone, press play, and enjoy.

Chapter Eighteen
You Can Overcome SEO Challenges

Jarod Spiewak, Founder and CEO of Comet Fuel, Manchester, New Hampshire, USA.

Courtesy of Jarod Spiewak

Most businesses are wasting a lot of money on search engine optimisation (SEO).

New Hampshire-based Jarod Spiewak, who is the founder and CEO of Comet Fuel and a digital marketing specialist, shares not only how SEO works for entrepreneurs but also how he uses Upwork to secure six-figure contracts for his agency and sharing his tools for free to generate leads.

The SEO Challenge

Jarod considers SEO as a bandwagon marketing channel. It has that appeal that everybody wants: Everybody uses Google to find anything and showing at the top of search rankings is part vanity and part revenue.

Many businesses consider SEO to be 'free', unlike advertisements wherein you have to keep paying for every click. However, it's not necessarily free to grow your SEO nor maintain it.

But while everybody wants it, the reality is that there's a limited amount of space. Once you earn a position, it doesn't mean that it can't get taken away from you.

What he found over the years (mostly through trial and error) is that a lot of companies who are investing in SEO either make slow and expensive progress, or make good progress and have it quickly taken away by somebody else in their business space.

One of the biggest hacks is to have a brand that builds momentum, which then starts a snowball effect. As an example, he cited working with a company that did an internal correlation study and found that in cities where they have billboards, the click-through rate (CTR) was higher on Google. Psychology 101 teaches us that people are more drawn to things they're familiar with.

By having a more recognisable brand, it's possible for a lower ranking company to receive more clicks than a competitor who ranks higher.

This plays into a so-called re-ranking. Here, a higher-than-expected CTR within a designated search position for a designated keyword may influence Google, telling the search engine that more people than expected are clicking on that particular result and that it should actually be positioned at a higher rank.

And it's not just about traffic. It also facilitates an easier move through top positions because the performance is better than what Google would expect to see from other competitors.

These are just some of the benefits of having a brand, which makes it much more difficult for somebody to compete against.

On Link Building

If you're selling something, being on the front page of Google is not the only route to success.

Large companies certainly have distinct advantages when it comes to building a brand and putting up billboards. Looking at the link-building aspect of Google, these companies are going to attract more media attention at a far less cost. Sometimes, they can achieve it without even having to do anything.

On the contrary, smaller brands may to try harder in order to gain that attention.

However, according to Jarod, it's still possible to beat out bigger brands. It's just that the methodologies that you have to use will be a little bit different.

How Comet Fuel Chooses Clients

Comet Fuel profiles clients based on experience. Jarod spends a lot of time talking to a lot of different people in marketing or those who are in C-level positions.

He only chooses a business that he thinks is going to be a right fit for their company. A business that would take the suggestions that they make; a business that is on the same wavelength as them.

If he and that business won't agree with each other, no matter how good Comet Fuel is, they're never going to make that connection.

Speed, Not Scale

If you go back to pre-Google, all search engines just looked at what you told them about yourself. And everybody wants to say that they're the best at something.

Then, Google decided: What if we use other people saying that you're good at what you do; that you're a reputable business through the use of hypertext links? Using hypertext links allows users to click on something, which would then bring them to a different page or site.

Because if other non-associated sources are recommending a resource, it's a stronger indication that resource is actually good at what they're saying – compared to them just saying that they're good themselves. This is similar to how people cite sources in journals.

During the episode, Jarod cited podcasting as an example to show the difference between a large and a small company.

Podcasting is a relatively new medium. If we're talking about how to get large organisations into podcasting, the scenario would look like this: A certain employee reaches out to their boss and says that they should guest on a podcast. Then the boss says that they'd look into that – along with several other things.

The deliberation can take weeks, months, or even years. Who's going to be the spokesperson? What if that spokesperson leaves the company? How are we going to record this? What are our key performance indicators? How can we get the budget approved?

If it's a smaller company, you can directly talk to a decision-maker. You can book them and do the podcast as early as tomorrow.

In this sense, the speed of execution can massively outweigh the excessive amount of resources that another company has. It's a matter of effectively deploying the capital. A big company would be investing in all the best equipment and making sure that it represents their brand. If it's a smaller one, they'd be fine buying a $50 Blue Snowball and just popping on with a webcam.

This way, you can compete with a larger competitor. They'd probably be a lot more professional about it. But if you're doing it at the moment, then you're going to have a year of experience before they even start.

For the unnoticed entrepreneur, it's actually speed – not scale – in the digital age that is a key success factor.

Going Mobile and Geography-Specific

With almost anything SEO, there's some ambiguity about crossing over from desktop to mobile.

Google has moved into a mobile-first index. This means that when they crawl most websites, they'd look at the mobile version first.

If you take out your phone and see how long your mobile loads, that's what Google is experiencing. If you try how the navigation works, that's what they're also experiencing.

When it comes to locations, there are local, national, and global locations.

If you're a national-based company that has several locations, you'd usually have some sort of location-based structure on your website. You'd also make it clear when it comes to what's relevant to a certain geography. You might have different languages on your site, for instance. Or you might have different top-level domains.

The type of content that you'll make then is all about intent.

There are contents that are not local intent-based – it doesn't matter where someone is based out of. For example, if you saw a bunch of ants in your house, you'll do some searching about how to deal with 50 000 of them behind your wall.

When Jarod did a search on this, the pest control article that he found was from a local pest control company that's nowhere near where he lives. Because he didn't search specific enough, Google just decided that that article was the best one.

If he'd change the search into what ant species are in New Hampshire, then he'd more likely find New Hampshire websites or any other article that other people have written about the topic.

One of Comet Fuel's clients who are focusing locally is in the cannabis space. Depending on where you are in the US, the use of cannabis can be completely legalised. In some, it's just recreational; in others, it's medical. There are also places where it's still completely illegal.

If they want to talk about getting a cannabis dispensary license, they'd have a general page about how to get a dispensary license at a high level. There could also be subsections or individual pages that will detail how to get your dispensary license in Michigan, California, or Colorado.

On Outsourcing Content Creation

SEO and public relations are always about content quality.

However, today, if you search for something that you personally know really well and look at what ranks on Google, you'll often be disappointed in the actual quality of content. Most of the time, it's fairly generic and it reads the same. If you look at the top five articles, you'd get 95% of the information. And when you'll search for another article, you'll find that it merely sounds spun.

Unfortunately, this is what's happening quite often: People simply outsource content to a professional writer who isn't necessarily aware of what's happening in their space. It's a lot cheaper to pay somebody to just look at what's currently on the web and essentially rewrite in a way that isn't considered plagiarism. The company will be legally fine and their content can rank.

However, it's still no more helpful than everything else out there.

It's considered more cost-prohibitive for you to have somebody who's not only a great and engaging writer, but also able to learn about your industry. It could also be somebody who's already involved in your space; somebody who's willing to sit down with you to ask you questions and understand your internal methodology. Because your approach is different, it would be hard for anybody to write about how you do things without having a conversation with you.

For instance, an article on the web could say that hourly based pricing is standard, but in reality, your business has never done that. So the content that your outsourced writer will write will only be irrelevant. Without that conversation and understanding, the only thing that you'd ever get is fairly generic content.

When it comes to Artificial Intelligence (AI)-based content production, Jarod said that he's not as well-versed. And at scale, it's usually all enterprise-level stuff. It's more about making basic content (e.g. writing about your store across different thousand locations).

How Comet Fuel Finds Leads

Comet Fuel has done a couple of things throughout the years in terms of finding leads. One of the more long-term ones is producing tools that they've made public and free. They've got hundreds of businesses using their tools as their internal main tool, which has often led to leads coming to them.

Another is through the content they produce. Their company would have people reaching out, saying that they first heard about them a few years ago and now they're ready to try and work with them. They also source leads from referrals.

However, what's interesting is Jarod's background itself.

Prior to owning an agency, he was freelancing for about six years via Upwork (the merger of oDesk and Elance). It was his primary source of leads and he was able to build a very strong profile that's still there until today. Now, he's still getting people reaching out, offering four- to five-figure per month contracts mainly because the profile was established enough.

Essentially, he just let things organically grow, turning something that is somewhere between an inbound and an outbound channel into an almost purely inbound channel.

Today, Jarod is able to land five and six-figure clients on Upwork. But when he first started on the platform, he was offering marketing services for $5 an hour. At the time, there were also fewer US-based people offering higher quality SEO services.

He aggressively used the platform and got a bit more and more competitive. Over time, the landscape has shifted as a lot of agencies started emerging (Now, when they try to hire somebody as a freelancer to help them with a specific task, it's hard to find someone that isn't an agency).

While there are a lot of lower end people, there are also plenty of enterprises client-wise. One of the clients that Comet Fuel got to work with was owned by a company worth $15 billion. What they essentially looked for was a one-time engagement for an initial project. But there are also clients wherein they've had multiple six-figure contracts with. If you stand out enough to attract that kind of attention, you'll find a good mix of opportunities out there.

Chapter Nineteen
Can You Overcome Stage Fright?

R Robinson, Advisor & Entrepreneur in Residence of Animoca Brands, Bali, Indonesia.

Richard Robinson, originally from Boston, has been an entrepreneur for his whole life, for most of that in Asia. Seasoned Advisor, Entrepreneur, Exec, Keynote Speaker, Professor & Investor based in Bali and Beijing.

Courtesy of R Robinson

Joining Industry Groups

Many entrepreneurs come as failures. And the road to failure is absolutely treacherous and miserable all the time. However, this should prompt you to have a terrific attitude and look at it as a way to build up your skills, experience, and network.

Richard regards himself as a keen student of entrepreneurship. He tries to take whatever he could from each venture and bring it to the next. And one thing that he always brings from venture to venture is being part of industry groups, like what he did when he first started his career in Hong Kong in the mid-1990s.

For him, joining industry groups is an incredibly powerful way to establish your career. It can also be helpful later on as you enter new areas.

For instance, he's currently involved in Web 3.0, which is a sub-sector of cryptocurrency. In this play-to-earn space, he found completely new friends. And similar to what he did around 30 years ago, he's now starting an industry group to bring like-minded people together. He works with a young professional who helps him organise that and bring speakers and participants to their networking group.

If you want to make a name for yourself and you're in a place where there's a lot of like-minded people in your industry, Richard also advises finding two or three things that you can cross over. For example, you can hold a networking event in London for people who are interested in e-commerce from China. Or an event in Singapore about social media for business-to-business (B2B) companies.

For the event, you need to start a newsletter and social media campaign. You can also do a fireside chat, which is a panel of sorts where you can be the moderator. You can ask your speakers two to three talking points – you can talk about their story, what they're working on now, and what they see in the future. Then, you open a question-and-answer portion with the audience.

Through this, you can bring together a group of people from the industry who'll be grateful for what you did. You'd become a node in the industry and you can get well-known and be seen as an expert for pulling together people around a specific topic. Most importantly, you can connect with senior people in the industry who are really making things happen. You can bond with them one-on-one, be with them on stage, and even open up opportunities for them.

Bringing Out Your Inner Extrovert

As an entrepreneur, calling yourself shy and introverted is an excuse. According to Richard, you can practise so you can bring out your inner extrovert.

Many are afraid because they can't be like someone who can stand up and speak. Or they might come off looking like Steve Jobs who, in the early days, was a lousy presenter.

He then cited a common friend named Benjamin Joffe who started Mobile Monday Beijing. Back when he was first introduced to him, he said that he was painful to watch and he didn't think he ought to be on stage. And he's never been on stage because he's a little introverted, though he has a great personality. But for Richard, he has become the best presenter on the planet when it comes to hardware startups.

The key is, you just need to go out there and do it more.

The Problem with Public Speaking

Most of the time, people fail before they even start a company; people fail even before they get up on stage. The number one reason is fear of people and speaking in front of an audience. Statistically speaking, if you are to give a eulogy at a funeral, you'd much rather be in the box than behind the podium.

The leading problem in public speaking is not about people judging or dissecting you; it's about people not paying attention and listening to you – it's when you've lost them already.

This is why you have to be you, times two. Meaning, you have to learn how to sell if you're an entrepreneur. If you feel like you can't do it, that's because you haven't done it enough. You have to sell to your investors, to people you're recruiting, your customers, and your partners.

Even if you're not an entrepreneur, you have to sell to your boss if you want to get that budget; you have to sell to your family; you have to learn how to persuade people and be able to tell a story. It's a soft skill that Richard pushes really hard even in the Master of Business Administration programme where he teaches.

It's an important learned skill. Another learned skill that you need to have as an entrepreneur is staying calm when things are going wrong.

Deliberate Practice is Needed

When it comes to presenting, it's not just about getting enough preparation. It's deliberate practice.

You have to film yourself and watch yourself present. You also have to listen to other people telling you that you use particular words repeatedly; that your body language and the cadence of your voice are lousy; that you talk every second because you don't want to have any silence, which would make you realise that you're naked on stage. However, in reality, one of the most powerful things that you can say before an audience is…

…nothing.

Once you get comfortable and you stand on the edge of the stage in front of a thousand people, then you throw some energy out there and say nothing afterwards – about 20% of your audience will look up and give you more attention.

And there are many more ways in which you can improve the way you present. These are things that you don't learn in school. Even if you gain just a 1% improvement in your public speaking skills, you can already make a big impact. Doing things for your improvement is how you can become more comfortable in doing that. It's not a sort of gift. It's something you improve on.

Becoming an Industry Facilitator

Based on Richard's experience, one of the most powerful things that he's done is to see to it that he's reaching out to an industry luminary who's coming to town. Then, he sets up a meeting with them and other speakers that he's previously gathered.

This is a good way wherein you can gain industry insights from them. If you can facilitate that, it will have a high impact.

When it comes to public speaking, the worst part for him is creating bespoke presentations because it takes a lot of time. Especially when it's your first time creating it and it's a sales pitch, it won't work so great.

In this aspect, he advises to simply build something up, offer some meat, and just practice. You could be just giving one slide or no slide at all. It's sort of a stand-up comedy where you do smaller gigs; then you do a stadium show only after you've practised.

Another thing that you can do is to be a moderator of a panel. This will allow you to coordinate with all the panelists.

If you're early on in your career, you can go to an event and say that you want to put together a panel of this new, interesting angle of the industry. Suggest a list of speakers and yourself as the moderator, and give a list of topics.

When doing an event, take note that the most expensive thing is an empty seat in the panel. When you're organising a venture, you might be working on getting people to the event, getting sponsors, and getting logistics done. But if you don't know what's going on in the industry, then you won't be able to give some kind of meat. On the contrary, if you know an interesting angle, then you can reach out to relevant people and invite them as one of your panelists (Richard recommends getting three to four).

For the panel, you have to prepare three interesting talking points. However, it's important to remember that when you're moderating a panel, you're not in a little league where everybody has to play. Not everybody has to answer a question. You're not there to make everybody agree but to give meat to your audience.

You also don't have to be an expert. You just have to be good at keeping things interesting and snappy. Being a panelist is a little bit easier because you can just show up and as long as you've prepared well, then you do a fireside chat.

On Emceeing and How You can Leverage It

In terms of connecting with industry figures, Richard cited emceeing as the easiest thing to do. All you have to do is show up, greet the audience, introduce the panelists, bring energy, and tie the insights you got from today's panelists to yesterday's. You don't even have to prepare because you'll be given a clipboard.

If you're at a big event, you can meet people before the show starts.

What Richard did at a web summit in Lisbon, Portugal, attended by 5000 people, was to sit down with panelists backstage. He introduced himself as the emcee and gave a little background about him (he's an entrepreneur then based in Beijing). During the conversation, he also asked about interesting things about the speakers that he could bring up (e.g. philanthropy they're supporting, a passion they're pursuing).

For him, it's a great way to connect with people.

Understanding and Working on Your Strengths

Towards the end of the podcast episode, Richard suggested checking out PrinciplesYou. It's based on the book called *Principles* by Ray Dalio, designed to help you understand – and quadruple – your strength. There's also a 30-minute video on YouTube that summarises the whole book in a high-end animation.

According to the test, he is an inspirer, entertainer, and impresario. And he uses all these skills to promote his companies as well as his personal brand, like what he did when he set up EO with me.

If you don't have the confidence to set up a whole new organisation, you can also take a group that exists somewhere else and be the host of that in your place.

For instance, Richard is currently running the Bali chapter of a blockchain networking group called Offchain. It was founded by Johnathan Hakim, with whom he started the group IandI back in the day. During that time, their organisation held events where they invited speakers and had hundred people showing up. Their attendees then included Jack Ma, who is now the richest man in China, and Charles Zhang, the founder of Chinese Internet company Sohu.

Chapter Twenty
Do You Have What it Takes to Be a TEDx Speaker?

Elaine Powell, CEO and Founder of Elaine Powell International Ltd, London, England, UK.

Elaine Powell runs a company called the MindSpeak Academy, coaching passionate innovators, entrepreneurs, and experts to grow their authority, credibility, and thought leadership. Elaine is a professional speaker, public speaking and TEDx coach, has spoken at several hundred events, trained over 30 000 people, and delivered 600 workshops. As well as running a TEDx event in London for three years.

Courtesy of Elaine Powell

Speaking on a Prestigious Stage

Many people love TED and TEDx but knowing how to navigate this world in order to get accepted to speak is not always easy. Elaine clarified, it is possible to be on one of the most prestigious stages and like a funnel: many people come into it but only a few come out the other end.

Getting onto a TED or TEDx stage is ultimately about having an idea worth spreading. Whoever is interested in speaking on TED or TEDx must spend time thinking about their idea. Is it unique? Is it innovative? Is it something that they've been living for a while? Usually, the people you'll find on the TED or TEDx stages are experts or those who have an experience that births an idea worth spreading.

Everyone can have an idea inside of them, though some ideas aren't meant to be birthed right now.

TED vs TEDx

TED is a non-profit organisation birthed in 1984 by Richard Wurman and Harry Marks. It was primarily a conference where thought leaders, especially those around Silicon Valley (because it was based in California), could share new technology and innovations. After all, TED is Technology, Entertainment, and Design.

At the time, it cost around US $4000 to attend the week-long conference. Thought leaders would speak for up to 18 minutes. In an event like this, it isn't just about the talks; it is an opportunity to network with other doers and shakers.

As time progressed, other people became interested in having that TED experience in their local community and so TEDx was born.

Think of TED like McDonald's, it's HQ and TEDx is like a franchise. The independent license holders have to follow TED's strict guileless or else their license will be revoked. TEDx events are run totally by volunteers. As a TEDx curator for three years, Elaine has also gone through the process of being a licence holder.

Unless you have an outstanding idea, you are more likely to get onto a TEDx stage rather than a TED stage, as each year they receive around 25 000 applications.

Many aspire to speak on the big TED stage, only a few get invited.

Even though most won't get onto the TED stage, Elaine noted that you can still have your talk hosted on the TED.com platform. This can happen if TED deems that your TEDx talk's content is of a high standard and they will then place it on the main website. (They also watch each TEDx talks to fact check everything before they get uploaded on YouTube.) Currently, 50 000 TED and TEDx talks have been given at 10 000 events.

How to Get onto a TEDx Stage

When you visit TED.com, you can find your local TEDx events in the menu that are happening throughout the world. This is where you can start. Though the dates are indicated, not all TEDx events organisers have a website. So you have to do a lot of research to find which among those events are actually open for speakers' applications. Some have year round rolling applications, others only open their speaker applications for a short time period.

Elaine remarked that as every TEDx talk event is independent, every application form is also very different. There are some key things that people will always ask for. Some will ask you to share your idea in a sentence or 15 words or less; then they will ask you to share your idea in 200 or 300 words. Some may ask about your credibility. Others will ask about your favourite TEDx talk. Some may also ask for a one- to two-minute video of you talking about your TEDx idea.

There's a process that you will have to go through once you submit your application for a TEDx talk. Keep in mind that every event is different and therefore may ask very different application questions. They will ask you to put your responses in writing. If not accepted, some events will let you know and some won't.

Some may also pick 20 or so of the best ideas and then come up with a shortlist. They may also get people to interview applicants.

TED also does well in providing all the guidance necessary for a TEDx curator to run an event. They give guidelines about how to pick speakers and how to work with them. They keep an eye out because, just like McDonald's, if a franchisee starts selling curry, they're going to revoke that license.

Elaine suggested that if you're not on a programme like hers to help you through the process, then apply first to your local TEDx event as it is meant to serve the community.

How to Prepare for a TEDx Talk

There are some passionate experts who are doing a lot of the work with Elaine before they've been accepted for a TEDx talk, as their game is to raise their visibility, credibility, and influence by becoming a thought leader. Overall, this gives them a better chance of not only being accepted but strategically leveraging their talk afterwards.

When you've been accepted by a TEDx event, the majority of them will give you a speaker coach. That speaker coach will work with you for three to six months ahead of the event.

There are people who are running a TEDx event for the first time; therefore, they will be on a steep learning curve. Some events won't have a speaker coach, most will. There are also those bigger events wherein you'll have a very experienced speaker curation team that will help you shift and mould your idea.

Take note that as TED and TEDx is a non-profit organisation, you and others do not get paid to speak and neither do you pay to speak.

At the MindSpeak Academy, they'd suggest you allocate 50–60 hours to craft and practice an outstanding TEDx talk. You have to give it the time and respect that it deserves.

The reason people hire coaches like Elaine is that they see a TEDx talk as a business investment; that it's a piece of intellectual property, an asset and a product that they need to make sure is the best. It's going to sit on YouTube and opportunities are going to come her client's way, which can all be leveraged.

It is a powerful vehicle to get you into the realms of thought leadership if that is your aspiration.

Tips for Your TEDx Talk

For Elaine, mindset is a primary. First, you have to believe you are good enough. You have to be internally confident that you are a thought leader and you have something credible to say. She only works with people with whom she has talked to and considers to be capable of winning with their idea.

Elaine suggests you get in touch with your why. Why are you doing this? It can be because of your passion or your heart to make a huge difference. Then, think about how are you going to make this legacy live on?

One of Elaine's taglines is that she helps people deliver presentations and TEDx talks so that they can advance the human race and transform the world. Because it's these ideas that transform people and the world.

When she's working with anyone who wants to deliver a TEDx talk, she encourages them to focus on the impact they will make when others hear this talk. You have to be really solid in why you're doing it so that when it gets tough, as it will, you will keep ongoing.

What Compelled Elaine to Be a Speaking Coach

In 2011, there were riots in the UK, which affected a lot of the big cities. Back then, Elaine was doing public speaking workshops in schools. She recounted how she kept hearing the young people say that they weren't given a voice, which is why they had to express themselves that way.

She had a history of working with young offenders and young people in public speaking. Given that, she thought running a TEDx event would give them a platform to share their voice. This is what she did in partnership with the BRIT School, which she ran for three years.

Over the past couple of years, Elaine has been a TEDx coach for one of the London TEDx events. Now, she's currently coaching people with public speaking (which is her area of expertise) and helping them to become a thought leader in their industry by delivering and leveraging outstanding TEDx talks.

Chapter Twenty One

Self-Publishing 101: The Book Broad Explains Self-Publishing Success

Julie Broad, President of Book Launchers, Las Vegas, Nevada, USA.

Julie Broad, based in Las Vegas, is an Amazon Overall #1 best-selling author and an expert in self-publishing books with over 30 000 subscribers on her YouTube account, and helps business owners get noticed through self-publishing

Courtesy of Julie Broad

The Mission of Book Launchers

Book Launchers helps you write, publish, and promote a non-fiction book. Julie started the company about four years ago after she self-published two of her books and helped real estate investors publish theirs (she was in the real estate space in Canada for quite a long time).

She has seen many people hiring the right people, such as editors and cover designers. However, once they put out the book – even if the book was decent – it wouldn't sell. And most of the time, it comes down to the fact that they weren't planning how they were going to market the book. And marketing has to get layered into the entire process.

It doesn't work to hire piecemeal unless you're an exceptional project manager who can communicate your vision and teach people at every stage.

With her company, what she really wanted is to bring that in under one roof; help busy entrepreneurs and professionals create an amazing book that people will read.

The Right Mindset

Marketing should be part of your book production process. If you're struggling with the post-production and publishing phase, it mostly comes back to what your expectations are.

Some see people out there launch into the stratosphere with their books. But what they don't realise is that it's similar to the old adage about how overnight success takes 10 years. Somebody whose book skyrockets to number one and becomes a best-seller has spent 2–10 years building an audience that was hungry for that book when it launched.

A lot of people are launching a book to build their audience, which is a different approach. It works but you can't expect to have an extraordinary launch if you have spent a few years building an audience in that space. Julie emphasised that it's about the mindset to begin with.

The Spine of Your Book

Right from day one, you also need to be crystal clear on who your audience is and what the outcome of the outcome is that you have for that audience.

As an example, Julie cited leadership books. A lot of people like to say that they have a book that's going to make their audience a better leader. The outcome there is being a better leader. But what does being a better leader mean for your specific reader?

Therefore, it's important to really know your reader intimately and dive deeper into what they want: When I become a better leader, now I'm going to have the admiration of people. Or now, I'm going to get promotions. Or now, I'm going to be able to finally get my important message out.

You have to dive deep into that outcome from the outcome, and that has to be the foundation and spine of your book. And everything in your book should hang off that spine. You don't need anything that doesn't contribute to that outcome of the outcome. You have to focus all your stories, tips, and strategies on that.

Writing for Your Reader

Many people write a book because they have something to say. On the contrary, it's actually about listening to what the people need.

For Julie, one of the biggest challenges people have is that they write a book because they've been told by others to do so. This sets them up to believe that the book should be about them. But even if you're writing a memoir and it's your story, you should take note that it's not for you – it's for your reader. You only need to tell the pieces of information that are relevant to them.

In particular, this has been a challenge for memoir writers because it's their story, and it's intimate and personal. If you write a memoir and include a little detail about your uncle, it might mean the world to you but in reality, your reader doesn't need to know it.

It can be hard to detach yourself emotionally and go straight into what your reader needs. But at every stage, if you focus back on your reader who needs the message and the outcome from the outcome that they're going to get – and what's going to happen if they don't get them – then you can drive your book forward and have a strong marketing plan in place.

You'll also make better decisions about your cover, the title of the book, and the subtitle. You're going to be less ego-driven but more service-based in the process. And from that, you can create a stronger book.

On Compilation Books

Whether you're authoring the book yourself or compiling interviews with entrepreneurs and experts (like how I did with my *The UnNoticed Entrepreneur* book), Julie pointed out that how you want to write for your audience all depends on your goals for the book. If anyone says that this is how you should do it, don't believe them. For her, there's really no wrong way. But, there are ways that will help you achieve your goals better.

What's great about compilation books is that if you have a thread that ties all of the articles, interviews, and stories together – and you have the outcome of an outcome – you'd still have a strong market.

Talking about my book, Julie lauded the concept, the clear benefit that it gives, and how the cover shows what that benefit is, which is standing out and finally getting noticed. When you're unnoticed, one of the things that you want is to be noticed. Because then, you can have more impact, and probably, make more money. It has that outcome of the outcome and with that, it's already off to a strong start.

What Should Your Book's Title Be?

Choosing the title of your book is an art and science.

What Julie always encourages people to do, first of all, is to not ask family and friends what's a good title, unless they're part of your reader base or they're professionals in the publishing space. She has seen a lot of really great books that get badly titled because their family was really hung up on one title.

Titling your book is about your reader and making sure that your book is clear for them. You don't want to be too generic. You need to be a household name before you can get away with calling your book something very generic. It's really about that hook – selling that hook and including that in your title.

Your title also has to be memorable, easy to say, and easy to spell. She brought up how she regretted titling her second book *The New Brand You*. Because when the book came out and she did a bunch of podcast interviews, 80% of the hosts called it 'The Brand New You'. They were already holding the book in front of them and yet, they were still reading it like that.

If she had tested that with people in advance, she would've discovered that for whatever reason, the brain doesn't just remember 'The New Brand

You'; it just doesn't stick. In the future, she plans to relaunch the book and package it up for authors specifically.

Drawing from what she considers an interesting experience, she underscores why it's important to title your book with something that's easy to remember, say, and spell.

For the subtitle, she advised getting keywords for Google and Amazon. Your subtitle has to sell your book to the reader and make your book discoverable for search engines.

There are brainstorming tools that can help you out. If you're stuck, you can go online and find title generators, which can be a good place to start. However, keep in mind that these generators aren't going to get you the end result. You have to get ideas and let your entire team contribute to the brainstorming process.

In Book Launchers, they have somebody who built a rating system for titles. This way, they can easily search up if a particular title is available. It also allows them to take a URL and analyse how many keywords are in it and present them in a top-10 order based on that.

Traditional vs Self-Publishing

You might think that traditional publishing is the better route because someone is going to sell the book for you. You can just show up, write your book, and they're the ones who'll sell it. However, it's actually the opposite that happens: You'll get a book deal from a traditional publisher and they'll see how you're going to sell 10 000 copies or more.

If you think that going traditional is the solution to your marketing problems, it's not. Julie mentioned that she herself got turned down for a book deal, and that's how she ended up in the self-publishing space. They said that she didn't have a platform strong enough to sell books. But she was able to gloriously prove that wrong by taking her book to the top spot on Amazon Canada.

She learned from the experience that you're still responsible for marketing, no matter what route. But for her, self-publishing was a great gift because she made way more money in her first year of selling books. She earned $86 000 in book sales, which is higher than the under-$10 000 she would've earned from the book deal. In the deal, she'd be getting about 86 cents per book sold. In self-publishing, she'd made about $6 to $7 per book. Financially speaking, there's a huge difference.

However, the bigger thing for her – especially for entrepreneurs – is intellectual property (IP). When you get a book deal, you're giving or selling that IP to the publisher. You won't have control over it. She got to learn this through the experiences of her friends.

One of them used to be in real estate and published a book through Wiley. Later on, Wiley republished it under somebody else's name because her friend was no longer in the real estate space. It was his book, words, and stories but somebody else's name went on the cover.

Another was a friend who got a production company that wanted to work with him on a television deal. He also got a book with Wiley, but Wiley wouldn't negotiate. He didn't own what was in the book or even the title so he ended up buying the book back from them in order to push through with the said deal.

Pricing Your Book

According to Julie, setting the price of your book depends on your goal.

If you care about how much money you'll make per book, you probably want to go exclusive with Amazon for the ebook because you'll make more money that way. You have to price it between $2.99 and $9.99 in order to get the most royalty from the platform.

However, if you want a wide distribution and you care more about reaching more people, then expect that you're not going to make as much money per copy of your book.

Around half of Book Launchers' clients go exclusively ebook first, then they go wide on print. The print book could be available everywhere but the ebook is only available on Amazon. This maximises their revenue and their reach for the most past.

But, ultimately, you have to choose what's more important to you. And based on that, you can price things out.

The Cost of Self-Publishing a Book

The cost of self-publishing your book is dependent on what you do and who you hire.

With Book Launchers, Julie's strategy can be considered as good or better than a traditionally published book. They have three different editors working on every book that they have, a professional cover designer, and professional interior layout people. A minimum of $10 000 will already cover the most part (some books are faster and easier to do while others are more complicated). They also do the marketing.

What you have to be particularly careful about are trade offs (e.g. quality tradeoff). When she did her books a few years ago, she spent $6000 for the editors and the cover. She did everything else, from project-managing to researching. The price varies and you can self-publish a book for a lot less than that. But you still need professionals to make your book great.

Building the Book Launchers' Brand

The foundation of your company is your personal brand. With Book Launchers, Julie started with 10 beta clients who knew her as a real estate investor.

She's previously built that reputation as somebody who does what she says she's going to do. When she said she's opening a publishing company and is in need of clients, she had those 10 people who knew her back when she's in the real estate space. They said that they wanted to write a book and signed on as one of her beta clients. That is a personal brand.

For her previous business, she also had a YouTube channel and a newsletter, and did speaking engagements. These are the things where she had built her brand on.

For her, your personal brand is who you are. In her case, she's also known as somebody who speaks the truth. She's not going to do anything shady to get you to work with her.

Her YouTube channel has also been fundamental to everything she's done, including the businesses that she's run. It's something that she enjoys; something that she considers a great way to help people who are going to work with her and people who aren't necessarily going to invest in her services. With the platform, she can serve, have fun, and grow her business.

On Managing Her YouTube Channel

As mentioned, Julie's YouTube channel has over 30 000 subscribers. For her channel's content production, she shoots eight videos and does two live streams per month. The latter is especially important for creating engagement.

When she first started on YouTube, she was struggling with getting people to comment and engage with the content. She found that by having live streams, she can do giveaways (e.g. mugs) and create a kind of community where she's essentially 'bribing' people to comment but in a more fun way. Her movement called #NoBoringBooks eventually became a whole community thing; everybody got their mugs after a while because they commented on the videos.

What also drives her content is her clients' and YouTube audience's questions. In fact, the first 10 videos that she uploaded were driven by questions that she got during her calls with clients (e.g. What's an ISBN?).

She's been writing down comments that she still doesn't have a video for and has been creating content that answers those questions. She focused on that – she wasn't watching the numbers nor worrying about it. The next thing she knew, her channel already had 2000 subscribers. The trick is that you'd better not watch it because growth can be slow if you do so.

Chapter Twenty Two
When Should You Use a Ghost Writer?

Nick Vivion, Senior Web3 Consultant of The 5th Column, Los Angeles Metropolitan Area, California, USA.

Courtesy of Nick Vivion

Ghost Works Communications' Nick Vivion has been living in a recreation vehicle or RV for about five months now. As a public relations person through and through, his story recently got featured on the BBC. But when not doing PR for himself and his RV lifestyle, he works at the forefront of the technology industry and helps new technology companies get noticed.

The Challenges

According to Nick, getting new technology companies noticed is incredibly difficult. One of the challenges is that you simultaneously have a geeky audience – those that know the technology – and another audience that knows nothing about it. Therefore, you have to be careful about what you say: The former will tear you apart if you say something wrong while the latter will require a higher level view to understand what you're talking about.

This type of dichotomy is challenging because you have to educate on one side and be very detailed on the other. If you have a basic message and you're pitching to a more technical outlet, you will look bad. On the flip side, if you delve too deep and you're going to a mainstream journalist, the news would go just right over their head. In both situations, you're missing an opportunity.

To help manage their clients' content strategy, Nick and his team use tools to implement an integrated communications approach. You can have social media content, newsletters, and blocks. With these, you can create your content and do op-eds at different publications to help different audiences. Personally, Nick loves to do thought leadership pieces because it allows him to go deeper and teach people what they need to know about his clients' brands and their expertise in their particular fields.

Building a Brand Through Content

For Nick, the first step is to cut through the buzzwords and figure out what everyone is trying to say. Once you know the core messages out there, it really comes down to setting expectations. However, he pointed out that there is no single solution. It takes a cohesive, integrated approach to build a brand. You'd need all these pieces and pillars to build your brand upon.

Most people believe that getting featured in *The New York Times* is going to transform their business. While it can happen, realistically speaking, your audience isn't going to stop what they're doing and tell everyone about a particular piece they've read in the said publication. Entrepreneurs, especially, are so passionate about what they're doing that they think everyone is going to care. Nick's core message is, no one really cares. You have to keep that in mind and start from there.

Helping Clients Working in Emerging Tech

Working with clients in emerging tech like blockchain is especially difficult because there aren't many outlets catering to it. For example, if you have five or six clients in one space, you can't constantly pitch the same story to 20 journalists. It takes a thoughtful understanding of what your clients are, where they're headed, and how your clients fit inside of those. If you can get that narrative across, it could be a powerful thing.

However, there will always be clients who'll keep wanting more. Based on his experience, Nick has had clients who'd call and ask about what his agency could do for them in that particular week. Immediately finding a larger place in the narrative can only create artificial pressure, which is not helpful for the agency. Because, sometimes, it's through pushing the little wins that can help you gain momentum and get the big one.

How can Clients Support Their PR Agency?

For entrepreneurs and businesses to support their PR agencies, Nick emphasised the need to understand that these agencies are here to help. You have to acknowledge that they're not here just to take your money and run away – they're in the same battle as you. The first step is to realise that you and your agency can do things together.

The second is to be responsive. If there's a quick inbound media opportunity, an agency would need a response within an hour. The sooner your agency gets back to the journalist (who has their own deadline), the more likely it is for you to get noticed.

Sharing your long-term plan is also helpful. And Nick is all about oversharing. He always tells his clients to give him everything and not hide or edit out anything (including the bad stuff), because editing is his job – especially as a former journalist.

For an agency to help you get to where you need to be, they have to know the truth. This is why it's essential to encourage this type of relationship.

Also, understand that, in most cases, entrepreneurs don't get rich or famous quickly. It's about investing in a long-term relationship, especially when it comes to PR. During the podcast interview, Nick shared that the more he understands about a business, the better he gets in coming up with a PR strategy. If he's writing blogs and placing op-eds for you, he'd know your voice better.

As a client, you have to take note that it's a long-term commitment. After all, building a brand takes time, patience, and a strategy.

Creating Audience-Centric Content for Clients

When working with clients, Nick starts with knowing their objectives. After understanding the bigger picture, he breaks it down into the audiences that would be involved in those objectives.

After identifying the audience, he starts creating content. He'd build all the content, PR blocks, and any other social media or external communications that need to happen. It's all about having a communication strategy for each of your audiences.

In reality, things often get complicated because most people don't want to do the audience work. But if you're doing that, you'd be like a sales team that simply sprays and prays.

The Importance of Teaming up with Other Industry Forces

One of the useful ways of introducing new technology is by participating in industry associations. To move an industry, you also might need to join forces with your competitors and participate in certain kinds of forums.

In the blockchain community, widespread adoption especially matters. Because when it comes to technology, finding these partners is key.

One of Nick's clients works with the Institute of Electrical and Electronics Engineers (IEEE), which is a global standards body. Together, his client and the organisation are building standards for blockchain and the Internet of Things (IoT). This kind of project is important because it not only gets you partners but also allows you to set your future. What's great about these associations is that they're always looking for content. And as a lot of them are paid organisations, they want to keep people happy. Your agendas are also aligned because they also want to press that narrative and want it to be successful. This is an important piece when you're trying to build your brand.

What About Going Global?

There are new tech companies, including startups, that want to do international PR. For instance, one of Nick's clients is in Canada's cryptocurrency exchange and has been recently launched in Europe.

Doing global PR is quite difficult because you're not only a small company in your hometown or home country, you're also a challenger brand in other countries. There will be different languages, preferences, and media outlets. You also have to have new relationships. In these cases, taking a geography-based strategy can help. Whether it's a country or a region, you have to localise all your approaches.

For example, if you're expanding to Europe, consider how and why is your product relevant to the French versus the Germans? Do you need to use a different and a more nuanced message or do you simply use your other message in another country?

What makes this further complicated is the need to work with a limited team. Nick noted that your expansion plans should be thoughtful and be inclusive of communications people who'd help you understand what something means – because nationalities are different from one another. Every country is different and localising your approach is the only way to success.

From a PR Agency's Point of View: Working with People with Different Roles

According to Nick, if you work in a PR agency, you're most likely to have a triple audience: The one who pays the bills, the one who hired you, and the one you deal with during day-to-day operations.

If that day-to-day person doesn't talk or report much to the Chief Executive Officer, you have to figure out what needs to be shared: How do you show that you're having an impact? You also have to understand that the internal person may have someone else that they're trying to bring in or that they simply don't want you. Therefore, you have to be really mindful – know who the actual decision-maker is and make sure that they're happy, and bring your strategy down to the PR person that you're dealing with. Keep yourself aligned with them to avoid any conflict.

Being resilient is also important because people within an organisation also change roles. You have to embed yourself in their organisation and be useful across all levels. This allows them to see you as a partner in their future success, rather than just a mere vendor who's coming in to provide a particular service.

Working with Sales Teams

One of Nick's biggest secrets is working with sales teams.

People often forget but it's the salespeople – rather than the marketing people – who know more about what's going on in their customers' lives. They understand customer problems as well as the new things that are emerging. With them, you can also get access to recordings of calls and get a good story out of a statement from a customer. And ultimately, PR is about finding good stories.

The same goes for product marketing. If you can obtain their near-term roadmap, you can have a creative feature or change a feature into more of a communication and PR strategy. This is better than just working alone or relying on a feature that was simply provided by your client. Working in tandem can help you make an actually newsworthy feature.

Sales decks and related presentations can also help you gain more insights that wouldn't typically surface in a marketing brief. Take note that sales and marketing teams have different metrics. And, ultimately, brand marketing needs to come from the problems that your client is solving and elevating them. You also have to know where the brand sits in the minds of their customers.

Having a Monthly Plan is Important

It can be tough when you're caught in between dry spells of major news announcements or when there are things that are a little more notable. This is why Nick always recommends having a monthly plan. Even if it's only creating a blog post and sharing it with journalists, or even simply reaching out to journalists. Though they won't always respond, it matters to have these little touchpoints in the journey.

This is when social media also becomes helpful. With it, you can always get your message out and participate. Nick's company, for instance, handles a lot of LinkedIn management. They go into the LinkedIn accounts of their clients' CEOs and other executives and manage them. For them, even these little comments and pieces of content can build over time. The cadence should be constant for people to be able to digest the content.

Owned vs Earned Media

Nick's preference is owned media, in the sense that it lets you control your content. When you look at venture capital firm Andreessen Horowitz (a16z), you'll find that they are also doing their own content. But while many people go directly to the consumer, he pointed out that owned media doesn't have the same cache as earned ones and doesn't build a full strategy.

However, each brand is different. If it's something wherein there's a need to educate and cover a lot of touchpoints, having a 70-30 allocation is recommended, favouring owned media. If it's a brand that is constantly releasing features and has a lot of organic growth in a buzzy industry, it's the other way around: 70-30, with earned media leading the way. Nonetheless, the choice all boils down to your personal brand preferences: Do you want to have more control over your content, or do you want to have external social proof?

As Nick's company also does search engine optimisation (SEO) for owned media, he attested how it's great being able to manage the SEO of your website content. But even with SEO, algorithms change. When it got an update in June, one of his client's sites lost 5000 monthly readers. In this sense, the owned media is not really fully owned because you're still at the mercy of someone else.

The Value of Good PR

For Nick, PR can be really valuable for the internal evolution of a company. People are too focused on external metrics, but PR agencies like his more importantly help understand brand narratives. They help coalesce your teams around a common vision and a shared messaging, which, in turn, will help you better craft the whole narrative that will go down to your sales teams. Once your sales teams know exactly where you stand, they can sell it better.

Ultimately, PR is about helping you become a better brand. It's not an external metric because, in reality, it is difficult to measure. Brands don't have metrics. You just know whether or not a brand is good. You just have that feeling if it's weak or if it's truly working.

Chapter Twenty Three
Who Can Run Amazon Ads for You?

Alex Strathdee, Owner & Founder of POD PR, San Diego, California, USA.

Writing a book out is just one part of publishing a book, but how you get it noticed is another thing. Alex Strathdee, a surfer based in sunny San Diego in California, and owner and founder of Advanced Amazon Advertising, helps authors get their books noticed in the largest bookstore on the planet, Amazon.

Courtesy of Alex Strathdee

Running Ads on Amazon

When you search on Amazon, you will see a 'Sponsored' tag underneath some products or books.

According to Alex, Amazon is a different ad platform than Facebook or Google because people are there to buy things, to begin with. When you place an advertisement on the platform, the conversation rates are often much higher. You're going to get a lot more engagement with your ads. And through Advanced Amazon Advertising, he helps authors get noticed on what is considered the largest bookstore in the world.

There are a lot of similarities between Amazon's main products page and their book category. However, the former has richer content. In the latter, what Amazon really cares about is the book's relevance to the consumers. The biggest difference between the two is the varying priority goals when it comes to placing ads for the items being sold on the platform. But there's a lot of overlap in terms of targeting and the overall maintenance of what you're targeting.

The Best Time for Advertising Your Book

I've recently published a book called *The UnNoticed Entrepreneur*. And everyone talks about how launching a book is really just the beginning – not the end. The question is, should people be marketing in advance the book that's going on Amazon?

As we currently live in a click-ready society, Alex doesn't personally recommend running an ad until the day that you actually launch your book.

If you have an extra budget, you can feel free to go for it and run it beforehand. But keep in mind that people want their stuff now. If you're running those ads on Amazon early and they go there, you might be building awareness prior to your launch but people aren't going to be buying your book out of those ads per se. So it's a lot harder to track the exact return on investment (ROI).

While it will help you build some long-tail marketing, he recommends you to get your ad up and running upon your book's launch. You can do the social media marketing in advance, but the sponsored ads for your book should be done once it's launched.

Keyword and Product Targeting on Amazon

One of the best ways to figure out what you should be targeting is to look at what Amazon is saying other people are buying.

When you look at your product page and scroll down to the bottom, you'll see that people who bought a certain item also bought this particular book. You can also do this with your competitors – you can go to their product pages and browse through the bottom part.

This is how you begin building your targeting list. You have assurance because Amazon offers real data on which items people bought together.

While geography affects targeting, what you want to be doing is to target customer search terms. This is what's called keyword targeting on Amazon. You should also do product targeting, which is targeting Amazon Standard Identification Numbers (ASINs) or the codes for ebooks and International Standard Book Numbers (ISBNs) or the codes for paperbacks. You'd want to have different campaigns running for each of these.

For customer search terms, you can get these by searching into Amazon's search bar. For example, if you type 'business books', you can see what else people have searched for. If what you're searching for is a competitive niche, he wouldn't recommend sticking to just one search term. You can backward-engineer Amazon to find your perfect target.

Alex advised thinking about customer search terms as a different kind of targeting than targeting books that are related to yours.

You have to find customer search terms that people are searching for in Amazon when finding books that are similar to yours. Then, generate a list of 200 or 300 of these keywords. For example, for *The UnNoticed Entrepreneur* book, I can use keywords such as 'building a business', 'growing a business', 'small business', and 'small business for people in their 20s'.

The key is to think of all the different possible ways that people could be searching for things on Amazon that are related to your book. This is how you can build up your keywords. The goal is to target searches that people are actually searching for.

This is different from the product targeting that you do on Amazon.

Product targeting is where you go out and find other books in your niche. To do this, look at your category. Know that not all of the books in there are going to be relevant. So place a filter to identify which books are going to be relevant. Then, build a list of the books' ASINs and ISBNs and target those.

Ads on Amazon show up differently. They don't show up on the customer search page, but on the actual product page. If you scroll down to the bottom of your product page, you will see a bunch of sponsored listings and that's where you're trying to show up with your ad placements.

The Importance of Book Codes

ASINs and ISBNs are important because these are essentially Amazon's tags for the products that you want to target.

When people go to Amazon and look for a specific book (for instance, they type in *Rich Dad Poor Dad*), what they do is click on that book on Amazon. If you targeted the book *Rich Dad Poor Dad*, which gets tens of thousands of searches a month, it's actually a chance for you to bring that reader to you because your ad will be placed on the book's product page.

The marketing rule of 7 states that you need to show up in front of your audience multiple times before you can actually get them to buy your product. A book's Amazon product page is basically just another place for you to show up along the way. And ISBNs and ASINs are your way to tell Amazon that this particular book is what you want to target.

These numbers can be found at the bottom of an Amazon product page. These are what you want to pull out and tell Amazon that you're targeting.

Targeting Books Outside Your Niche

You can also target the ones that aren't your category. For instance, Alex shared that there's a spiritual book that they're working on and it works well targeting alien books.

Sometimes, you have to think about what your reader is reading. It's not just a matter of finding out who your avatar is but also thinking about what books they might be reading.

This will help you reduce the cost of running ads. If you target an entrepreneur and you assume that that person is also interested in fitness, then, you might also be getting them once they look for fitness books and you've previously targeted fitness books (or any other books outside your main category).

Fortunately, Amazon provides data in the form of click-through rates. If you have a click-through rate that's above 0.36, then you know that it's something that's relevant. If it's below that, it's otherwise. It's fine to test these things because, in the long term, you'd want to really focus on relevance.

A lot of people make the mistake of going after category ads, which is where you just target a whole category and run automated campaigns. If you have no sales history, Amazon is just going to take your money because they don't know where your book is particularly relevant. You really have to build that yourself with the right targeting out of the gates.

Tools You can Use

About 90% of the work will take place in Excel spreadsheets. Beyond that, a lot of work takes place in something called Amazon Ads. This is Amazon's self-service portal that actually runs your ad campaigns.

Any self-published author can run these campaigns themselves. Alex and his team have worked with publishers such as New World Library and Morgan James Publishing. They've worked with these publishers' authors and they're able to set up ads accounts that are separate to themselves so that each author can run ads for their own books.

If you're traditionally-, pseudo-, or hybrid-published, then you won't have access to your own ads account. Your publisher will need to set up one for you.

However, don't think that just because you are a self-published author, you won't have access to this. Through your Kindle Direct Publishing account, you can access this portal even if you're a self-published author. You just need to click on the marketing tab and you'll find the directions to get there.

The Cost of Running Ads on Amazon

The cost-per-click on Amazon rose by about 50% over the past year.

Over the years, Alex has already worked with a lot of authors who make thousands of dollars from their books. However, he and his team don't undertake authors who are simply after that because the cost of the ads is getting too high. Who they care about are people who see the value in a reader.

This is why a lot of authors that they work with will have coaching programmes, courses, and speaking opportunities. What they're trying to do is to help build their business with their books and not necessarily make money with them.

There are top 20% among authors who make a living out of their royalties. It shows how people can still make a whole living on their books on Amazon. However, Alex encourages clients to make sure that they have other opportunities for readers to go deeper with them. If you're able to turn a reader into a $10 000-client, then your ROI on the ads that you run will be much better for you.

In this sense, the book becomes the biggest business card that you could ever have.

But how do you make a book into a sales funnel?

Alex said that it's going to depend on what your branding is – who you are as an individual. Some authors have readers who are a bit more open to more spammy stuff. For instance, if you open up the front page of a book by Pat Flynn, you'll get access to a complimentary video course where he will literally walk you through the book himself. What he's doing is collecting email addresses.

Every author is different. Alex mentioned Mike Michalowicz who has a book called *Profit First*. He's not spamming because his audiences are not interested in someone who's just going to sell. He has a much more subtle approach to his book. In his book, it says that if you implement the profit first system, he'd want to hear about it – he'd want to be your champion, so he gave his email address for you to reach out to him.

Putting on free courses, putting out your email address, and including extra resources in the book are all different ways that can further drive traffic from the book. It really depends on you and your reader. If your audience is going to be very adverse to more direct marketing, then you have to take a more subtle approach.

Enticing Non-Amazon People to Buy Your Book

When asked about talking non-Amazon people to go to Amazon to buy an author's book, Alex stated that it's all about controlling the process.

Amazon takes all their customers' email addresses, but they don't provide authors with those to help build their books. It's no different from traditional publishing. If you've sold your books at Barnes & Noble, you won't get the email address of the person who bought your book. Amazon works the same and they're intentionally the bad guy. They're just taking the place of traditional bookstores.

If you have the means and the right publishing resources, you can print on demand yourself, send traffic to your book, and even get higher royalties. But if you're someone who doesn't have those kinds of resources, then what you'd want is to publish on Amazon and let them handle all the distribution of your book. Most people in the US have Amazon. While Australia is a bit behind in sales, they're slowly getting there. In the UK, Amazon is also a big platform.

On Building Your Amazon Author Profile

For Alex, promoting your book entails taking one thing at a time. The first thing that he advises to focus on is running ads; it's going to be more important than building out your Amazon author profile through the Amazon Author Central.

Keep in mind that people are more interested in your book – they click on it, they read it, they hear about you through it.

There are people who put a lot of time into their author page. But, essentially, it's the same thing as having lots of rich content that you want to put on your product page – you spend a lot of time on it.

Though he doesn't have the data to tell which works or not, he recommends that if you have the time, feel free to build your author profile. When doing that, you have to include links to your social media and website among others. In my author page, I've included RSS feeds, which is an easy way to take your blogs and Medium articles to your author profile.

Putting himself in the shoes of the consumer, he posed the question: Have I ever clicked on an author profile on Amazon? And the answer is, no, he hasn't done it. However, he made it clear that he's not a representative of everyone else. There are other people who do visit an author's profile, though they're going to be a smaller percentage.

Personally, he said that he'd spend his time elsewhere rather than polishing his profile up. However, he didn't discount the fact that the Amazon Author Central is really useful for marketing. You can look at your rank over time among other things through it.

How Much Should You Spend Promoting Your Book?

To determine how much you need to spend to promote your book, it comes down to your goals. If your goal is to drive traffic into the backend, you're going to spend more. But $400 is usually what Alex recommends when you're starting out.

If you're an independent author and you want to take a more gradual approach, you can get away with $200 a month. However, it might take you a year to actually build up your Amazon advertising.

Clients who come to Alex want their book to be selling now. So they need to be able to aggressively test things. In the first month, they recommend a $400 starting budget. Over time, some authors tend to spend more (up to $3000). In fact, they have an author who spends $6000 a month because he has $10 000 in sales. If you have the sales to support it or if you want to accomplish your goals, it makes sense to spend more.

Often, authors simply want to break even on their ads. But, in the end, it's basically the readers who want to go further with your book that will really give you value.

Getting His Business Noticed

To get his own business noticed, Alex said that getting on podcasts is a wonderful tool. So does having your own podcast.

When people ask him how to start getting clients, he answers that they have to interview and talk to them. So if you start a podcast with a focus on your prospective client, then you can get more clients.

For instance, Alex wants to work with authors. So he started a podcast interviewing the best authors out there. This is how he got connected with Mike Michalowikz who wrote *Profit First* and Michael Watkins, the author of *The First 90 Days*.

Interviewing your ideal client is a great help. About 50% of authors that he interviews end up becoming his client. During his interviews, he doesn't talk about Amazon ads at all – he genuinely loves interviewing authors.

When promoting your business, you can't just make it spammy. You have to genuinely enjoy what you do. In his case, it's only by the end of the episode when the guest asks what he does, that he introduces he's doing Amazon ads. Then he'd be asked if the guest could hire him.

This is how he gets clients and how you can, too: Start a podcast, interview your ideal client, and get noticed by the exact person who's going to pay you for your service.

Chapter Twenty Four
What to Look For in a Virtual Events Platform?

Sonali Nair, Executive Producer & CEO of Segment Agency, Toronto, Ontario, Canada.

Courtesy of Sonali Nair

Having organised over 2000 hours of successful events, Sonali Nair is a Certified Meeting Professional who is the perfect person to talk about digital events strategy, as that's what she does for tech company Opentext.

For small and medium businesses, when it comes to events and the strategy or marketing associated with it, the primary goal is to engage with customers. Especially during the pandemic where meeting people in person can't really take place, that's where virtual or digital events come into action, as it gives businesses the opportunity to create an experience, to create a story about the brand, and to connect with customers.

For digital events, one engagement tool Sonali can think of that actually connects with the brand and the overall virtual event experience is ON24, of which she is a personal user. Apart from the fact that they recently improved their entire user interface experience, which Sonali says has made using it even better, it creates and it helps companies deliver an immersive experience for customers through the visuals and resources they have available at your disposal.

Make Sure Your Virtual Event has These Three Features

Before diving into the key functionalities of ON24, it's first important to keep in mind that everyone is receiving a lot of digital event requests. With that said, determine at the start how long the event will be, then you can pick the right engagement tools. What works for Sonali is the CTA option, wherein one can customise visually and identify the call to action for attendees as soon as they exit the event console. This lets them create their experience after they attend the event, which is really helpful since the goal is to encourage customers to take the next step.

Another key feature is the related resources that can be added within the console. Sonali suggests not making presentations PowerPoint-heavy, but rather to keep it conversational, allowing the sharing of additional resources like PDF documents or links where they can be redirected for additional information, such as customer success stories or product testimonials. This is another great way to redirect attendees to a place where they can read more about a brand or hear from people like themselves who went through the same journey and whose problem was solved by using that company's products or services.

The third key feature would be the Q&A portion which is redirected to the host or the speaker. Instead of the typical scenario where the speaker answers questions from members of the audience, in terms of on-demand virtual events where the speaker doesn't address questions live, redirecting them to one live person available is another great way to keep attendees engaged when they're watching the on-demand event, because they know that there's one person on the other side of the computer, who is reading their questions and is available to answer them.

How to Get Your Brand to Stand Out in Virtual Events

In in-person trade shows, it was easier to attract the attention of passersby who unintentionally ended up checking out your booth. Now, with everything done virtually, this is where the choice of event technology comes into the picture. Before doing so, however, first identify the objectives. What is it that you want to accomplish? In trade shows or virtual conferences where the business aims to get sponsors, what is it that sponsors or the exhibitors are looking for? Sonali's example was how Cvent launched this Virtual Attendee Hub, which gives so much power to exhibitors and helps them create an entire journey of the experience. So, companies should always take into consideration what happens when an attendee logs into the console and the virtual environment, what they see, how they can customise their experience, whether through chat, visuals, or other resources. Don't forget this important element of virtual events: identify what you want to achieve out of that experience, and then pick your technology, instead of doing this the other way around.

What it took a company to stand out in trade shows is no longer relevant in the virtual world, so to make a brand more appealing over others is a challenge, which is why their experience matters so much. Having an in-depth understanding of the target audience will help businesses anticipate their customers' expectations of the brand and determine what steps need to be taken in order to meet those expectations and create that experience. In in-person events, swag bags or raffle draws (which can be done virtually as well) drew a lot of attention, and so it's all about finding out what the attendees will connect with so businesses can gamify the entire experience and differentiate themselves from their competitors.

The Five Strategy Boards Your Business Needs According to Sonali

Sonali has these five strategy boards. When it comes to this, she says to think of it as a business plan. Without it, no company will be able to function for a very simple reason: there is no goal nor clarity on the target audience. She likens it to having a recipe without an ingredient list. The most important strategy board is brand DNA, followed by the target audience persona, then the messaging used to connect with them, the tools, strategies, and tactics to grow and market the brand, and the tools used to sustain the business. These five strategy boards go a long way, because these will bring together all the aspects and elements of a brand's organisational goals. These also help communicate the relevance of the event to attendees and keep them engaged, so they come back to you and your product.

One example she provided of a successful event she managed was for the Spelling Bee of Canada, a non-profit organisation that hosts spellathons for kids. What usually took place in person, they had to make virtual within two months. They wanted the parents and kids to be able to connect with each other, and so they used an array of event tools to market and host that spelling bee. They used YouTube Live, Twitch, and Twitter, to name a few, and they were able to attract 40 participants, 10 winners, and over 150 attendees. Those numbers were amazing to them, because everything was transformed digitally at the last minute. For her, it really comes down to how the attendees are kept engaged and made to feel that it's not just a computer screen, that they're sitting in front of, that they still have the support from the other attendees.

To sum it up, Sonali Nair shared about the impact of virtual events, how you can look at five different strategy boards and then blend these different technologies to create a truly engaging experience for all attendees, which is the key message. With that, think about the experience and the joy that you're going to be creating, rather than just your own outcomes.

PART TWO
TOOLS

Chapter One
Introduction

There are over 8000 marketing tech applications[1], but don't worry I will not list them all but introduce you to 16 which cover some of the basic content creation, measurement, and customer service functions you will want to deploy. Artificial intelligence is proving to be a boon in this sector as it is making these tools more and more powerful and across many categories. It's not just in text creation but also in social and video too that a simple web app can produce results which make even a small company look like the largest in the market.

Founders and their representatives of these technologies have come onto the podcast to explain how they are enabling entrepreneurs and enterprises with their new tools. This is a field moving quickly, all moving so quickly that I'll ask you to check the individual websites for current details and prices, and their details are in the appendices. What you will see is that technology is available which can make a great difference across the whole customer journey; from building your funnel to engaging your team, to customer service and back to the funnel. It's really liberating and empowering; and these are all easy to use.

So let's see who you can read about in the coming pages.

Joe Schultz in Sweden details Adplorer, delivering context relevant advertising across social media.

Jason Weekes from London explains how to bring good 'CARMA' to your sales funnel through proper measurement and media monitoring.

---

1   For more detailed listing see https://chiefmartec.com/2020/04/marketing-technology-landscape-2020-martech-5000/

Holland-based **Erwin Lima** is 'eating his own dog food' when using Storylab.ai.

Kate Bradley Chernis in America explains how Gary Vee uses Lately and increased engagement by 12 000%.

Dhriti Goyal from India introduces Pepper Content which has over 60 000 writers.

Fabian Langer in Dubai, UAE shows us his AI writer for a citation-rich, SEO-friendly content writing.

Jonathan Mall introduces neuroflash, software which includes 'emotion mapping algorithms'.

Matthew Stormoen in California shares how an entire company can contribute content on one social account.

Colin JG Miles in Singapore introduces the concept behind Zilliqa, and bitcoin sponsorship.

Luke Fisher in London is putting employees at the heart of organisational communication with his mo.work application.

Chase Palmieri is building Credder, the Rotten Tomatoes for news, addresses credibility in the digital space.

Michael Sieb in Germany introduces a free online text-to-video editing platform.

Vancouver-based **Michael Cheng** explains his platform for making free videos.

Michael Hoffman in Boston introduces 'Gather Voices' for collective video contributions.

Dr. Frank Buckler in Germany says, "most companies are basing their decisions for tomorrow on the invalid customer experience."

CEO **Scott Sandland**, based in California, introduces 'AI-powered empathy analysis', and his platform Cyrano.ai.

Chapter Two
Advertising: Creating Consistency Across Franchise Networks

Joe Schultz, SVP of Global Sales of Adplorer, Greater Malmö Metropolitan Area, Sweden.

Courtesy of Joe Schultz

Joe Schultz from Sweden is the Senior Vice President of Global Sales for Adplorer. Apart from their headquarters in Cologne, Germany, they also have offices in Paris, France, and Atlanta, United States. Adplorer provides an all in one solution for local, digital advertising campaigns across Google, YouTube, Bing, Facebook, Instagram, and more.

Helping Franchise Organisations and Multi-Location Businesses

A lot of Adplorer's clients are franchise organisations. They help multi-location businesses maintain the same brand voice across the different markets that their clients are working with.

They guide business owners on how to live up to their brand guidelines. This allows their customers in different places to get the same feel around their brand. They do this while providing local business owners certain freedom: They let them run lead generation the way that they see fit for their situation. This helps them focus on business areas that they consider to have great potential. It further ensures that they can adapt to local competition and the local culture.

Joe is passionate about this because it allows small local business owners to run state-of-the-art marketing campaigns. He has been in this space for a while now and he has seen several small business owners go to marketing agencies. While these agencies may be good and may be trying their best to help these business owners, the digital marketing space can be rather complex. They need to spend a lot of time learning the business and setting up campaigns before they can drive leads to their clients.

Adplorer works by helping central offices provide templated campaigns to local business owners. These local owners can also select which campaigns to use and adapt. This way, they can start generating leads more cost-efficiently.

It's a great way of allowing franchisees to embrace the franchisor's corporate identity and messaging. It also helps them keep all assets up to date.

The Case of a German E-Bike Manufacturer

Adplorer works with different businesses – from large companies such as Volkswagen down to franchises with only a handful of locations.

Joe cited e-motion technologies, a German manufacturer of electric bikes, as an example. The company has had a really good growth journey in the last few years. However, they were struggling with their local marketing as the different local owners tried to find their own way of doing it. They started competing against each other and because of it, they weren't able to see the results that they wanted to see.

When e-motion sourced the markets, they found Adplorer and started working with them. About 90% of their franchisees jumped on board, helping them continue to grow.

In this kind of work, Joe also emphasised that you have to incorporate geographical targeting into your digital campaigns. This is to make sure that there's no overlap. Because, unlike the franchisees' physical geographical boundaries, the internet doesn't have those.

If there's an overlap, the only entities that would gain are Google and Facebook. Though they're considered a great partner, you don't want to give them more money than what is necessary. Therefore, there should be no competition among your franchisees. Every pound spent by a local business owner should maximise the return of investment (ROI) of their marketing campaign.

How it All Started

Adplorer's current Chief Executive Officer (CEO) and the Chief Technology Officer (CTO) started the company as a small agency in 2008. At the time, they were selling digital advertising to small- and medium-sized businesses (SMBs).

They were passionate about helping these SMBs compete against big organisations. However, they encountered scalability problems: It wasn't easy to manage hundreds of campaigns. This prompted them to build a technology that will automate parts of the process and make them more efficient.

When Google found their technology, Adplorer got introduced to other like-minded agencies. And partly because of this, they realised that there's a lot more potential in working with other SMB agencies. It will be more beneficial if they help them through their technology rather than compete with them as agents who sell digital advertising.

This is how Adplorer morphed into a technology company. Initially, they focused on reselling their technology to the SMB space. But when they started building a self-service interface, they realised that their technology is perfect for franchises and other multi-location businesses. Now, they're growing more quickly in their multi-location side than their SMB reseller side.

But while they have two business areas, the end game for both is being able to help local business owners drive marketing with good ROI.

How Adplorer Works

With increasing demands, Adplorer now has partners in multiple locations. When helping clients, either their headquarters or one of their partner's works with a franchise store to develop assets and templated campaigns (e.g. for Google search or Facebook advertising).

Each franchisee can log into their own dashboard and select among the available templates. Then, they can adapt the template within the guidelines set by the franchisor.

The franchisor can also choose to subsidise the marketing budget and share the cost or let their franchisees pay for it themselves. However, based on experience, Joe said that it typically works better if the budget is subsidised. This way, the franchisees will be keener and more enticed to log in.

Once a franchisee chooses a template and activates a campaign, Adplorer generates and manages the campaign on an ongoing basis. They do this with the help of the Application Programming Interface (API) of Google, Facebook, and Bing among others. Whenever the franchisee logs in, they can see the exact results achieved.

Adplorer prides themselves on working closely with their clients. Additionally, if they get integrated into their client's customer relations management (CRM) systems, they'll be able to determine which part of the revenue they can directly attribute to their campaigns.

By doing that, they can automatically tweak and move the budget to the campaign elements that generate the best ROI. For instance, if they see that a certain keyword generates better value than other keywords on their search campaign, then they would steer more of the budget towards that.

For Joe, the beauty of working with a franchise system is that they get to work with very similar campaigns. Instead of simply looking at the post-click performance data for one location, they can aggregate all the data. This allows them to be quicker at responding to different search behaviours and trends, ensuring that all the different franchisees benefit from that.

If you have a new franchisee who goes online and if they haven't done any local marketing before, Adplorer can utilise their learnings to better serve that new franchisee. They call this 'Collective Intelligence Marketing'. And this very term is one of the reasons that compelled Joe to join Adplorer.

On Local Franchisees' Web Presence, Language Use

In most cases, the local franchisees that Adplorer works with have local websites of sorts. It comes in the form of a standalone landing page or a subdomain of the main website.

If you're a local consumer looking for a local business to help you with something, a local-looking page will be good for you. It will provide you with images and references that are local.

Adplorer also has clients in countries with a different language. And when working with a client in Greece, for example, they have to adapt to the Greek alphabet.

Joe shared that it's a privilege to work with a different alphabet. He's also working hard to adapt to other languages because it's important when finding clients in other parts of the world. For instance, in Arabic, everything is written and read from right to left, rather than from left to right.

While the different languages are not a big deal for their engineers, he considers it beneficial to work on those from a business development standpoint.

How Adplorer Markets Itself

According to Joe, the best marketing for them is by word of mouth. They typically see clients who bring Adplorer's technology with them when they move from one organisation to another.

They also have clients who are multi-brand franchisees. These franchisees get to utilise their technology through one of their franchisors. Then, they also introduce it to another franchisor.

This works in the kind of markets where they already have a presence. The downside, however, is that it takes a long time to build that.

In the UK, which is a new market to them, Adplorer joined the British Franchise Association (BFA). The BFA pulls together a large number of franchise systems and gives support to them. Adplorer feels welcomed to have joined it, and now they're looking forward to taking part in their annual event to be held in November 2022 in London.

Joe said he's also hopeful that they can start attending events again as the world copes from the pandemic. He noted that events have always been good for them because, in that space, you can meet, talk to, and connect with people. You get to know the problems that they've faced and how they've come up with solutions for those.

A More Proactive, Dedicated Strategy

An agency reached out to Joe on LinkedIn. As he tends to get a few of these enquiries, he didn't reply at first. After a couple of days, he received a follow-up, which was apparently done by the CEO of the agency. Because he thought it was quite good to receive that, he set up a call with him. However, he ended up talking to someone else. It turns out that the agency was using the CEO's LinkedIn profile to do outbound activities.

He learned that the agency has a whole programme that they use to qualify prospects, do outbounds, and generate calls. This is something that Adplorer is working on now.

Joe shared that it's a good strategy because if you're a business owner, you need to do something to stand out. The world is getting smaller and more crowded. And to be able to personalise and be persistent is what counts.

Also, as sales get more specialised, he said that it's important for sales and marketing people to also specialise in the areas that they are best in. According to him, it's rare to find salespeople who are really good all the way – from opening the door to making it close and working with the client afterwards. He considers himself as not much of a door opener, and this is why if you're as such, it's good to surround yourself with people who are good door openers (whether they do it via email, phone, events, or whatever avenue).

When it comes to the marketing and sales process of a business, it's important to bring in the right people and technology to help you to amplify your message across multiple markets. Today, there are tools that can help you automate outreaches in platforms (e.g. ProspectIn for LinkedIn). There's also Adplorer, which you can use if you're looking for a multi-level, franchise marketing platform.

Chapter Three
Media: Bringing Good 'CARMA' to Your Sales Funnel Through Proper Measurement and Media Monitoring

Jason Weekes, Commercial Director, CARMA International, London, UK.

Making a noise in public without measurement is going to lead to wasted money, time, and creates a reputation risk. After all, we don't start manufacturing something and never check on quality or output at any stage, so why would that work for what your company says about itself; and increasingly what others say about you.

Courtesy of Jason Weekes

Why Measure

CARMA is a client-first, expert-led, and data-driven company. These are factors that are important in relation to media monitoring, measurement, and evaluation.

They help public relations agencies, marketers, and communicators demonstrate the value of PR and the work that they're doing.

As a business grows, the owner finds it hard to know what people are thinking and saying about their business and its market. In the process, a lot of marketing, communications, and PR teams also fail to make that transition from tactical execution to strategic thinking. The problem is that their measurement is all tied in with that.

Any marketer or communicator will measure stuff in some form. At the start of that measurement journey, people will have to count stuff, but typically only count the data points that are easy to count, not necessarily the elements that matter. And the issue with 'counting stuff' is that you can end up in a sort of a perpetual cycle of not really achieving your business objectives and not thinking about how you can drive your business forward.

However, with proper analysis, you can understand your audience.

Back when you first started your business (when there were three or four of you in an office with five or six customers), doing this was very easy. But as you grow, so does your audience. They – along with the touchpoints you have with them – change. You'd also need to understand your competitors better as the competitor landscape is also changing. And there are many different touchpoints that can't necessarily be done in the ways that you've been doing it as a small, agile business.

If you want your business to grow, you need to think more strategically than just counting or doing stuff.

How the Monitoring Landscape has Changed

Nobody gets into PR to do measurement. People get into PR to do the fun stuff. But over the past years, monitoring and measurement have changed.

Back in the day, you would have had clippings from newspapers and magazines land on your desk. You would report what you've achieved for a certain month, typically in terms of volumes or reach of coverage, in an attempt to demonstrate the value of your work. But do quant-based metrics really demonstrate the value of your work? Does counting volumes or reach demonstrate success if it's the wrong audience you've communicated with, or if the messages are wrong, or if the coverage you're generating is negative in terms of sentiment?

Now, the way we measure things and the metrics that we're looking at have changed. We've moved on in terms of channels – there is digital media; there are paid channels, earned channels, and our own channels.

This change is about moving beyond just measuring the content that gets printed in newspapers. While the majority of media is still traditional media, there's a lot more going on. This is why Jason emphasised the need to think about how media and PR link in with the rest of a business' communications strategy and other touchpoints as well.

Monitoring Helps Make Future Decisions

Jason said that we're at a point where we can really do proper and expert analysis from real people; not just with automation that's talking about likes, subscribers, and shares. Today, we can dig into different metrics that allow businesses like you to understand how your content is performing.

It's not just about how much you're doing, but the value of what you're doing.

A lot of people won't have the time and money to be doing stuff that doesn't matter and doesn't generate results. So it's through integrating measurement in the planning process and thinking about the success of your campaigns (and reevaluating them) that you can do the stuff that matters.

If you're putting out content, ask yourself: Is it getting to the right people? Are the messages landing? How are we faring compared with other organisations? How are our spokespeople performing? Which people do we need to be using more and less?

Digging into these can save you a lot of effort and help you deliver what matters.

Beyond Metrics

Today, there are different digital and artificial intelligence (AI)-powered platforms being used to analyse content. While this technology is a foundational building block, you still need sociopolitical and cultural understanding when analysing the content of your campaigns. You need context and empathy.

Simply put, technology is good for data, but you need interpretation of that data to give Insights. This is why at CARMA, they have analysts on the ground who'd derive insights from those metrics.

Though media metrics tell you so many things, by looking at additional data points you can learn more about what people think or feel as a result of seeing coverage. What do people do now because of the activity that you've done?

CARMA's experts and analysts have at least 10 years of experience. They're not just salespeople trying to sell you reports, but consultants who help you prove and improve the effectiveness of your communications programmes. They understand that broader environment and apply those insights to your business to help you make organisational decisions.

Though many of CARMA's staff have worked in PR roles before getting into the wonderful world of media intelligence, they're not PR consultants; they're not there to tell you how to do your job. What they provide you with are insights on how to make better decisions.

If you have a campaign (e.g. you want to lead people into entering the top of your sales funnel), they'd show you how their PR campaign is influencing website traffic; where people do go once they get to your website.

Before, it was just about content going out into the world. Now, it's about thinking about the entire end-to-end process—from putting a piece of content out to monitoring how it affects the share price. It's about looking across the whole spectrum and producing reports for clients to help them make decisions while having that micro-focus at every single point of the process.

On Content That Directly Leads to Engagement and Traffic

Digital PR provides solid benefits – digital linking, for instance, has a huge impact on increasing search rankings.

But when it comes to content, he noted that it's always going to depend on your organisation. If your prospects are getting into the middle of the funnel (i.e. they're now aware of you, they've seen your social media updates and infographics), it's now those educational resources that would move them to the bottom of the funnel. These are content that would help them understand and provide them value more broadly. Brian Clark, the author of *Copyblogger,* has also talked about the changing nature of what we produce as PR people – from being less promotional to more informative; from sell to tell.

AMEC or Association for the Measurement and Evaluation of Communication (https://amecorg.com) is a great resource on this topic. By integrating measurement at the start of the process, you'll have your objectives in mind and those objectives will keep you on track. This all comes back to doing what matters. By deriving insights that show the value (or the lack of value) in what you're doing through an integrated framework, you can look at your activities at every step of the process and tie them back to your objectives. Ultimately, it will help you keep thinking about what you need to do better – what's working and what's not.

Adapting to Changing Trends

We now live in a weird post-COVID world where everything has changed. Everything that you thought you knew about your audience in early 2020 has changed – the way they consume their media, the days they go to work, their objectives, the way their businesses operate. It's really important to keep your research up to date (be it market research, focus groups, or doing proper evaluations of your campaigns). There really isn't a particular trend. So whatever you do, you should make sure that measurement is running through your veins. Know your audience by touching base with them and by properly researching.

A Necessity Even for SMEs

Historically, people thought that research and media monitoring are the preserve of multinational corporations with a big corporate department; it's outside the budget parameters of average small- and medium-sized enterprises (SMEs).

However, this doesn't need to be the case. In fact, CARMA has recently launched a service for SMEs.

Today, we're seeing more automation, which is fantastic. But what that misses is that client service, that consultancy that you need to set up a measurement framework. According to Jason, another way to look at things is that it's costly not to do measurements. It's detrimental not to know your audience.

If you're a PR agency and you're missing clips and you're not able to prove your value, or you're trying to monitor everything, you won't be able to cut through the noise. And there are two angles there: One, it's expensive not to do monitoring and not doing it properly. Two, it doesn't need to be expensive if you can find the right partner to work with you; a partner who can create a service that's not just out of the box but one that matches what you're trying to achieve for yourself (if you're in-house) or for your clients (if you're a third-party agency).

Depending on your measurement maturity, measurement can go from a few hundred dollars to tens of thousands of dollars a month. If you can afford to spend a few hundred dollars on Facebook advertisements every month, you can also afford to be monitoring them as well.

Measurement is an area of marketing that most business owners put off a bit. It's not the glamorous or fun part of creating something. However, it's ultimately the acid test of how well a business has done.

Chapter Four

Text: Create Better Copy Faster – Without Losing Human Creativity – With This AI Copywriting Tool

Erwin Lima, Co-Founder & Chief Storyteller, The Randstad, Netherlands.

Holland-based Erwin Lima who is a published author and storyteller is eating his own dog food, and it's a great part of the StoryLab.ai narrative, a new company he co-founded.

His company uses their Artificial Intelligence (AI) tool to help you create better stories – about your company, your brand, and the services you provide – faster so you can get noticed by the right people.

Courtesy of Erwin Lima

How Do You Start Creating Stories?

A blank piece of paper is difficult. A blank screen and a cursor are no easier.

When using their tool, Erwin said that you just have to have an idea of what you want to write about. This idea could be just the name of your company or a description of the service or product that you want to talk about. Your idea could just be two, three, or five words.

Then you need to expand on that idea and describe it with one or two more lines of text. If you go into their generator, you'll see exactly how that works.

For example, when he was trying their Google Ad Headline Generator (they also have Facebook Ad and Blog Generators), he was trying to come up with a good ad copy about how to sell the Trust gamer mouse that his son is using. He keyed in 'Trust gamer mouse' in the idea or topic box of their generator. In the description box, he said that the mouse is something that gamers need to be super accurate and quick.

When he clicked on the button that says 'Inspire me!', what came back literally surprised him. It gave him two options that were decent, but one of those was pretty good: 'Trust your movement'. As a copywriter who has a bunch of experience, it gave him goosebumps that the AI tool that they've come up with has come up with a creative headline for a gaming mouse.

A Big Help in Idea and Content Generation

For Erwin, the main thing that any AI copywriting tool can help you with is idea generation. It's the ability to start not with a blank page but with something to go off.

Many people use their tool for content idea generation. When you key in a topic that you want to write about and hit the 'Inspire me!' button, it will come up with a couple of ideas for headline generation. It translates and directs your input into usable headlines.

Their tool also has a sequence called Blog Story Generator. When you click that, it will ask you to put in a topic and give you headline ideas. Upon selecting a headline, it will give you a blog intro. Once you select that blog intro, their tool will give you an outline for the blog. This really helps you in the process of creating a blog story out of nothing. You have to simply know the topic that you want to write about.

Keeping Long-Form Content Relevant

Often, AI-produced content gets farther and farther away from what you want to say the longer it becomes.

To keep long-form content relevant, Erwin shared two things. One is that the AI engine that they use is GPT-3, which is the largest natural language processing AI in the world. It does what it does really well.

In general, he remarked that their tool comes back with copy or content that is good and on-topic. However, keep in mind that the AI itself doesn't literally understand what it's saying and what the topic is all about. It may veer off the topic a little bit – and that's where the second part comes in.

Erwin always advises anyone using any AI copywriting tool, especially theirs, to get something to help them start off. But still, there's a need to keep the human element. You have to keep your own human creativity to check and balance and make sure that what the tool is saying is what you want to be saying.

Their aim is to provide you maximum help with their AI copy generation and use it as something to create content and improve as you go along. Think of it as something that augments rather than replaces human creativity.

Analysing Content Performance

There are tools like Headline Analyser from Coschedule that allow you to evaluate a piece of content for style and engagement among others. And analysing content performance is something that Erwin and his team are working on for a handful of months now.

They've started creating the basic tools. His tech-savvy buddy is on the backend, pushing buttons, turning whatnots, and tweaking everything to get it to the point wherein they can guarantee a 95% quality assurance in what they provide.

In the back of their heads, they have a tangential roadmap of sorts that covers this analysis service. One of the directions that they're heading to is to be able to give you instant feedback on the copy that you're creating to give you an indication of how effective it can be.

Storifying Your Brand

One of the elements of my SPEAK|PR methodology is storification. But how do you pin down a story for your brand?

During the podcast episode, Erwin mentioned the hero's journey. It's a story structure that a lot of storytellers reference. Depending on how you look at it, it has 12 steps or has three to four phases. Erwin likes to layer it into three: Need, solution, result.

Need. The first step is that if you are the founder or one of the founders of a company, look at what you feel needs to be changed – what needs to be different?

Solution. The second step is the solution. What did you come up with? What's the solution to the thing that needs to be changed? It could be your value proposition or your overall promise to the world. You can also talk about a product or service that you're offering.

Result. The third one is the result. What does your solution bring to the world? How will it change the world? You can talk about your vision for the future or about how your brand sits in that future. You can talk about how it changes the initial problem that you saw; how you're trying to help your customers and your audience.

This is the most basic structure of storytelling that you can use to talk about your brand. You can then dive in and create subsections (e.g. the history of your business, your personal history as a founder, the specifics of your products or services).

From the top-level structure, you can get down into these smaller tiers, dive deeper into them, and use those to create content around every step with the help of AI tools like Storylab.ai.

Amplifying Your Content

For now, you can't use Storylab.ai to distribute your content. You can, however, use and reuse every bit of content that you get from their tool; copy your content from their editor and paste it onto whatever platform you're using.

On their tool's interface, after you've put in your topic and a small description of it, you'll be taken to an editor where you can edit the content generated and write more.

There are two buttons at the bottom of the editor. One says 'Save', allowing you to save whatever it is that you've been working on. The other button remains blank and Erwin noted that it's something that they're reserving for the future.

They plan to make it a connector to platforms, letting you automatically publish your content from their system to as many platforms as you like. He said that they're not planning to put any restrictions on how you can use the content made through their tool – you'll get it all.

On Your Content's Visuals

Today, text has increasingly become inadequate when it comes to generating enough engagement. Integrating multimedia within Storylab.ai is something that they're also thinking about, according to Erwin.

Towards the slightly longer future, they're planning the integration and easy creation of graphics off of the copy that you created through their tool. But for now, you can solely focus on your copy, texts, and words. You can create your story there and use that to go on another platform to add visuals. Because, as he reiterated, it's important to add visuals to your story.

Storylab.ai's Pricing

Storylab.ai is available through a freemium model pricing. This model gives you 25 AI runs each month. According to Erwin, this is already enough to help you get a feel about how their platform works for you and assess if the copy that they've given you is valuable.

Once you max out those 25, you can upgrade and get 250 AI runs per month at $7. To most entrepreneurs, this is something that's already worth considering.

To get Storylab.ai noticed, Erwin is creating a bunch of content. Their Chief Marketing Officer also creates a ton of content by using their content generating and editing tool and their own guidelines on how to make better copy. He does marketing and search engine optimisation (SEO) so that as many people as possible get to see their content. They're also active on social media, including Facebook, Twitter, LinkedIn, and Instagram.

Chapter Five
Text: AI-Powered Tool Increases Engagement By 12,000%

Kate Bradley Chernis, Co-Founder & CEO of Lately.AI, New York City Metropolitan Area, USA.

Courtesy of Kate Bradley

Former Sirius FM DJ Kate Bradley Chernis has launched Lately which has just delivered a 12 000% increase in content engagement for one of their clients, Gary Vaynerchuk. They are able to repurpose blogs, press releases, newsletters, white papers, video and audio transcripts, and other evergreen content into dozens of pre-hashtagged and pre-short linked social media posts.

The problem Lately is trying to solve for entrepreneurs is twofold, Kate says. The first problem is the pain point of writing and the fear of the blank page. Believe it or not, not only is that a problem for most people, but marketers especially have a problem with writing. Kate says they don't like it, so they hire consultants to do it or they push it off to other people. On average, it takes 12 minutes to write one single social media post, so that tells you what goes into it. The second problem they solve is the unlocking of the content they create. Generally, long-form content like blogs, videos, podcasts, or newsletters takes several hours to create, and then most of the time, nothing happens with it. Maybe there's one public shout out, "Check out my blog," which Kate believes is the most vapid call to action on the face of the planet, and then that's it. And so, that's what Lately magically solves.

How does Lately solve those problems? Initially, Kate did this manually when she used to own a marketing agency for Walmart, and she got them

130% ROI year over year for three years. At the time, it was just her. Now, it's automated. With a blog, a newsletter, a press release, a video, or a podcast, you can put it into Lately, connect your social channels, and then Lately analyses everything you've ever published. They study your analytics, they look at the highest engaging posts, and they create a writing model based on what they learned that your customers like, respond to, or share. They take that long-form content and examine that for that same content. They look for those magical keywords and phrases that light up your audience, and they pull quotes into social posts based on what they've found. In only 1.8 seconds, you get hundreds of pre-vetted social media posts that they believe your audience is going to want to watch, read, or listen to.

How to Effectively Repurpose Your Content Using Lately

Companies always want to know what's trending in the world, and more often than not, it's not what's trending with their own target audience. And so, they create these word clouds that show you, again, what words your audience are engaging within your own content, and they create clouds of hashtags, too. That allows you to look at what's trending with your audience on a daily basis, which is very valuable, especially before coming up with more content. One observation they've had was that in order to scale, especially for smaller businesses, you need to be everywhere all the time, and you need both quantity and quality. This is why Lately recommends two things. First of all, you don't want the AI to run on its own. You want to put your human eyeball on each of the posts Lately has generated. Take a few minutes to go through and grab around 30 that are really awesome. Crack a joke. Maybe add a different hashtag. Throw in something that showcases your personality. Kate says that's the difference of starting at third base and getting the home run or not. On its own, Lately is awesome. On their own, humans are awesome. But when you combine humans plus Lately, that scores the run, and that's the most important thing.

Another thing Kate recommends is that you schedule all, let's say, 30 or 40 you decide to use, but do them out over time, which is otherwise known as producing legacy content. Say you're publishing on Twitter for the next 10 weeks or so. What's amazing about legacy content is that because none of them are the same, you get a much higher re-share percentage, even from the same people, because people love quotables. They love to share. It's like getting to sample the food at a grocery before buying it. You're giving customers a sneak peek of what's really inside that content you have prepared.

In terms of integration with other platforms or having multiple systems to manage, Lately replaces all of them, because it is a really robust and powerful platform where you can do everything you did on those other platforms. When Kate developed this idea for Walmart back in the day and got them that 130% ROI year over year, what she started with was the organisation of the marketing. It was Walmart's corporate company and the foundation, so non-profit for profit, the IRS or the government in America, and then the National Disability Institute, United Way Worldwide, Bank of America, AT&T, and these national and global companies all had franchises, and then they also had tens of thousands of other small and medium businesses and non-profits participating. There was a good cause that everybody wanted to help market, but in order to do that, she wanted to know more about these companies. Auditing all 20 000 was a tall order, so she created an easy way to quickly understand what was happening and what their skill levels were like. She discovered that, whether it was a library down the street or the largest retailer in the world, they all had the same problems.

First, she organised everything from the calendar to what content they were pushing out and where it was going. She made sense of it, and that helped her uncover the redundancies. This lack of consistency is the key in marketing. That also helped her understand the writing problems and then unlock the content, which are all the things that have gone into Lately. Like what happens to all entrepreneurs, they had built an organisation system, because that's really the meat of what she had done, but it turns out that that's the unsexiest sell around. Nobody cares about organising, but they did care about this little feature that they had that let you push a button and create 100 social posts in 1.8 seconds. They learned to redesign and remarket the product around that, and so everything else in the background comes as a second 'Aha' moment which takes their customers aback.

Lately can Work with Text, Audio, and Video

When it comes to audio and video, Lately can use that to create content too. Kate shares that she asked one of their interns to take a podcast and transcribe it for her by hand, and then they would go through and run the transcription through Lately and push a link back to the full podcast by hand. She then asked the intern to select the best parts by hand to see if that could be done. It took a year and a half, and it never got done. Kate had all these podcasts lined up, but they were collecting dust. Eventually, some customers started asking for this to be automated, so now, they can also take podcasts and videos, and run through them through the same system. Again, you upload your content to Lately, push a button, and they automatically transcribe the whole text, which you can then use as a blog post if you want to, and they will instantly find the smartest quotes that they know your customers will want to read, hear, or watch, and they will match the video clips up with that, so you get 100 mini movie trailers to promote this podcast for the next year.

What Lately is Doing for Gary Vee

That's an amazing opportunity, since you can publish everything straight from Lately. You can download it and put it where you want to, or you can publish straight through them. The kicker is that they're working with Gary Vaynerchuk or Gary Vee, and he launched an entire Twitter channel that's fuelled 100% with Lately's AI. Currently, they are getting him a 12 000% increase in engagement, which is quite impressive. If Gary Vee wanted to grow his audience in China or Japan, Lately also works in different languages. Surprisingly enough, Kate and her team didn't know at first that this was possible, because they hadn't tested it. They only found out it worked when their customers tried doing it. Once they found out, they optimised it for a better customer experience. It's important to them, because most social media platforms don't always cater to the rest of the world. Apart from superstars like Gary Vee, Kate shares that they've also been working with SAP, Microsoft, AB InBev, but also small customers, like small business solutions. Gather Voices, which I've talked about before, is one of their customers as well. They work with mid-sized businesses like Amerifirst and Husky.

Lately enables companies to have a multilingual campaign with a central technology platform. That is a glorious solution for companies that are taking content every day and repurposing it across different regions. One of the things they did with the Walmart project was they started to write social posts in Spanish. They weren't very good at speaking Spanish, so they had to bring someone in to help them. That was almost a dozen years ago. They were just discovering that the population they were trying to reach largely was Spanish-speaking. And so, you can do that now with Lately. They don't have a translator built-in yet, but Kate says not to worry as that feature is coming soon. When it comes to integration to apps like WeChat, Weibo, and Yoku, Kate says those are also on their roadmap.

Pricing and Other Features

As Lately is a growing company, they've pulled the pricing off to be mysterious, but also because they're consistently testing it out. They have clients that are small, medium, and large. Essentially, she says the pricing starts at $300 per month with annual contracts per license. They also do a sliding scale fee, and it really depends on the qualifications of the customer. It depends on the depth of your usage and how many licenses you plan to buy. If you're going to buy 100 licenses, that price will go down and you could get a bulk deal. They're still studying their customers, and that's why Kate says it's really important to get on a call. They treat their small customers the same way they treat their very large customers, which is with lots of love. They're very nice and fun, so it's a painless 20 minutes.

Another awesome feature of Lately is that you can stack accounts upon each other. There can be a national or global account that acts as a puppeteer for all of its local franchises, and you can use the AI content to syndicate across thousands of channels. That's how they work with their larger customers. For agencies like EASTWEST PR, Kate says that one can buy a license and have multiple clients, but it'd still be a single login, so that makes it really easy to bounce between different clients without that pain of coming in and out and then keeping the logins private on the client's behalf. As far as the limits, they've made Lately very friendly, and they're always playing with it. Again, that's something they cater to per customer. She says they just changed it, so she can't rattle off what they exactly are.

One of the most important things for them over at Lately is not only does the AI require a human to make it awesome, but that marketing runs on emotion. From the five-stage SPEAK|pr methodology which is Storify, Personalise, Engage, Amplify, and Know, this is personalisation at scale, content creation, and amplification. Lately seems to be a really useful tool to help you not only come up with lots more content from one simple piece but distribute it as well.

Chapter Six
Text: What if You Don't Have Time to Write?

Dhriti Goyal, Sr. Product Marketing Manager of Pepper Content, Mumbai, India.

Pepper Content aids businesses in democratising content. Content creation is a part of the whole task of running a business. It's required but most of the time, with bandwidth crunch and having a lean marketing team, content creation becomes a little difficult and tricky. This is where they're helping.

Pepper Content enables businesses to create quality content quickly and efficiently. With the help of their large pool of writing talent allied to artificial intelligence (AI) technology, it's more like getting them together and offering them a one-stop destination for content creation.

Why Outsource Content Creation from Pepper Content

The good part about Pepper Content is that you can get any sort of content done. Be it any written content, any design, or any translation project. They're also coming up with video projects. Any infographic that you want to get created, you can get it written, designed, and translated into different languages by their content creators.

Established international platforms like Upwork and Fiverr have a good pool of creators and it's up to you to choose. However, there is no standardisation of the quality or the kind of service that they provide. With Pepper Content, creators are rated and are given a series of tests. Based on your requirement, they assign a creator to the project. Dhriti said that this is how they make sure that you get the quality of the content and the right creator for you.

As I experienced on Upwork, you put out a bid and you check what the creators have done before, but you won't necessarily get a standard metric.

There are two models in which Pepper Content is working right now. One is a self-serve model wherein you can simply sign up and do it on a per-requirement basis. The other is enterprise. If you have a bulk project, then they will assign an account manager to you. The billing also happens once – either on a monthly or quarterly basis, depending on the contract.

Ensuring Domain Expertise

One of the main challenges for people looking for writers is determining if they know the subject matter already.

To overcome this issue, Dhriti said that whenever they onboard a creator, they give a series of tests. In those tests, they evaluate them on the basis of different parameters. These include grammar and style of writing. Industry or domain expertise is also one of the aspects that they evaluate them on. When they get onboarded, their industry expertise is assigned to them so that they'll fit the requirement.

For now, the majority of their creators are from India. But they're also looking for creators from all over the world as they're expanding their operations in the US and in other Asia–Pacific countries. The primary language of their content is in English and they also translate into different languages.

Pepper Content has a network of 60 000+ creators in different fields. Talking about data, Dhriti said that they've already solved more than a hundred industry verticals. This shows that they have creators from almost all industries.

They also have their own AI content writing assistant tool called Peppertype. This is being used all over the globe, not just in India. And most of its users are creators, writers, and even content managers. This tool, which is based on GPT-3, will help you write for your specific case. So if you're writing for an Amazon product description, it will give you different content. If you're writing for social media posts, it will give you another piece of content.

How to Use Their Platform for Content Creation

To use their services, you have to sign up on a Pepper Content account. Once you sign up, you can create a project.

There's a structured or a guided brief process or flow where you can add your requirements. It asks the smallest of details that are required in a brief (e.g. tone of voice, the structure of the article). Once you submit that, you'll be given a schedule telling how many days it will take for them to finish the project. If you choose the self-serve model, you'll also be given the day when you have to make the payment. In the case of the enterprise model, you can do the payment at a later date.

Once the project comes to Pepper Content, their AI-powered recommender engine will see which creators are available and are fit for the assignment. Then, it will get assigned to the particular creator and the project will be given to them. They will then write it, design it, and submit it.

There's also a layer of quality check. They have editors who check the content. They also have their own curated content audit system, which is AI-powered. It checks the readability, grammar, and language correctness among others. Then, the project will go for submission for you, the client.

You will be notified and you can approve it, reject it, or send it for revoke. Pepper Content allows up to two or three free revokes. If in case you didn't like it at all, the project will be rejected and will be assigned to a different creator. Then, the process will start again.

If there's a bulk assignment – for example, you have a hundred blogs that need to be done in 10 days – then you will be the one to give the deadline (i.e. in how many days do you need the assignment submitted?). They will next give the project to a different set of creators. This is how you can say that with Pepper Content, you'll never miss a deadline.

How Pepper Creators Get Chosen for a Project

The creators don't have to bid to get assigned to a project. Dhriti mentioned that it's on the basis of priority. For instance, this is the preferred writer as per their recommender engine. If the writer doesn't accept it (they may have something else to do or they don't want to do it), then they will go to the next recommended writer, and so on. This is purely based on their own profile.

In Upwork or Fiverr, creators bid and have different prices. It can be per hour or per project, which is a fixed cost. When it comes to Pepper, the pricing is quite standard.

When the creator gets onboarded, there's pricing discussed or finalised with them. While creating the project, they also ask clients the level of the creator that they're looking for. Are they looking for someone on the basic level or someone experienced? Based on that, the project will be assigned to a creator; the pricing is determined according to the creator's level of expertise.

If you do a project with Pepper Content, you can start at around $20. Just like what companies face whenever they hire a freelancer, there's a minimum amount of money and words. With their company, you can start with the smallest of the amount. You also don't have to have that contract or something with them before they start the project.

Dhriti highly suggested that you check out their platform yourself and see that it's affordable for any sort of business or individual.

Content Trends

Dhriti revealed that most people come to Pepper Content for blogs, which are mostly search engine optimisation (SEO) blogs. They're getting orders of a hundred blogs that have to be completed in 10 or 15 days. They've done such scale for brands that are not just in the business-to-consumer (B2C) space but even in business-to-business (B2B).

A lot of the content requirements that they take on are website content. They also have projects about designing eBooks or white papers. And they have companies who are coming for translation into different languages.

One of the things that she found interesting is that a lot of new-age technology companies are coming to them for content. And the primary reason is that the things that they're building are very new. It's why they need more content to be created and pushed out so that people become aware. They want not experts to write it, but general writers. Because if these writers are able to understand and write it, then it will be easy for their content to be consumed by others.

These are some of the things that she found while studying data from the audits that they're getting. And, for her, it's really interesting to see how people are trying content in different ways.

On AI Writing

Peppertype, their AI writing assistant, is a really interesting tool that individuals can use – even by social managers who need small captions and all that.

There are instances when a passion project comes into the picture. It's something that's very close to the company; something that everyone is looking forward to. Then there are those regular projects wherein you just have to send an email or produce some infographic. You'll always stumble upon both of these things. The question is: How should you go about it?

For Dhriti, there are a few things that can be taken care of by Peppertype – those that need little refinement or tweaks. But sometimes, you need to go at scale and also take care of the quality. This is when you need that human intervention. A mix of both is always a good combination.

Talking about passion projects, she shared that these are projects that you sometimes want to keep with you. But as their company is trying to help businesses stay lean, they extend their creative squad team to you. You can even have your favourite freelancers working on your passion project and serve as your extended arm (Pepper Content allows enterprise clients to use the same content creator again. Whoever they're liking, whoever they see whose writing is something that resonates with them, they can favourite them. Whenever your next project comes, it will go to that particular creator).

Then, she reiterated that a mix of AI and humans is required to scale your content with automation. It's really about augmentation rather than replacement.

Pepper Content's Portal Experience

An assignment will get submitted on Pepper Content's platform. They have a so-called Pepper Editor, which is their own writing tool integrated on their platform.

Before they only had integration with Google Docs, then they switched to their own editor. The reason is to get a certain kind of liberty in terms of versioning (Keep in mind that there's a writer who writes the content, there's an editor who puts comments, then there's also the final client). In their company, there's also not only one person who's going to approve the content. There are a bunch of people – including people from branding and product teams who will look at the content from their perspective.

So the versioning – the comments and what has changed – is better in Pepper Editor.

On their portal, the creator and the client can also see the project brief on the side. They also have a video brief component. A person who's giving the brief can record a video; the creator can also access that on the side. This makes the whole information exchange easy.

I use video a lot (with Loom and Screencast-O-Matic). And I can say that these explanations done by video save a lot of time and misunderstandings.

On their platform, you can also see the stage of the project (Is it approved? Is it under 'writing' or 'editing' status?) in real-time.

With a platform like Pepper Content, you can create content of all forms at a very low cost – very flexibly and with guaranteed quality.

Chapter Seven
Text: Citation-Rich, SEO-Friendly Content Writer

Fabian Langer, Founder of AI-Writer.com, Dubai, United Arab Emirates.

Courtesy of Fabian Langer

Fabian Langer, the founder and creator of AI Writer, shares a very simple way to get noticed through content writing.

If you want to get noticed, you need to be found on Google. The answer to getting found on search engines lies in writing content that Google can find on your site so that people can find you. This is where AI Writer can help you. Fabian's app can help you create content more efficiently and search engine optimisation (SEO)-friendly.

Citations for Verification

How is AI Writer different from all of the other artificial intelligence (AI) writing tools that have been cropping up?

According to Fabian, the whole approach is a bit different because as an end-user, you will get citations. Everything that the AI is writing can be traced back to the original source.

This is the main difference. Most of the other AI writing tools just make stuff up on the fly; they pull all the knowledge from one AI, and the AI just keeps on writing. With his tool, however, you can verify everything that's written by going to the sources where the information came from. Basically, you can trust what the AI Writer is writing.

This is especially helpful if you're filing things for journalists for stories.

If you have a perfect article but you can't check what is written there, can you even use it on a website? In his opinion, you can't because you'll never know if it's true – except when you're an expert in that domain. However, usually, you don't need an AI writing tool to write for you if you're an expert, because you can just write it yourself very quickly.

You Don't Have to Start from Scratch

The only thing that you need to use AI Writer is your headline, the topic that you want to write about.

Then the AI does the same thing that you would as a human if you start writing about a topic that you're not familiar with – it goes to Google, puts in the topic in the search query, gets the sources, reads up on the topic, then creates an article.

However, the AI Writer can do it a lot more efficiently than you can. It takes the first 100 results, and it goes through all this information. Then it tries to get the essence of the topic for you.

So it tries to write a final article that has a lot of research. But it's far from perfect. What it really does well is that it gives you some kind of brainstorming – it helps you research faster so that you can write about a new topic a lot faster than if you'd go there and read all the articles yourself.

When you give the AI Writer a headline, you'll get back an article. It's a very simple process. The article that you'll get is basically a draft to help you speed up. The main selling point is that you don't have to start from scratch.

Knowing Intent and Perspective is Key

The AI Writer saves you a lot of time scrolling and becoming a subject matter expert, which is helpful, especially if you're a public relations firm or a career writer.

The question now is, how can this tool help someone get an article with a corporate view on a topic? Because when a company asks someone to write about a topic like the environment or 5G, they actually already have a perspective or attitude about it.

To be honest, Fabian noted that it's a hard thing to do. If the company has a lot of content published already, however, it can be fed to the AI as the source material. But as he mentioned, the AI writing process starts with a Google search. So if you want to write very favourably about a topic, then you need to adjust the query so it yields the right source materials and writes in the perspective that you intend to.

This is a bit like Googling; it's an art form. You need to know what the query needs to look like. Though it's a trial-and-error of sorts, you can still do it pretty fast.

Currently, the AI Writer has a new feature called Keyboard Reports, and it's still in early beta testing. This tool can go out to Google and if you type a topic on the search bar, it provides some suggestions for you so that you'll know what other people are searching in this field. Then, the tool takes all these suggestions and analyses which content is ranking for these keywords. It also evaluates how hard it will be to rank for this keyword; how much traffic does this keyword generate.

With it, you can analyse all the different subtopics in your domain and see which one you'll be able to rank in Google and how much traffic you'll be getting. By examining these, you'll know what to write about to get the most out of your time – and to get the most traffic.

On Controlling Length

In terms of helping control content length, Fabian also said that it's quite hard to get right. At the moment, his AI decides itself. For instance, if it finds a lot of information, it writes 1000 or 1500 words. That is the maximum because, after that, the quality degrades as there's not enough information from one search to write more about a topic.

If the AI decides that it didn't find enough sources to write a lot of texts, it just cuts the content short.

The AI is trained in a specific way to maximise quality. If you train it to write 1000 words and you suddenly say, "Okay, I just want 500," it wouldn't be as simple as cutting the length down. You have to train it to know what is the most important 500 words. Synthesising information is harder than you think.

To ensure quality, Fabian has trained the AI Writer on hundreds of thousands of articles in the past. And this is basically the AI part. The AI learned how to do it and it's a black box. As a developer, he gave it a lot of information about the sentences, how they're connected, and how they look.

Though he can't disclose it, there's a huge model that learned this task and it's the AI part – the black box, the magic.

On Avoiding Plagiarism

Plagiarism is a huge issue if you're using AI to write.

In America, Fabian shared that there's a so-called Fair Use law, and it states that it's fine to use about 10% of a source. Abiding by that, he stated that his AI Writer will never use more than 10% or so from a source.

But, on top of that, everything that his AI is writing is heavily rewritten. There's nothing that is just copied from anywhere. It's always written in the AI's own words. Because there's a huge focus in the research, there'll be no plagiarism in the final article.

If you take the content to a plagiarism checker like Copyscape, the tool will only find about 5% of the whole article. Additionally, the AI Writer can also trace back to any source at all. It's very heavily unique in the end.

To show his trust in what his AI writes – that it doesn't bring you any problems – Fabian shared that he is using AI-produced articles on his website.

Pricing

The AI Writer starts very cheaply. At $29 a month, you can get the first package. From that, the pricing basically goes up.

There are people who need thousands of articles every month and they can get a huge package. But the average user only pays on a monthly subscription basis.

For the $29 subscription, you get 40 articles. This fee is very cheap compared to what you spend on time to write an article yourself. It translates to less than $1 per article, plus it also saves you around 20–40% of your time.

Price point-wise, the monthly subscription is very affordable.

Producing Content in Another Language

Currently, the AI Writer is only capable of producing English content. Fabian explained that for this kind of AI to work for various languages, you have to train all the models from scratch again to get into another language.

With English, you already have a big advantage because you have a lot of data, open-source libraries, and models that you can build upon.

He also pointed out that it costs hundreds of thousands of dollars to train models from scratch. Given that the AI Writer is a one-person company, Fabian needs to focus on the biggest market by far. He also mentioned that there are research and open-source models that you can build upon in

English that aren't available in German. So it's a matter of resources and their allocation.

He shared, however, that he has a lot of customers that use translation tools like Google Translate on top of the articles from AI Writer to get them into their target language. These apps have become pretty good at translating texts.

Being a One-Man Entrepreneur

To get himself noticed as an entrepreneur, Fabian uses SEO. Most of his traffic comes from Google directly. As mentioned, he uses his own AI-written articles. He also uses keyword research. This is basically the main source of how he gets noticed by people who are looking for a solution like his.

His marketing is SEO-focused. If you want to use his AI, you can go to Google, find his AI tool, and try it yourself. He also offers an easy process of getting a trial version to see if the tool works for you.

On Making Shorter Content, Checking Grammar

Unfortunately, however, the AI Writer can't help people to make shorter posts, snippets, and headlines like what other tools such as Headline Analyzer can. He mentioned that there are a lot of other startups that use GPT-3, for instance, and they work quite well for creating short content that his technology can't offer.

The GPT-3 is an API that everybody can tap into and get their own AI writing app commenced in just a few days.

However, he mentioned that this is a solution that makes stuff up from thin air. And as he said, that's something that you can't use on your website because you can never trust it. Also, it makes a lot of stuff that's just false or incorrect. You need to fact-check your own AI, which is a lot of work.

He emphasised a really good point because there's an AI writer that I used and the grammar was so shocking that it took me longer to correct it, though it creates a huge volume very quickly.

While Fabian stated that the AI Writer has no grammar checker, it has a model that is trained to write English. It's the same thing as choosing what information to put into it; there's a huge black box and he tried his best to train it. He's still working on it all the time so it's only getting better and better. But then, in the end, it's never perfect.

He clarified that this is not the main reason to use an AI writer – to get something out that's perfect. Instead, it can help you be more effective in perfecting your writing.

In my case, I've used his tool to create the first draft of a certain piece of content and do the resource investigation. Then I added in my quotes and localised the content.

What the Future Holds for AI Writer

Fabian shared that he's always working on the models; he wants to make the app better every few months. The AI Writer is the only product that he's working on and, for him, it's the one-on-one method that can make it perfect.

Chapter Eight
Text: Predictive Text Writing Tool

Jonathan Mall, CEO & Co-Founder of neuroflash, Hamburg, Hamburg, Germany.

Courtesy of Jonathan Mall

When you understand how people think, you can write the words that make them click.

Jonathan Mall is a Doctor of Psychology. He's also the founder and Chief Executive Officer of neuroflash, an AI copywriting software that predicts how people think and feel about words. Helping copywriters to separate fresh copy from trash copy to make more cash copy. neuroflash also helps tongue-tied, pen-tied, and keyboard-restricted business owners create great copy.

What is neuroflash?

neuroflash is an artificial intelligence (AI) software that automatically generates and optimises short-form marketing text. It helps marketers find messages that resonate with their consumers.

The big difference between neuroflash and other tools is accuracy. Their unique selling proposition is that their proprietary semantic approximation and emotion mapping algorithms can predict consumer associations and feelings in 17 languages with up to 99% accuracy. This means that if you're a brand and you have a persona that you want to address, the software can ensure that your message is effectively conveyed. When you write something, people will understand what you want them to understand. You won't only get higher conversion rates, but also make people connect your brand with their lives.

198

How it Works

The software works in three steps. First, you have to provide a brief that describes the content that you want to create. It could be one or two sentences containing words that will help the machine understand who you are and what type of business you have.

Based on that, the AI will then create the text. If you want an email subject line, it will create 10–20 email subject lines. If you want a slogan, it will produce 20 slogans.

The third step is about differentiating plain text from a text that gets clicked and helps people understand your brand. It's a crucial one because it's anchored in the ability to trigger certain automatic thoughts and emotions.

In marketing, if a short-form content is highly emotional and has a clear topic that is in line with your brand values, then the message is considered effective. It allows people to understand who you are. With those few words, you can make them feel that everything is congruent, enticing them to go right into your longer form of content.

Going Beyond What Headline Analysers Do

Today, there are tools that analyse headlines. And they're all about using powerful and emotive words. However, neuroflash goes beyond those because it is very flexible when it comes to conveying certain types of associations.

If you have a topic that is highly specialised or your brand has some special features – these things have to be conveyed in order to get people to click on your headline. Additionally, your headline should also be able to convey that you're authentic.

Many businesses will say, "I'm an authentic brand, click this headline" or "This is a great product." But, in reality, nobody will click those. With neuroflash, their engine can see words such as 'true', 'original', and 'traditional', which are strongly associated with authenticity. And if these words are utilised and people get to read them, they'd get the idea that the content comes from an authentic source or brand.

Apart from the words themselves, you also have to ensure things like emotionality. If a piece of content is exciting and on-brand, it will entice people to click.

Predicting Automatic Thoughts and Emotions

neuroflash is able to predict two things: automatic thoughts and emotions. For Jonathan, emotion is relatively easier to explain because they've already done over 60 000 surveys involving 17 languages in over 20 countries. In the surveys, they asked people how they feel about a certain word. Through that, they're able to predict any other word that they didn't ask. Their algorithm has an accuracy of 93% to 99%.

In terms of associations – on how opinions are created – they reverse engineer.

Talking a bit about psychology, Jonathan mentioned how politicians and brands convince people that they are great. They do so by doing public relations, by being seen in certain situations, and by having articles and headlines written about them. These are content that connects words and their brand or product name to something positive. For instance, "This tape is super strong." They use 'strong' because people trust the strong. If you have a brand that says it's strong and they repeat that messaging over and over through marketing, people will think that it is really strong. Consumers will have that automatic thought because they've heard the message over and over again. In their brain, these two things have already gotten connected.

This is also seen in this age of COVID-19. In Germany, for example, Jonathan cited how there are a lot of headlines about the AstraZeneca vaccine and its side effects. There are also headlines about BioNTech, but there are fewer. With it, people became more reluctant to take AstraZeneca than BioNTech because the former had way more headlines associating side effects with the vaccine brand.

200

This goes to show how opinions are created. And it's the same for brands, products, and even politicians.

Knowing that what people read, hear, and consume influences them because it creates associations, neuroflash looks at texts that audiences would potentially read. Then, they extract from them the likelihood that a single word is indeed associated with another one. If you want to express authenticity or trustworthiness without saying the actual word, the software can tell you which words are closest to those terms. Implicitly and subconsciously, you give people the idea that you are being authentic and trustworthy.

In essence, it works almost like a giant thesaurus that has your goal in mind. You can simply set certain things in their engine (e.g. you want your brand to be associated with authenticity, you want to have more trendy terms for your audience), then the software will check for any generated text – and how easy it would be for people to get from that text the idea that you want to convey.

When you simply say, "Hey, trust me." It will never work because people would say, "Why should I trust this guy? His message is too straight." There's conscious thinking that goes on. However, if you tell experience – for example, you're a guy who always gives presents to his mother for her birthday – you can better gain trust because the word 'mother' is highly associated with trust. By painting that picture – and using that word – in context, you can help people understand that you are trustworthy.

Helping Your Business with Positioning

There are so-called industry leaders in different categories and sectors. For example, Hertz for automobiles, Apple for computers, and Pfizer for pharmaceutics. According to Jonathan, you can use neuroflash to identify what these leading companies are doing and help position yourself in similar ways.

When you use the software, you have to define it as a goal. Put in a brand name and the engine will look at words that are closely associated with it. For instance, if you want to be more rebellious, you can key in Adidas or Nike.

These brands speak in a certain way and they use certain words. With the help of neuroflash, you can use words that are closest to the words being used by the brand that you are trying to emulate.

Creating Channel-Specific Content

Recently, neuroflash had a client who used the same brief to create a slogan for a Facebook headline and a Google advertisement. Through the software, he was able to create both. In the sidebar, he also saw how strong each of the copy was in terms of brand values and the emotions that they're trying to trigger.

With neuroflash, you can create channel-specific content that has the appropriate length. The software can also incorporate other features like the use of emoticons, which are more prevalent on certain channels.

You can also ensure that the tonality is similar across all your channels.

Keeping the Software Updated

According to Jonathan, they also make sure that neuroflash is up-to-date. For example, if you want to be like Adidas (who, two years ago, had certain campaigns that are quite different from what they have today), their engine is updated to reflect the brand's current zeitgeist.

If the meaning of a word or the positioning of a brand changes, neuroflash can automatically and immediately show it. Despite societal changes and cultural zeitgeists, you can stay accurate about how you can show that you're a truthful and authentic brand.

However, in terms of topicality, Jonathan recommends looking at a newspaper instead. For instance, if you're talking about American athlete Simone Biles pulling out of gymnastics at the Olympics, the context is different now than what it was a month ago when she was still in the tryouts. However, the association remains that she's working hard and she's one of the best.

neuroflash uses around 12 months of text data from mass media, social media, and other platforms to create semantic approximations and understand certain topic associations. This means that the grander things are always updated. But, as Jonathan noted, if you want to know exactly what happened today, looking at a newspaper is what is recommended.

For him, if you're changing your marketing positioning every day, your strategic foresight is questionable. After all, the best communication is one that changes very slowly but has a strong core. And even though that core also changes gradually over time, the key remains in trying to be consistent. You have to be consistent and not simply transitory with whatever the latest fad is.

On Humility and Trust

One thing that Jonathan – and many people in his team who have a scientific background – values is humility.

When you make mistakes, you should disclose and correct them. This is something that neuroflash does, and it has actually surprised their clients. Today, many people are all about working with businesses that are always right and do everything perfectly. However, once that business makes a mistake, the tendency is for clients to switch to another.

This is why Jonathan and his team have always tried to be very open about that. If they made a mistake, they will be the first to say so. But they will also offer corrections. In the end, it leads to them gaining more trust. And it's trust that carries businesses forward. While these could be situations wherein a relationship is put to the test, they're also a way to show how strong and reliable that relationship is.

As neuroflash builds itself as a brand, they also make sure to carry a certain set of values forward. These include reliability, trustworthiness, authenticity – and a healthy dose of playfulness. In the end, while they're obviously dealing with money, the best content out there is one that makes people smile; one that makes people feel something. When they write newsletters and headlines on their website, they always try to incorporate these values whenever possible.

How neuroflash Attracts Leads

In terms of bringing a supply of leads to their funnel, neuroflash uses a dual path.

The first is through referrals. In the past and to this day, they've been working with different brands. And if we talk about brands like Adidas, Nivea, or Volkswagen, it's a lot about trust. Thanks to their relationships with other brands, they're able to get referrals.

When you're in the enterprise sector, the best way to grow is through those. Because it's through referrals that you get to meet another Chief Marketing Officer (CMO) and talk to them. There are other ways to get to them but those are more costly, time-consuming, and not always reliable.

For inbound leads, they use the normal mix of search engine optimisation (SEO), conferences, PR, and anything that will help them get the word out.

Currently, neuroflash can rate content in 17 languages and produce content in German and in English. Over the next months, they also plan to add more languages.

Chapter Nine
Social: Mobilise Your Whole Team With Shared Content

Matthew Stormoen, Founder & CEO of Mobibi, Santa Monica, California, USA.

Courtesy of Matthew Stormoen

Matthew Stormoen, based in Santa Monica, California, is the founder and CEO of the company called Mobibi. Mobibi is a crowdsourcing-type of content system or platform to help entrepreneurs get noticed. They use technology to empower your employees to create content, share important company news, and, more importantly, be engaged in the mission of your business.

The Whole Company as a Marketing Team

One of the challenges for many companies is that they talk about their vision and embed that onto their team; then they have a marketing manager or people – in charge of being custodians of that vision online – who are kind of being swamped with that task.

As he discussed how he helps businesses become an army or a whole marketing team of sorts, Matthew shared a little backstory.

He spent 15 years running a digital agency. He has a lot of experience working with those in charge of marketing operations within different companies. One of the biggest things that he noticed is that in content creation (whether it's a blog, a video, or a social post), it's typically relegated to one person or a small team. This leads to your content tending to take on a limited point of view.

If you look at brands, startups, and entrepreneurs on social media, they're very good at one thing or at a small niche. What happens is that after 6–12 months, the same message comes out over and over and over again. This is why you see engagements decline. The follower growth stalls because one person has a limited perspective.

The idea with Mobibi is that they want to collect content from the entire organisation – content with different points of view, with a diversity of voice. When you start publishing that kind of content, it doesn't only engage your audience with new ideas and concepts, but it also gets your entire staff thinking: How do I grow this business?

Now, instead of having three people thinking about that, you've got 25 or 50 people doing that. It's a multiplier and you can get your business an amplification army.

Controlling Content

Many companies, especially those bigger ones with shareholders, are terrified about what gets said by their people that might not be compliant in some way. And it's a common concern that Mobibi addresses right away.

Their technology has user roles and permissions. Employees who will join their programme on behalf of your company are called contributors – they're contributing content to be reviewed, approved, or rejected. Nothing from a contributor can be published without a manager hitting the approve button.

In relation to this concern, Matthew pointed out that a lot of companies make a big mistake thinking that they have to stay right in a specific brand lane; they can't deviate from a message, a concept, or a design. This is why he challenges companies to focus on their audience and target market – those who'd say if their brand is right – other than delving into political and other issues that are not to be touched.

Typically, companies get a brand manager that comes in and says, "This is our brand. This is what we're going to be." This entails dictating to hundreds of thousands of customers. Matthew asks companies to flip this convention and send a bunch of different messages and then see what resonates with the customers.

The challenge now, however, is that generating crowdsourced content under some degree of control can create a large bottleneck for whoever it is that has to approve content.

Matthew acknowledged that artificial intelligence (AI) still hasn't come to a point where it can actually understand the subtleties of content. In their platform, they do use some AI that performs text analysis. It's a tool from Amazon called Comprehend. Through it, managers can efficiently scan content, look for flags, and search for certain words.

He also pointed out that at the basic level, your company's employees, in general, should all be gearing towards promoting your business – especially if you're a startup – because their employment is at stake. What Mobibi gives is not the ability for your audience to create content but for your employees to do so.

How Mobibi Works

The starting point when using Mobibi is the so-called brand channel.

Mobibi has a mobile app. And it harks back to the old days of client-server relationships, wherein you have your server and all these nodes connected.

If you have 50 employees and you sign up for the Mobibi platform and every employee downloads the app, they'll have a content creation tool in their hand. If they see an article or if they have a thought or an idea, they can simply open the app, type that in, indicate where they'd like to send it, and then submit. That will be their contribution.

When your manager comes in and they look at the platform, they'll already see, for example, 25 ideas.

If you will be that person, you don't even have to think of 25 ideas. It'd be the best editorial job imaginable. If you're publishing even just one tweet per day (which means 365 tweets per year), a lot of creativity is already put on one person only.

Today, many companies are resorting to AI to create content. And there's a danger in the sense that it's becoming more kind of anodyne – there really isn't much personality to it because it's created by AI that's not invested in your business. With Mobibi, Matthew and company are exploring a whole new source of contribution from people who are going to have different yet relevant perspectives about the business.

Matthew then related it to how he, as an automotive enthusiast (with Audi as one of the brands that he likes), would love to hear from someone in Audi's engineering team about some advancements they made – instead of some information about a summer event that they're holding.

If you use the Mobibi platform and empower people in different units within your business, you're getting different perspectives and content. And what this does to your customers, partners, and other members of your staff is provide them with a 360-degree view of your business.

Motivating Employees to Create Content

When Matthew and company started creating Mobibi, one of the issues that they immediately thought about is how to motivate someone to create content when it's not their job to do so.

Looking back in his career, Matthew shared that there was one company that had a loyalty programme based on performance. They offer a magazine and products and you can only get the products and other gifts by using points that you get from the magazine.

Around 15–20 years later, he still remembers that programme from that organisation. With that said, he mentioned that for Mobibi, they've built a point system. They employed gamification and they have leaderboards.

There are two things that you can get from this one. One, you get the desire to compete together with your employees and get that natural camaraderie. The second is that it allows you to offer small gifts to the winner of the month or quarter.

From an organisational standpoint, you're not just getting great content to drive your demand generation, but you're also actually getting your employees excited about doing it. And this is the power of the platform: It's not just about sales and revenue. It's getting your employees engaged about your mission as a company.

Sharing Company Content

The reason they call their users contributors is, because, on the flip side of them creating content to publish on the brand channel, they can also add their personal social media. This way, the brand channel can send out content that they can also publish on their own socials.

For instance, when your company is recruiting, typically, the human resources (HR) department will create a separate campaign. The campaign would say anyone who brings a new recruit gets $500, then the HR department would provide a recruiting message.

Through Mobibi, your employees can add their personal social media accounts. Then, your brand can send them recruiting collateral that they can publish on their account (for example on their personal LinkedIn). You can also do it at scale because you could have a hundred people on your brand channel.

With this, you're not only promoting from a brand point – you're also promoting from a personal, employee level. Mobibi also has a tracking feature to help you monitor which employees published your content, where it was published, and whether the people who signed up or sent their applications came from that post.

This personal level of promotion is powerful because, today, it's the accounts of Chief Executive Officers and other individual employees that are followed and not the corporate pages. In platforms such as Twitter and LinkedIn, it's the individual network where the content is getting engagement.

This makes sense because why would people follow corporate channels if they only publish the same kind of content. They're simply promoting their products. And these are what corporations are told to advertise, as opposed to what the company's mission is or what the contextual relationship between their company and their partners, for example, is. Because, today, it's also essential to talk not just to end customers but to partners as well because the supply chain is mission-critical. There are many companies recently, in fact, who have had their supply chains disrupted.

Sticking to Brand Guidelines

Businesses have their brand guidelines. For instance, logos must appear on the left or the right. There's also an element wherein some people got a high-quality phone camera; some have a low one. Some might also be posting poor infographics and some are not.

How does Mobibi address quality, consistency, and balance?

When talking about point systems and gamification, Matthew stated that it's all about the interactions within the system. For instance, your approval rate. It could be that out of 50 ideas, only one gets approved. While it's a terrible approval rate, it'll be immediately apparent if someone among your contributors is not qualified to be doing content creation.

Matthew also emphasised how incredibly important brand guidelines are. Many of us have become a little bit cynical of our brands and just how clearly crafted the messages are – to the point that we don't even understand who the brand is anymore. This is why today, many businesses sound the same.

If you look back at breakout brands such as the Dollar Shave Club, who did weird commercial videos with bears, back then someone might have said that it's not brand-appropriate. But in five years, they were able to sell the razor company for a billion dollars to Unilever.

This goes to show that as a marketer and as a company leader, you have to break out of the box that everybody's playing in. If you want to grow your business and capitalise on a market, some risk is required. And the higher you go, the more understanding you get of that risk.

On Pricing and Promotion

Most software as a service (SaaS) companies today charge a per-user basis. According to Matthew, this poses a terrible problem because it means that you and your assistant could be paying the same cost.

The packages that they created at Mobibi range anywhere from $49 to north of $500, depending on how many contributors you want. You can have, for instance, one manager and five contributors for under $100. When asked about how they get Mobibi noticed, Matthew mentioned that the process of finding people and reaching out to them is a very manual one. And it depends on the stage of growth that you're in.

Unless you're venture capital-backed, it's very hard to be bootstrapped and profitable if you're paying for your leads. This is why he advised leveraging all the free tools and generating content upon content upon content.

The typical idea is that you can only post one tweet per day. But if you refresh your Twitter feed, you'll see how many tweets come in. There is nothing wrong with posting three tweets a day.

In fact, when clients have used Mobibi and enabled this contributor concept, they've ramped up their publishing by around 200% and it's paid off in spades. And it's because they're getting much more inbound marketing content that's going out in different channels.

Matthew and his team at Mobibi address a real problem by getting the whole team to contribute to what the company is doing and share content. This concept of content creation can raise enthusiasm and creativity from the organisation.

Chapter Ten
Social: Blockchain-Powered Hashtag Service

Colin J G Miles, Chief Commercial Officer and Co-CEO of Zilliqa, Singapore.

Colin JG Miles was at the time of the interview the Chief Commercial Officer and Co-CEO of Zilliqa, which has introduced a blockchain for a social media product called SocialPay. SocialPay provides incentives for #amplification by rewarding people with bitcoin-like currency delivered by their bitcoin wallets underpinned by blockchain. It all sounds like sci-fi but SocialPay delivered 15 million tweet engagements and cash donations for the Singapore Red Cross #CovidHeroes within 24 hours.

Courtesy of Colin J G Miles

There are two problems that Zilliqa and SocialPay are solving together: blockchain and social media. Zilliqa was born in the National University of Singapore three to four years ago as a white paper trying to solve one of the biggest problems in the blockchain, which were the bottlenecks that were created on both Bitcoin and Ethereum due to slow processing. The logic of sharding, which is splitting up transactions across multiple nodes, was put forward academically and then brought into the real world as an exploratory startup. It raised a large amount of money on a token-generating event, which funded the build out of the company and the technology to its mature state now, whereby they can bring all these applications onto the blockchain and know that it can process thousands and thousands of transactions per second.

How Zilliqa Works

Zilliqa makes use of what the blockchain does really well, which is incentivizing good behaviour. They use $ZIL, which is Zilliqa's token, to give people rewards for promoting content, branded information, or a Corporate Social Responsibility (CSR) campaign which they've done with the Red Cross to drive interactions on Twitter. They have other channels as well, but Twitter is the first point of call, because they've found a great response from it as a community. In using SocialPay and rewarding people for promoting hashtags, particularly, they've driven phenomenal engagement. Their numbers are off the charts. It's a simple process, but it works brilliantly, so they're very excited to see the impact on social media marketing.

To be able to use Zilliqa, people will need to first have a crypto wallet, of which Zilliqa has several key partners: Atomic, Trust, Moonlet, ZeroPay, or Zeeves, which is their play on the butler name, and all these wallets can receive $ZIL. If you go to the SocialPay landing page, click once, twice, three times, add your wallet and your Twitter account, as soon as you send a tweet, retweet a tweet, or click their automated templated tweet which makes it really easy, you are given, say, 30 $ZIL for doing that. In terms of the value of $ZIL, 1 ZIL is equivalent to roughly $0.02. It depends on the day, and it's been as high as $0.03 in past months. It's worth having, especially for those in Southeast Asia, as it's a really decent incentive to get $0.15 or $0.20 or even higher for promoting something. And of course, if you hold it, the value can go up, so there's no downside to it.

The key part for them is to push it out in a viral way to socially engage as many people as humanly possible. They started as a proof of concept with their own Zilliqa hashtag and their own branding campaign, and it was quite a shocking number for them. Colin says they hit as many as 45 million social media engagements in the Twitter community in a span of three days. This was measured by LunarCRUSH, which is a free service you can use to measure and monitor all of your activity. It's a brilliant company that works tirelessly to monitor the crypto community. And when they saw those numbers, they were absolutely astonished, because the cost of $ZIL to make that campaign work was in the low thousands, so they were able to get a monumental number of engagements for a really small fee. It was then that they discovered that Zilliqa was going to be a powerful tool. They applied this same method to a CSR COVID heroes campaign with the Singapore Red Cross to help drive donations to their fundraising campaign. They used the #CovidHeroes hashtag, and anyone who retweeted that got paid in $ZIL for doing so. They made a corporate donation to the Red Cross as such, and so it was a win-win for the community and for the Red Cross. That campaign got as high as 15 million engagements. It was only 24 hours, but again, it worked tremendously well numbers-wise. The third campaign they ran was completely unbelievable for them in terms of its impact on the social dominance ranking, which LunarCRUSH also provides. They hit 80% dominance on Twitter for their #ZIL3 hashtag. This was in honour of Zilliqa's third anniversary, which they celebrated with a virtual event and promoted using SocialPay, and it absolutely smashed the numbers to an incredible level.

What to Expect from Zilliqa in Their Pilot Phase

It will soon be possible for companies to use Zilliqa to promote their products and get people to come back to their website or landing page. For this, they are currently in the first phase of development. This is their proof of concept, and it has shown to be incredibly successful. What's being built now is what they call SocialPay 2.0, which should allow individual companies to self-serve. It will give businesses the ability to create their own campaigns through a web portal, issue their own hashtags, and then drive traffic under their own brand name. They believe this is the best way to scale. After that, they can go slightly more neutral. Retail outlets will be able to offer vouchers and coupons for those who wish to claim them either online or in-store where permissible, and that enables a different level of engagement, because the crypto part may still be a little bit rarefied for mass adoption, so this allows them to cover both bases. They can offer $ZIL as an incentive, or companies could offer their own loyalty points or miles, whatever it is you want to drive transactions with.

Part of their pilot phase includes working out what the attack vectors are when it comes to possibly getting hijacked. Bots were definitely an issue, which they realized early on. People were trying to create false accounts to get the number of likes needed, so they set the first number of likes at five, then they've tried to increase it up to 30 likes in line with their event on three weeks later. After that, they brought about it down again to make it slightly easier. For Colin and his team, it's something which they're finding to be an iterative process. They also reset the conditions that Twitter accounts had to be more than a month old. You couldn't create an account on the same day and claim. So, they've been toggling quite a lot to avoid bot interactions. They added Captchas on the web pages to stop bots signing up too. Clearly, they have a lot of mitigation in place to protect the process, the brand, and the spend.

Hashtags are not limited only to Twitter, so Colin says there is a long strategic pathway for the SocialPay disruptive marketing logic. They already have an integration with Telegram, which apparently is huge for crypto communities. They have a bot called Zeeves that enables Zilliqa to reward people with $ZIL if they answer quiz questions on AMAs, which are abundant in Telegram crypto communities. They have a partner as well who's integrating the reward system into Twitch, and they're working very aggressively with a company based in London to do YouTube, which to Colin is a huge potential upside for the SocialPay logic to reward people for doing good things on YouTube. For those creating content, they need a huge boost and a lot of help to get people to promote the content enough to get into the YouTube algorithms to get a sizable audience, and it's not easy if you're just starting from scratch. So, how do you get that audience? Zilliqa is one great way to do it.

Zilliqa can be Used on Any Platform Anywhere in the World

When it comes to the content or the payload itself, it could be hosted anywhere. It could be a podcast link which they would then install into a Twitter or Telegram campaign, then they would tell people to listen to this podcast, and then do an Application Programming Interface (API) integration. Specifically, they can confirm that someone did listen to the podcast and then send them maybe an even bigger reward. The interesting part is watching the shear crush that takes place when the campaign goes live and how many people try and create wallets to receive the $ZIL. Colin says 4000 wallets were created in three hours for a campaign that was run initially. Now, they have gone up to 10 000 wallets. The objective is to reach 100 000 wallets for that one campaign. So for them, the number of wallets created increased. They went from around 100 000–200 000 wallets in a very short period of time of running these campaigns. This proves that if the incentive is there, people will do it.

In terms of Zilliqa's use globally, Colin says doing the geographical analysis is really important. They looked at the campaign hits of the last campaign, and more than 50% of the activity was from the United States of America, then Europe was next, and Asia was third. They were mildly surprised by that. Within Asia, it was quite compelling, he says, because Indonesia and India were overwhelmingly involved. To Colin, it showed that they are truly universal. They could promote to any part of the world that they wanted to, and there were no restrictions. It really is a global product, a global service, and a global solution. Depending on how you wish to do the engagement, how you wish to do the consumption, where you want the target audience to come from, things can be tailored accordingly. For instance, if the payload and the return is for a high street in London, that's okay. People in California aren't going to follow through with that campaign. There's a natural filtering that's going on.

For brands or charities, it can be looked at as a CSR component. Zilliqa is happy to give back in that sense. If there is the opportunity to drive donations, that's even better. That could potentially be a sponsored campaign, whereby a lead sponsor for a global United Nations campaign could actually cover the cost. It would be something similar to the 'One Love' campaign with the re-release of Bob Marley's song for UNICEF. So, there are many ways to work with sponsors and to provide this technology to underpin a much bigger social impact.

For them, the way to get adoption is to simplify it as much as possible and not mention jargon, technology, or any of the issues which people perceive as complicated in the blockchain environment. If they say, very simply, that you can run your hashtag campaign, you can issue tokens or coupons just through this web interface in three easy clicks, and it's as easy as AdWords or Facebook campaigns, then they've got something unique. People don't have to know what's going on behind the scenes with the technology at all. They just want to see and manage the results, and this can be done in real time, which is exciting. You can see the spikes going up dramatically on your engagement, and then you can see what the end result is: performance marketing, how many people were converted to buy a product, promote a service, or increase brand impact. There are so many ways to cut it, but their goal is to make self-service simple.

N.B. Since writing this Colin has taken a role as CEO APAC @TzAPAC.

Chapter Eleven
Social: Engaging the Team With Internal Social Recognition

Luke Fisher, CEO & Co-founder of Mo.Work, Greater Guildford Area, UK.

Courtesy of Luke Fisher

Luke Fisher is the CEO and co-founder of Mo.Work, a platform for employee engagement and recognition. The brand itself is actually just two letters, 'Mo', because it stands for 'moments'. They believe moments are at the core of building relationships and enhancing the productivity of a team. They focus on how the team is motivated and how they are brought together so that they are more productive and perform better for the organisation, because employees get much more from work if they're experiencing moments and having a great time with their colleagues.

Increase staff engagement with Mo.Work

As people transition to working remotely and not going back to the office, Mo's time has come, because people are lacking energy and a sense of connection. All of those little interactions in the day-to-day work life in which people learn are lost. Conversations are now so task-orientated online that meetings are solely to discuss a certain agenda and then that's it, and so this is where Mo.Work comes in. At a practical level, it is a SaaS platform, which can be accessed on their website with a user account, on a mobile app, or integrated into a system like Slack. People can post and share experiences that matter to them, and these are the moments that are worth celebrating from one end of the employee lifecycle to the other. From the moment that you first get your job, the first day in the office, when you pass your probation, when you get promoted all the way through to when you leave, these are the things worth sharing. You can also link it to other things to elevate the moments like rewards or experiences you might want to make or improve, such as for someone delivering a significant contribution.

People in their personal lives are familiar with segmenting communication channels. In the same way that WhatsApp, Facebook, Microsoft Teams, Instagram, and other platforms serve different purposes, Mo is for those high-quality moments that are much more emotional than functional. This is what sets them apart. The functionality is consistent, along with the posting and interaction, but more than that, there's this level reserved for high quality that creates distinction. The aim is to capture the memorable experiences, not the everyday interactions.

Recognition from the company to a member of the team is gratifying, as is recognition from team member to team member, and this is another big part of the company culture that's missing when people are working from home. Most leaders of an organisation don't see everything that happens, and so there's a visibility and context gap the larger a company gets in understanding how somebody is really contributing, and that contribution, often at a leadership level, will only be visible if it's related to a performance or strategic objective or an operational plan. However, there are a million things that people do each and every day that aren't captured in terms of a value contribution in those relatively fixed measures. Those contributions when somebody makes your day helps you out, or puts in a little bit of effort to help you overcome a challenge feels good for them, but it also feels good for you and enables both of you to grow. Those interactions when working in a modern team aren't necessarily driven by the company, because it's a team of experts driven to achieve a goal in a different matrix-like structure compared to a command-and-control type of organisation.

Mo.Work: a global solution for businesses of all sizes

In terms of the kind of companies that use Mo.Work, it's not so much about how big the company is, but rather how much care there is. If you are a people-orientated leader and you know that you can't do everything, therefore, to deliver the outcomes in which you aspire to achieve, other people have to help you get there and be compensated for their contribution, then Mo.Work is perfect for you. Complexity, scale, and multiple locations add to that difficulty, and undoubtedly, the larger a company is, the less awareness there probably is, or the more countries that you operate in, the harder it is to create that sense of connection, energy, and momentum within the company along with the atmosphere, the conditions, and the culture being one in which people thrive in. But with Mo.Work, their service works well internally regardless of company size.

As companies go global and have offices or even outsource teams in different countries with different languages, Mo works as a transnational, multilingual platform thanks to third-party services that can access the codebase and do machine translation with a human check within weeks. Mo.Work uses Smartling which can translate 15 different languages. Mo.Work also helps companies with the ideation process. The key thing when it comes to employee engagement is that employees feel like they have a say. Most research talks about it in the context of employee voice, meaning these people have the opportunity to speak up in a safe space for them to share ideas and views on how to improve something through simple voting mechanisms like a thumbs up or thumbs down to give a sense of something's significance. Employees can layer on their comments and suggestions and let the idea evolve. A recent addition to their platform enables leaders to put forward specific challenges, so employees are encouraged to come up with ideas related to their challenges. It's a nice way to align top priorities and suggest improvements for the organisation.

Companies have become fairly savvy when it comes to employer brand, employee value proposition, and articulating what it means to be associated to the organisation. As much as you might design a beautifully looking web page or as much as you might pen down the perfect words that summarise what it's like, there's nothing that represents the company better than the experiences that the people share, and there's nothing better than taking content which is being shared and celebrated by the people and bringing that to life and adding more credibility to the business.

Meaning Over Money

People invest in this market for either moral improvement and investment or economic investment and economic gain. Many just want to create the environment for people to succeed and, therefore, don't seek to measure. Others aren't measuring because they're not commercially savvy enough to measure the impact, but the few that are measuring impact see results across what they call a value ladder. They'll get a level of sentiment improvement first, then see a level of reduced churn wherein staff are less likely to want to leave, and they will see improvements in employee engagement. They have countless examples of surveys conducted to measure the level of employee engagement or satisfaction, and the opportunity there is figuring out how to motivate people such that they become more productive and perform better. Proving that with confidence and good, solid attribution to productivity improvements is the challenge.

With their focus being meaning over money, they steer away from the traditional prize-type reward structure. To understand what's important to somebody comes down to individual circumstance. How something might be motivating and meaningful to one person might be very different to someone else, and they apply this to how people should be rewarded, because it should be about what matters to each one. An example of that might be the ability to take a day off or to take a course that gets that person accredited. These are means to creating a moment and elevating it with financial enablement from the company.

Their pricing plans are based on the number of people, and it's around the price of a cup of coffee (or less) per person, so it really is a low-cost solution for companies, which is why Mo.Work is used by companies like William Hill whom they work with across five countries and SHL, a company in the HR tech space, whom they work with in 25 countries around the world.

COVID has acted as a catalyst for many of the changes that were bound to happen in the workplace. Many people have been wanting to work flexibly, work for a company they care about, work for a company that makes good decisions and has values that they could stand by, and COVID has somehow let that come into fruition. The level of digital acceleration to support working from home means that all of these things have happened a lot faster than most people expected them to. This becomes the chance to help people find the right balance between productive work, collaborative work, and the level of social connection one gets from work. The opportunity depends on where these things wash out. Hopefully, this means that employees continue to work more flexibly in a way that allows them to make the best out of the work experience and see it much as a means to an opportunity rather than just a means to an end.

Chapter Twelve
Social: How to Evaluate the Credibility of Content in the Digital Space?

Chase Palmieri, CEO & Co-Founder of Credder, San Francisco Bay Area, California, USA.

When journalism moved online, it was kind of forced to chase clicks to satisfy advertising partners because that is the underlying revenue model. This is the problem that Credder is trying to solve.

Credder Chief Executive Officer (CEO) and co-founder Chase Palmieri and his team are on a mission to move the news industry from clicks to credibility. And they do so by building an open review platform for news where both journalists and the public can share their reviews.

Courtesy of Chase Palmieri

Even before the term 'fake news' became popular, they had already started their work. Personally, they're not huge fans of the term because it's not a helpful label in their opinion – anything can be called 'fake news'. However, they acknowledge that the popularisation of the term (especially during the 2016 US elections) has helped build awareness of what the company is working on.

The Rotten Tomatoes for News

The simplest way to think about Credder is to think of it as the Rotten Tomatoes for news.

When you think of Rotten Tomatoes, you know that there's a critic score and an audience score. The same thing applies to Credder. They have journalists reviewing under one category and the public under another.

You might also notice that when you buy a movie on iTunes or certain streaming platforms, you can see the Rotten Tomatoes score next to the content. This kind of licensing deal is how Credder wants to make their money, according to Chase.

Later this year, they're planning to begin licensing Credder scores for individual articles, authors, and outlets to third-party platforms including social media, search engines, web browsers, news aggregators, and programmatic advertisers – those who are trying to address content credibility on their platforms without having to make several editorial decisions.

Communicating with Different Stakeholders

When it comes to their communications, Chase shared that they have to be something different to a lot of different people.

To attract journalists to review on their platform, they need a different set of value propositions (e.g. bringing additional traffic to your site, building up your Twitter followers because your Twitter handle will be featured next to your reviews). These different types of value propositions are geared towards them; there's a different set aimed towards the regular reviewers.

Additionally, Credder's different customers to whom they're going to license to – for example, social media and search – are using ratings in varied ways. And even with two search engines, they might also be using ratings differently. Therefore, there's this need to change their language, copy, stated value propositions, and brand promises based on who they're selling to.

In the process, what Chase found to be helpful is to create different one-page brochures. They've created a one-page brochure for their ratings licensing strategy for social media, plus a separate one for news aggregators.

Because their enterprise application programming interface (API) can give different platforms access to their ratings, they need to express why it's a good fit for every particular type of platform.

On Their Corporate Identity

For Chase, it's a challenge to address their corporate identity when they've got so many servants and masters at the same time. He said that, in fact, they're making missteps.

For instance, when I mentioned their gold cheese logo, he revealed that they're actually currently addressing what they think is a branding misstep in Credder's early days. When they went with the cheese, they got a lot of people who would stop reading their name as Credder and start seeing it as cheddar instead.

Now, they're correcting it and they're going towards the more traditional way of showing good, not-so-good, and bad rating icons. They consider it important because if they're going to display their rating icons and scores on third-party platforms, they have to be simple for their readership; their branding must not overpower the readers' newsfeeds or search engines. Taking these into account, they're now aiming for a much simpler iconography.

In the beginning, Chase said that they were being 'cute' for a while with the use of the gold cheese icon. After all, what they wanted is to differentiate themselves in the media rating space. They did not want to use those simple green, yellow, and red check marks or shields. What they're eyeing is to create a timeless, loveable brand like what Rotten Tomatoes has done in the movie rating space, wherein they appear to not take themselves too seriously.

However, it has become a problem for them, because now it looks as though they're not taking themselves too seriously. And yet, they're trying to sell to third-party platforms.

They've figured this concern out with months of getting feedback from their passionate community of Credder reviewers. The reviewers were rather very upfront with them, saying that they should stick with the logo; that people said the same thing about Rotten Tomatoes in their early years and, now, they've become an iconic brand because they kind of broke the norm.

In the end, Chase thought that it became too big of an uphill battle for them to fight. Especially when they're also fighting many other uphill battles, they've decided that it's better to retreat on their initial goals there.

When asked about how he thought Rotten Tomatoes got across that divide of keeping that branding and iconography, he shared that the folks over there also have no idea how it was able to work. It's like how Craigslist is able to get away with their outdated user interface. For Chase, it's just that these early internet companies were providing a lot of value that they became the go-to spot for that. People, the consumers, just kind of learned how to deal with it and even love it.

Chase was able to tell that because Rotten Tomatoes' founder and former CEO Patrick Lee is actually their first advisor at Credder; he helped them raise their angel round of investments. And it's another reason they consider themselves as the Rotten Tomatoes for news.

Solving Credder's Distribution Challenge

Everybody should know that building a product doesn't necessarily mean that people will come and buy it. According to Chase, you have to have both sides of the issue worked out: You need to have a great product and you also need to have a product-focused approach to your distribution.

Luckily, Credder found a successful approach without spending, and that is through their search engine optimisation (SEO) strategy. Every single article, author, and outlet on Credder has a public rating page (similar to what IMDb and Rotten Tomatoes have). They've optimised all those different pages for Google search results. Because of that, they've managed to achieve 13.7% month-over-month growth last year all of which came from unpaid search traffic.

However, he pointed out that this might not work forever. If there are more media rating sites to emerge with more public rating pages, it's going to be more competitive. But as Credder is currently the only site that offers ratings for articles, authors, and outlets next to search results, they have a click-through advantage. If a star rating is found next to a search result, it becomes more attention-grabbing and clickable.

With their SEO strategy, which Chase considers an absolute flywheel, they get people to click on the pages. Then, a certain percentage of them leave their reviews. They index those reviews onto the rating pages to make them even stronger for Google to index in their search results. And this virtuous cycle continues.

Apart from their SEO strategy, they're also implementing a new feature wherein each time you leave a review, you can share that review on Twitter. Credder makes sure that every time you write a review, you can call out that journalist or outlet directly on Twitter. This is made possible by their database of the Twitter handles of journalists who are on their platform.

In my SPEAK|PR program, this falls under the amplification model.

On Upsetting Journalists

In the podcast, Chase shared that Credder will definitely upset some folks in journalism – like how Yelp upsets some restaurant owners and Rotten Tomatoes upsets some movie and production studios.

Their team doesn't expect to make friends with everyone. What they're trying to do is to create that level playing field where even a small, independent outlet can get good traffic if they have created a great piece of work (e.g. investigative reporting). They don't have to be on a level like *The New York Times* to capture that traffic-based attention.

In terms of mitigating the risks of gamifying ratings or reviews, Credder has a lot of internal measures. First off, they have a specific review process. It's not a simple one- to five-star rating; you have to label a specific reason for your review and add an explanation about it.

This then gets upvoted by the rest of the community as helpful or not helpful. This, in turn, creates the reviewer rating, allowing Credder reviewers to also be held accountable and have their own scores appear next to them. It's similar to how the Apple Support Communities works: You can give ratings for people who are giving the support, which has become an amazing kind of social validation.

Chase considers these measures as a built-in immunity system that they have to keep improving. At the very least, it already allows for the best review on any piece of content to bubble up to the top of the page.

Investments on Credder

Credder has raised a total of $495 000 worth of investment to date. Currently, they're in the middle of a pre-seed round where they aim to raise up to $600 000.

Chase regards themselves lucky for having Rotten Tomatoes' Patrick as their first advisor. Patrick was able to make key introductions to some heavy-hitting Silicon Valley angels, allowing Credder to raise their angel round. They've also met certain milestones and product rollouts, which led to their bridge round.

For their company, it's also been a matter of convincing the investor community that there's a need for the solution that they're offering; that the problem is getting bigger and, sooner or later, social media platforms, search engines, web browsers, and news aggregators are going to need to address that problem. This issue is already kind of playing out given the increasing pressure from users, the media – and now, regulators – to address content credibility issues.

There are other content credibility solutions out there, but Credder convinces investors that the one that will have the most staying power, most brand loyalty, and most adoptions by the said third-party platforms in the future will be the one that can create decentralised reputation – not just mere media ratings as decided by some small, select insider groups.

Credder argues that there's a need to create Yelp and Rotten Tomatoes for news consumers, and that a brand like that could actually have an important seat in the media landscape.

Media Relations for Credder

Chase has a background as a media watchdog for Project Censored, which is a non-profit partisan watchdog founded in 1976 in Sonoma County in California. He also continues his basic radio and podcasting skills through The Credder Podcast.

The podcast has been, for him, an interesting way of bringing in journalists and featuring great pieces of reporting that they did. Through this outlet, he also gets to invite key decision-makers of certain platforms (e.g. social media or web browser) to talk about how they're addressing content credibility issues.

At Credder, folks are very open and easy to get in touch with. They're also trying to have conversations with different stakeholders and assure them that they're not here to pick on anyone; that they and the stakeholders need to agree that there's a problem: Trust on online media is at a record low. The US, which is Credder's main market, has the highest rate of distrust of online media out of any country in the world. About only 29% of Americans say that they trust what they're seeing on online media.

The problem is big and it is hurting and will continue to hurt publishers' bottom line. Through Credder, they can access a communication tool that will, at least, allow them to understand how and why they're gaining or losing a reader's trust.

Talking about adjacent marketing and partnering with other industry associations, Chase said that what they prefer doing is working directly with publishers through their Partner Programme. Through this partnership, the Credder review process can be placed at the bottom of the articles on the publishers' own websites.

This offers publishers a great way to capture feedback and scores from their most loyal readership. It's also a way of telling that they, as publishers, are willing to be held accountable; that they want feedback at a time when a lot of people are getting rid of comments sections and moving in the direction of not understanding why they're gaining or losing trust.

Besides partnering with publishers, Cheddar is also working closely with social media platforms and social engines.

Also, instead of venturing into convention circuits, they use The Credder Podcast to target specific high-profile names in the industry (for instance, they've already featured Craig Newmark and Jay Rosen as their guests). They're diving into an hour-long discussion also as a way of introducing themselves.

Raising Brand Awareness

How does Credder get consumers to look at their logo the same way that consumers do on logos like Rotten Tomatoes and Trustpilot?

According to Chase, addressing this is the focus of their rebranding. Before somebody reads an article, they want people to check the Credder rating first, or check if the article has even been rated on the platform. They want readers to ask themselves the same way that somebody checks Rotten Tomatoes or Yelp ratings before watching a movie or dining in a restaurant.

This long-term challenge comes with a lot more brand awareness and SEO. But if they're going to achieve that status, it will be helpful for news consumers to save a lot of time.

The challenge, however, is that with movies, consumers have around a two-hour commitment. Therefore, they will have more incentive to check a score. If it's about restaurants, there's about an hour-and-a-half to two-hour commitment, plus the cost of paying for the meals and the risk of a bad taste. For that, there's a little bit more reason to check a rating first.

When it comes to news, there are 20- to 30-minute articles about great investigative reporting that people don't just read anymore because they're afraid to commit to a long article and end up with just a piece of clickbait, press release, or false advertising. The challenge for Credder is to show readers that seeing what others say about a particular article will help reduce the risk of diving into bad long-form content. It's about rebuilding the very concept of editorial integrity into the media.

Editorial integrity is an important part of what is being done in the public relations world. And if you're going to read something in the future, look out for that little golden piece of cheese because it will give you the credibility rating of a particular article.

Chapter Thirteen

Video: This Free Text-Based Video Editing Application Developed by Four German Students is Worth Considering for Your Content Production

Michael Sieb, CMO & Founder of Type Studio, Berlin, Germany.

"The vision at Type Studio is clearly to democratise the whole video production. The way how video is produced and really empowers people to actually create great content by their own even though they don't have much knowledge or like a huge editing background."

Courtesy of Michael Sieb

So says Michael Sieb, one of the four German students who developed Type Studio, an online audio and video transcription-based editing service with over 20 000 subscribers.

How Type Studio Works

Today's advanced video editing software lacks functionality. Michael and his co-founders started the project because they themselves have struggled to create video content. With their app, they lower the entry barrier so that everyone can create great, outstanding content.

Though they're still university students, they're mostly concentrated on building and enhancing Type Studio, which now has 20 000 users.

Type Studio supports both video and audio files. To use it, you have to sign up, make an account, and drag-and-drop your file into their editor. The file gets automatically uploaded and transcribed, which then makes the text editable. It uses Google's speech-to-text transcription application programming interface (API) to help them transcribe spoken words into text.

If you have bloopers and mistakes in your recordings, you can simply highlight the text and click on the delete button. The deleted words in the text will be automatically removed from your audio or video file. You can also add subtitles or translate your transcript into different languages.

Currently, Type Studio is only capable of editing recordings with one person speaking. However, Michael shared that they have a huge roadmap and they intend to implement new features soon. One of these is allowing users to edit files with two speakers. They consider this feature valuable because the direction now is that podcasts and many other recordings have more than one speaker.

Simple Tweaks Matter

Type Studio caters to content creators from all kinds of industries. It's a horizontal business model rather than targeting a specific niche.

In general, what their users have in common is that they're creating content-focused videos and audio podcasts. Mostly, they have people from the marketing space, such as influencers, publishing their content on different social media channels like YouTube.

According to Michael, simple tweaks can significantly leverage the quality of your output. For instance, when you add subtitles to your video, it can perform much better because most people on social media watch content without turning on the audio. If you add a nice frame and a proper headline, it can get attention from the people who are scrolling through their newsfeed.

Type Studio allows users to do that. It's not just about cutting text and cropping video files. You can also put images and headlines and any other element that you'd want on the canvas. You can also change the background colour. Their video editor enables you to really interact with and design your video.

Creating Multiple Content

Another feature that Type Studio offers is to help users easily repurpose a single video. You can create more content from a video and use it for different social media channels that have different requirements (e.g. aspect ratio).

With their application, you can upload one video, duplicate it, and create multiple versions out of it. You can create snippets that you want to post and change their aspect ratios accordingly.

While they're still working on users being able to share Type Studio's output directly to social media after editing, they have already implemented some integration features. For instance, if you want to upload a video for editing, you can simply drop a YouTube, Dropbox, or Google Drive link.

After rendering your output, you also get access to a sharing page, which lets you embed the video to your website or your blog. It also features an interactive transcript below the media file. With that, you can simply share links – nobody has to actually download the file.

Apart from the social media-sharing feature, they're also planning to launch a feature that enables you to schedule your videos for posting on your channels.

What Michael and company want is to build the whole process and make everything doable online. This prevents you from having to deal with downloading and uploading files.

Trends and Observations

In 12 months, Type Studio has gone from zero to 20 000 users. Most of their subscribers are influencers and subject matter experts in their fields who are publishing content.

During the pandemic, Michael observed how the whole education sector has switched into the digital world. This required teachers to do online quizzes and create more online video content. These users are happy to have a lean and easy-to-use video editor that gives them the power to create the content that they need.

Most of Type Studio's users come from Europe. In the beginning, it only supported the English language. This has expanded to almost 30 different languages. Now, there are people around the world with all kinds of languages that use Type Studio. However, their main target group would be those in the United States.

As for trends on content created on Type Studio, Michael observed that many are creating talking-head videos wherein you have a certain personality. Now, many brands are starting to have people in their companies create this type of content – as opposed to simply using stock images, footage, or animated things. They want to have that personal feel.

To get noticed, Michael shared that there's a need to post content more frequently. And Type Studio, as mentioned, can help with that because you can easily create multiple snippets or different kinds of content from one video. You don't have to hire a big agency to create all that content for you.

Type Studio can also be used for internal presentations. For instance, it could be used to trim Zoom recordings of your team and share them with the whole company. Rather than sending PowerPoint presentations, an edited video of you presenting that – alongside a document – can be more remarkably successful.

Democratising Content Creation

Type Studio uses a subscription model. It starts with a free plan where you can upload up to 10 minutes of audio or video per month. It has all the major functionalities except the translation feature.

They also offer a basic plan, priced at $12 per month; a pro plan at $28 per month. Discounts are available if you're subscribing for an entire year.

They have also already released an enterprise plan at $45 per month. It targets companies who want to use the application with their entire team.

Two weeks after they rolled out the enterprise plan, some companies have already reached out to them. Michael considers it a big help, especially when they're able to onboard a company with 20 licensees. With less work required, it can bring the same amount of money as getting 20 single creators.

However, Michael still emphasised how they built Type Studio for business-to-consumer (B2C) users. They're focusing on the end-consumer level because it allows them to get user feedback directly. With that, they can implement features that people want to see on their app. This is why they plan to stick with that kind of customer: They like to interact with their users rather than simply developing a video editor.

With this technology, Michael and his co-founders are helping entrepreneurs become content creators themselves. And it's delightful to see how technology can democratise content creation.

Chapter Fourteen
Video: The PowerPoint of Online Video Creation

Michael Cheng, CEO & Co-founder of Lumen5, Vancouver, British Columbia, Canada.

Vancouver-based Michael Cheng is the Chief Executive Officer (CEO) and one of the three founders of Lumen5, a video maker built to supercharge your content strategy. In this article, he explained how their video creation platform helps entrepreneurs get noticed by offering 'the PowerPoint of video creation'.

Courtesy of Michael Cheng

Lumen5: The PowerPoint for Videos

Video is one of those things that everyone wants to get into right now. Everyone wants to watch videos, but not everyone knows how to create them.

For many people, video production is very daunting; it seems like a complicated thing. Lumen5 is an online platform that Michael considers as the PowerPoint for videos. In PowerPoint, you can easily make a presentation, slide by slide, through point-and-click and drag-and-drop actions. He and his co-founders created Lumen5 as the video counterpart, so that anyone – even those without experience – can create engaging video content for their brand.

Lumen5's Beginnings

A lot of the best origin stories involve co-founders coming together from diverse backgrounds.

In Lumen5's case, co-founders Chris Bowal and Nigel Gutzmann both have a software background. They come from the world of engineering and building digital products. On the other hand, Michael has a background in multimedia and interactive design. He studied things such as video design, video editing, video production, and 3D modelling among other complicated creative tools.

He cited Adobe as the brand that has largely defined that software industry for the past 10–15 years. Many of their tools, including Adobe After Effects and Adobe Premiere, were made for video professionals. Together with Chris and Nigel, he saw that there was something missing. What about everyone else?

This wasn't really relevant until around five years ago when video content really took off. Today, there are different formats for this content. For instance, there's Instagram Stories wherein you can post a video that disappears after 24 hours. In this regard, it no longer makes sense to go out there and hire an agency to produce something that goes away after a day.

How Lumen5 Works

Lumen5 only requires very basic skills. If you know how to use Microsoft Word or PowerPoint (which entails point-and-click and typing text actions), that's all you need for you to be able to use the video creation platform.

Michael shared that Lumen5 users who are busy marketers or entrepreneurs love to use their nifty feature that turns blog posts into videos. They can simply copy and paste a link from their blog and then drop it straight into the Lumen5 system. Their system lays out the storyboard for them. They can pick and choose sentences directly within the platform.

Lumen5 also offers stock media (they have partnered with Shutterstock and Storyblocks). This way, users won't have to go out and capture some footage. They won't need a camera or a microphone. They simply have to search for a topic (e.g. coffee beans, cups of coffee, and baristas if the video is about coffee), then drag and drop the stock videos. This already takes care of the visual component of the final video output.

Generally, the average user can complete a video that they're satisfied with within 10 minutes. Meanwhile, first-time users can get it done in under 20 minutes.

If you use their platform, you'll get a bit faster with every video that you create. Over time, you can become a power user and familiarise yourself with all the different tools that Lumen5 has to offer.

Keeping Your Lumen5-Produced Content On-Brand

According to Michael, Lumen5 does a lot of work with Fortune 500 companies, which have branding requirements. Most of their work is divided into two major categories. First is the creative side – How you do create enticing and engaging videos and make the production really easy? The second one is branding.

Within Lumen5, entrepreneurs and business owners like you can upload your own fonts (including proprietary fonts, as long as you have the font file). All of their colours are also customisable to ensure that every video you create on their platform appears as your brand.

Lumen5 also offers a number of themes and templates for you to choose from. If your brand requires the design elements to have rounded or hard edges or the transitions to be smooth or quick, you can also choose such options in the platform. This way, they make consistency really easy. And this is how teams come to collaborate.

If you have 20–50 different people creating videos, they can tap into these same brand settings. They'll be able to use the same font and same template to produce similar-looking videos together. They can localise them for a particular geographical location as well.

Localising for Language

Michael shared that Lumen5 is also designed to be somewhat like a text editor. It's easy to get rid of or type text, and in this sense, using the platform is very different from using something like After Effects. In the latter, you'll have to navigate a timeline and find a certain element at a precise point in time.

Going back to his analogy that Lumen5 is the PowerPoint for videos, he emphasised their goal of designing a simple video creation platform.

Lumen5 offers two ways to do localisation. First, someone produces an original English-language version, then it gets distributed to localised teams or to a different individual who knows the target location better. These people can then simply edit out the text with their own language and tone. They can also tweak the settings to make sure that the colours reflect what the geo-demographics require.

The other way is more of a Canadian thing. Because Canada is a bilingual country (they speak English and French), users create two tiers of text to produce a bilingual video.

Through Lumen5, you can clone a video multiple times without interrupting the original version.

On Sonic Branding

According to Michael, Lumen5 supports audio in four ways.

First, they have a music library for all people out there who are stressed out at the thought of music production and are not quite ready for it. Similar to stock media, they've partnered with Storyblocks to offer thousands of audio tracks built right into their system. You can search it by mood (e.g. happy, bright, dark, ominous). Whatever it is, a keyword search will allow you to find the music that you're looking for.

For those who have their own tunes, Lumen5 also supports audio file uploads. It could be a jingle that you can put as an intro or outro of your video.

With Lumen5, you can also record a voiceover for your videos. Once you hit their voice button, you can read the script of your video out loud so you can give your audience that audio angle.

The last piece is artificial intelligence (AI) voiceover, which is still in its beta form. With Google Home and Alexa, most people are familiar with AI voices. Currently, Lumen5 is experimenting with different application programming interfaces (APIs) to see which is going to work better for the users. Now, there's only one voice available for you to add to your video, but over time, they plan to add more. This feature is something that they're creating themselves because creating a voice is a business in and of itself.

More Efficient Content Repurposing

Lumen5 has been around for about five years now. And Michael remarked that much of their time has been invested in solving problems like exporting your video into different sizes for different platforms. How do they make it easy for the average marketer and entrepreneur to be able to do such repetitive daily tasks?

When you create a video for desktop viewers, it will have a landscape orientation. You also want a square for your social feed. You may also want a vertical video for Instagram Stories, Snapchat, TikTok, or for mobile audiences in general.

On Lumen5, there's a tab on the left side of the system once you're done creating your video. You can change your video's dimensions using this one-click aspect ratio switch feature. It's a very important and unique value proposition that they bring to their users. If you were to use Adobe After Effects, Adobe Premiere, or iMovie, it's not going to be that simple. You're going to have to change the entirety of your video and shuffle everything around.

Lumen5 is beneficial because it has a structured approach to video creation. There are templates and building blocks. And when you switch aspect ratios, your video will automatically adapt to the aspect ratio that you chose. All of the images and the texts will be resized and moved to make them fit in the new aspect ratio. This all happens with a single click.

You can republish your video if you want to create a square version. You can also opt to duplicate your video, change the aspect ratio of the duplicate, and then publish. You can repeat the process to change the aspect ratio to vertical. After that, what you'll have are three project files for each different platform.

If you want to adjust the length for some of your project files to adapt to the local channels (e.g. YouTube videos should be longer, Instagram Stories should be 15 seconds or less), simple editing in Lumen5 also allows you to do that.

The Best Technology is Invisible

At Lumen5, Michael and company have always believed that the best design is invisible; the best technology is invisible. You can go through the entire video creation process and not know what happened.

For example, with regard to scene length, users have control over how long each of their video's scenes will be. But it's actually automatically calculated. Lumen5's design philosophy is all about great defaults: If they create great defaults, their users won't be able to feel the need to tweak those things.

Talking about scene length, Michael mentioned that as users compile their story and add a bit of text, Lumen5 calibrates all of that with the average reading speed. The magic really comes when the words-per-minute differ from language to language. Using their approach to design, you can create a video in Chinese, Japanese, or English, get different words-per-minute defaults, and still feel like all the videos are natural (i.e. you won't feel the need to change the scene length).

Another example is scene composition. Scene composition is something that you might study in photography school. But with Lumen5, the system will automatically position things in such a way that they look good. If you drag a photo as a background and the photo features a human face, then add text on it, the text will never be placed on top of the human face. Their system recognises that the human face is a visual subject and that the text is the content subject. They will be automatically placed on somewhat opposing ends to make them complement one another.

How Lumen5 Grew Their Subscribership

Michael and his co-founders started the company five years ago. Recently, they celebrated reaching the threshold of a million users. Back in the day, there used to be zero users. It was just him poking around the beta version.

One thing that they've always been passionate about as a product and design team is prioritising customers. During their first two years, they didn't really think at all about how to get a lot of users. Their emphasis was how to make five or 15 people really happy with their tool?

In the early days, what Michael did was tap into communities. He went into Reddit and Facebook groups of entrepreneurs and founders who were just starting their projects. He started simple conversations about how their Lumen5 can help these entrepreneurs create videos for their kickstarter campaigns. It's almost like being an unpaid contractor.

Before he knew it, he got 50 to a hundred people asking how he was able to do video content in just 10 minutes. Then, the conversation shifted from him creating videos to: "Here's how I did it. Here's an account, go ahead, and check it out".

This customer-centricity has created a lot of advocacies over the years. A lot of Lumen5's growth can be attributed to folks like myself who enjoy and appreciate the platform and tell their friends and family about it.

Lumen5's Freemium Pricing Model

When companies reach a certain stage, they start thinking about building on what they've previously had.

One of the things that Michael and his team did was to deploy a freemium pricing model. This allowed them to hit two birds with one stone.

The freemium model has let them offer Lumen5 for free – anyone can create videos without paying anything. The trade-off is that when you create a free video, it will have a Lumen5 watermark on it (the end part of the video says, "Video created using lumen5.com").

While people can call it a public relations strategy, it's also a sort of viral growth strategy. All of the free users can then create videos, post them, and share them with their followers. If thousands of their followers watch the video, they'll be able to see that the video was made using Lumen5. At least one of those followers will undoubtedly think about making a video for their business, just like what they saw.

Through the watermark exposure, Lumen5 has virally grown, gaining users that, in turn, bring in more users.

How Many Videos Should You Make?

Michael and his team find it hard to keep track of the content being made on Lumen5 because their users create unique videos. For example, there are many repurposed videos with different aspect ratios. But according to their estimate, the amount of content created through their platform is now in the seven-million range.

Often, he gets asked by clients about how many videos they should create. He usually answers one of two things. Number one is that every audience is different. So you really have to know your audience – How often are they spending their time on social media? How much content do they consume? The other thing is that you have to know yourself. Don't commit to creating 10 videos a day if you're not going to have time for it. You're only going to burn yourself out.

In the end, the best strategy is the one that's consistent over time. As a brand voice, you want to be consistent and persistent. You want to be able to do what you do and deliver value. You won't be able to do it if you over-commit and you only have fewer resources than what you need to actually deliver on those promises.

Lumen5's Affordable Pricing

By far, Lumen5's free plan is the most popular. They're able to offer their tool for free because they're confident about the product. If you try it for free, you'll see for yourself that they're not trying to deceive anyone.

They also have three different plans apart from their free one.

Creator plan. This is designed for individual creators. It starts at $15 per month and removes the Lumen5 branding. It's a very simple upgrade. It's suitable if you love creating videos and you want to take a bit more control of your brand, removing the 'Created using Lumen5.com' phrase at the end.

Premium plan. This is for professional video storytellers and is available at $79 per month. It gives you access to a lot of their system's premium stock media. You'll get the premium library courtesy of their Shutterstock partnership. You'll also be able to get a lot more control over colours and styles. Additionally, you'll be able to start storing what they call brand kits. If you're an agency producing videos for multiple clients, you're going to want to save multiple brand kits for different brand guidelines.

Business plan. This is for brands that are running a team. At $199 per month, you can get a lot more enterprise features. These include the ability to add multiple team members and to implement workspace permissions for editors and administrators. This plan is more collaboration-focused.

Chapter Fifteen
Video: 'Gather Voices' to Make a Compelling Story

Michael Hoffman, CEO of Gather Voices, Greater Chicago Area, USA.

Michael Hoffman is an expert in the use of video in marketing and digital engagement, and the CEO of tech startup Gather Voices, which is a software that makes it easy to create or collect videos from anyone anywhere in the world on any device and to easily manipulate that media, edit it, add branding, add a call to action, and be able to publish it.

Courtesy of Michael Hoffman

There are two reasons why that's interesting. One is that video is the kind of content that's dominating online, and video gets 1200% more shares than text or images. Traditionally, video has been expensive and slow, and so especially for organisations without large budgets and the ability to have large in-house production agencies, video is important but it hasn't been solved, so that's where Gather Voices comes in.

According to Michael, another factor that has fuelled their growth that is very relevant to PR professionals is that, today, things need to be real and authentic. It can't be made up. When Michael started a marketing agency 15 years ago, at that time, production quality was the most important thing and so was cleverness. Today, that's not it. It's about real, authentic stories. Companies are now figuring out that when they ask their community of customers, members, or fans to tell their own stories, those people come up with things they could have never imagined, never invented, and that's the best material. That's the material that people want. At Gather Voices, they're unlocking that opportunity to collect those stories with video to create a powerful new stream that supports what PR professionals really want to do.

How Gather Voices Works

The way Gather Voices works is that the contract can be with the company or with the agency that supports the company. Every instance of the software is fully branded, so if it's your company, everything's going to look and feel like it comes from your company, not from Gather Voices. They're simply powering this activity. They're not creating some kind of consumer brand. The company creates a request for video on their platform, and that request is basically a prompt that gets somebody to make a video; that somebody can be an employee, it can be a customer, it can be a thought leader, it can be anyone. The request has branding in it, of course, but it also has a time limit and talking points, because you don't want somebody rambling on for 20 minutes, which you will then have to edit, and that creates a tremendous amount of more work and slows things down.

With time limits and very clear instructions, the content you get back is much more focused. It's that piece that you want. You can even assemble different pieces together into a bigger piece, but giving that user some real narrow clarity helps a lot. That request for video can also include a video introduction. Imagine that Mike's asking you for a video, and when you click on something, you see him saying, "Hi, thanks for coming to make a video. Here's what we want you to talk about." What they found is that video request actually creates more engagement, because the psychological thing that's going on is, "Oh, that's a video. That doesn't seem so hard. I can do that," and that makes sense. So, the software bottles that request up into a link that can be shared via email, social media, text message, or it can be embedded directly into a website, form, or existing workflow. For example, if somebody's purchasing something, that Thank You page can have one of those requests for video built-in, so that you're collecting content in a passive way all the time and finding those gems of stories. This allows you to get real-time customer testimonials with video, which is golden.

You can also ask questions that aren't necessarily just self-serving questions. Something PR professionals might know better than marketers is that you need a hook that is relevant and interesting. It can't simply tell them to buy your products. It has to be a story. It's about being able to ask people about the first time that they experienced something or things that ladder into your company and your product, but aren't necessarily that direct self-serving testimonial which, of course, there's a place for. This software can do that, but Gather Voices is thinking in a much broader way about creating a story environment that supports a brand.

Gather Voices is new to the market, having only started in 2017. Since then, they have managed to acquire both an eclectic group of customers and a lot of traction. They work with leading hospitals, large law firms, big consumer packaging companies, and other professional service organisations. A lot of their traction has come from member organisations and those doing virtual events, because for member organisations, their whole reason for being is their members, and so the members' stories have value that maybe is higher than customer stories for a company, because they're subscribers themselves to the organisation. They fund the organisation, and they want to be part of a community of members. Thus, building that community becomes really important.

Why Gather Voices is Unique

With everyone focused on Zoom and audio-video conferencing these days, what sets Gather Voices apart is that it's not just one aspect of communications. Zoom is a synchronous medium, which means the participants all have to be on it at the same time, which is great if everyone's timezones match up, but it's also not something people want to spend all day on. It's also not possible to communise on Zoom with a group of thousands of customers or members. There's a large world of asynchronous content that is recorded in advance and used later on on websites and social media, which Gather Voices helps produce. Most video content is asynchronous, so companies need this ability to collect video that they're going to use possibly in a virtual event, because no one wants to run an event where they have to worry about everybody's internet, not just their own. Collecting content in advance also enables people to be more engaged in the event. One of the things that they've discovered at Gather Voices is that when you ask people to tell their stories and you include their stories in your content, people pay attention differently. They feel much more like co-creators than they do if they're being talked at. That, in turn, creates a deeper sense of connection and community, which is a very powerful thing for brands.

Many of Gather Voices' clients are those who run events, virtual events now, of course, and also membership organisations. An example of that is the Emergency Nurses Association, which represents emergency nurses around the world, and this is obviously a very important time for them. Emergency nurses are on the frontline of the COVID crisis, and they need to communicate a lot of important information to their membership. How do they do that? Well, instead of sending an email with content similar to what people get all day long, an email that people don't want to read or open, their leadership, experts, and thought leaders make videos using Gather Voices, and then share those videos out on their website in an email and on social media in a way that's much easier.

In the old days, those experts would have to either hire a camera crew or go to a studio to create content. With Gather Voices, they can record it on their own device, but what's different about just recording on your own device by yourself is the content's automatically routed to your communications team. You don't have to learn how to do Dropbox or other complicated things. All of the content's in one place, and there are a set of tools that allow the team to put the company branding and a call to action on it, edit it, and do all of that easily. This is extremely helpful as one of the major problems with any project with more than one contributor is compilation and the editorial work that takes place in post-production for video.

Let Gather Voices Guide You on the Path to Making Great Videos

One of the insights from Gather Voices is that if you give people very directed instructions, you get back shorter pieces of content that require less of that post-production effort. And so, part of the way their system is built is to guide people to talk about the part that you really want, give them time limits that enforce that, and make them give you that sound bite or that short piece of content that you don't have to pull out of some larger video. Anyone can see the value this kind of service brings to any content creator, especially an entrepreneur strapped for time.

On a commercial side, most of Gather Voices'clients are organisations that have in excess of $5 million revenue or budget, and so they're not yet able to serve the lower end of the market yet. Most of their clients purchase annual or multi-year subscriptions to their product which averages around $18 000 per year, which clients themselves found to be less than what they would spend on professional production. When Michael ran a marketing agency, that annual subscription amount was the average cost of a single video.

Gather Voices also has a different model with agencies as well. The way that they are servicing either one-off event video or smaller organisations is through their agencies. They have models that allow agencies to purchase a license which they can sub-license out to their clients. Any software is great for what it does, but it doesn't contain the intelligence that agencies and practitioners have on how to use it, how to make it effective, what to do with the content, and the like, and so that's what practitioners bring to the table. What Gather Voices is trying to do is create an ecosystem of folks who believe in video and its significance, and create whole opportunities and services around what the software enables. All of a sudden, you're able to get a lot more video content from a lot more people. Well, what do you do with that? How do you weave that opportunity into all of the initiatives that you're taking?

Under digital storification, which is part of the five-stage SPEAK|pr methodology, the value and the power of Gather Voices is truly evident.

Chapter Sixteen
Customer Service: Better Insights From Customer Feedback

Frank Buckler, Founder & CEO of SUCCESS DRIVERS, Cologne, North Rhine-Westphalia, Germany.

In a nutshell, businesses around the world make huge mistakes in decision-makings and they don't even know about it, but causal artificial intelligence (AI) can solve that. Through CX.AI's innovative AI technology, founder Dr Frank Buckler helps business owners improve customer experience.

Courtesy of Frank Buckler

'Causal' is Something Fundamental

'Causal' is a term commonly used in the academe, but it goes back to something very fundamental. Every business needs and does this every day: They try to find what they should do to be successful. Is it a cause-and-effect relationship? What should I do to achieve a certain outcome? Why do I need AI for that?

Normally, if someone comes to you and smashes you in the face, you're sure that that person is the cause of your pain. However, things are different in business. You're basically smashed by 10 guys in the face at the same time. And the pain could come minutes or even months or years later. It's virtually impossible to look at your data and experience and find out who caused you the pain. This leads businesses around the world to make mistakes in their decision-making without them even knowing about it. What is Causal Artificial Intelligence?

In terms of making decisions, businesses mostly look at today's data to make decisions for tomorrow. But for Frank, it's wrong to believe that fact means truth because fact is just a single thing. What you should be looking for is the consistent relationship between actions and outcomes. And this is not in the data – it's something you need to extract from the data. Therefore, you need machine learning technology.

Decades ago, there were already simple statistical techniques that tried to do this. But there were strong limitations as you need to put in lots of assumptions. This is what machine learning frees us from. It frees us from unrealistic assumptions and helps us gain insights into what drives business outcomes. This is the new era ushered in by AI.

Frank started his journey 28 years ago when the first AI wave began. He was then a student and he saw how AI was used to predict stock markets. This inspired him to develop his own AI-powered technology.

Causal AI tech has different applications, including marketing and sales. But it focuses on one specific problem: How to have better insights from customer feedback.

It starts from getting customer feedback and categorising them according to what people are saying. Then, you need to qualify what's important. You need to interpret what they really mean and you need AI for that.

Frank's company offers the solution you need. With their technology, you can run your data and be provided with a dashboard where you can simulate results. You can even simulate fiscal outcomes by inputting the different actions you can take. Their technology is used by companies and enterprises that have a lot of customers (they could be in the business-to-business or business-to-consumers space). Currently, Microsoft is one of their biggest customers.

On Getting Noticed as an Entrepreneur

When Frank was just starting, he did strategies that didn't work for his company. For instance, writing a book. In the latter part of the podcast episode, he detailed his experience of being an author. As going to a big publishing house takes some money, he opted to spend his money on a PR agent to market the book that he wrote and published through a not-so-famous house. However, good PR agents are also rare and you have to have connections to big newspapers. He was not saying that writing a book is a wrong tactic, but there are other ways to gain something for your business, especially online.

For CX.AI, he also did direct marketing, LinkedIn automation, and mailing. There were outcomes but he and his team couldn't figure out how to scale as a business just yet. Because in reality, it's hard to get the right people on the phone, speak to them, and make them interested in what you're selling.

Their causal AI tech started gaining traction and big enterprises as customers through referrals from friends – people who already trust them. For instance, Frank got to work with Deutsche Telekom through a friend there. The company then got fascinated about what their product can do and referred them to T-Mobile USA. Then T-Mobile referred them to Facebook, then to Intel, and so forth.

Having people who trust you works. However, it is hard to scale. This is why Frank further recommended engaging in speaking because you'll have an audience who are like-minded and are interested in what you're talking about.

You can also work with a reseller because such an agency has already built relationships with their customers. It will be easier for them to sell your service because people already listen to them.

The core of these is, you need to gain the trust of the people. With trust, you can sell even the things that they may need but are not understandable for them in the first place.

Building Relationships

Apart from their friends who give good words about them, CX.AI also got exposure in a scientific publication as they were cited by professors.

Through their software that they provided for free, they have also helped graduate students write their masters and doctoral theses (He got his connection to these students through a professor who loved the software). In return, they asked these students to give them a lead into their companies, because they were also working for organisations while writing their theses.

Basically, it starts with building a relationship with people and giving them benefits. From there, you can go up the ladder one step at a time. In Frank's case, it took him two to three years before he started to see some fruit from his relationship with these people from the academe.

Content Marketing as a Scalable Strategy

Trust is important especially in an industry where new technologies are being introduced. Your customers need to have trust in you and your product.

As their strategy, CX.AI now focuses on content marketing. They want their target audience to see them as an authority in their field. This also helps build trust over time. And compared to referrals, this is more scalable.

Currently, they do a yearly industry study. They also publish thought leadership articles bi-weekly. They've also opened a group for clients to provide exclusive content for them daily. They've also put out a course with interactive sessions.

Apart from the mentioned content formats, they also do webinars.

For Frank, the whole philosophy around content marketing is giving everything for free. And people will hire you because, at the end of the day, they won't have time to digest everything and do things by themselves.

Future Plans

Frank shared that they further plan to hold a virtual summit and hope to conduct a physical counterpart in the future. He believes that trust can be built better through physical interactions than through virtual ones.

For the summit, the idea is to have clients speak as well. They also plan to invite vendors who are offering great solutions to their target audience. Every speaker is related to tech or tech marketing, especially customer insights (If you are interested to be part of their speaking list, you can already reach out to him).

Apart from providing speaking opportunities, the other idea is to generate revenue together through a summit offering (i.e. selling different products at discounted prices). If the speakers who are part of the event promote the event themselves, they can also earn a revenue share.

Currently, you need to pay first before being able to speak at conferences. And the payoff is hard to justify. Though you may get an audience, it would be challenging to do a follow-up and get in the funnel. This is why they're aiming to hold a summit that's not just an educational event. It must have a funnel to capture the interest of the audience.

Frank shared that every small tech vendor has a group of people who trust them. If 10 small, brilliant tech vendors join forces, the number of people who trust them will be 10 times more compared to their individual audiences. They all can benefit from that pool.

Trust is the Key

For Frank, trust is a key component in any business. And it becomes more and more important because information is now everywhere. Plus, the ability to reach out to a prospect costs almost no money.

Because people are spammed with information and other free content, they actually don't need to consume it anymore. They only reach out to their peers and people that they trust.

However, when it comes to big players, this is less important because they have already established themselves as a trusted brand. As the old belief goes, you can't get fired by hiring IBM because everyone trusts IBM.

Chapter Seventeen

Customer Service: AI Software to Analyse Sentiment of Digital Content

Scott Sandland, Founder & CEO of Cyrano.ai, Newport Beach, California, USA.

Courtesy of Scott Sandland

Scott Sandland, based in California, is a thought leader in Artificial Empathy, contributing to best-selling books on AI, speaking on the subject at the United Nations AI for Good Summit, and CEO of a company called Cyrano.ai, which uses artificial intelligence (AI) to help businesses understand people better.

The name of his company comes from the play titled Cyrano de Bergerac. The story revolves around an eponymous guy who writes effectively. He uses his skill to tell another guy what he has to say to make a girl fall in love with him. In movies and television shows, there's a cliched scene where there's a person telling somebody what to say through an in-ear radio receiver. That cliche's original version is Cyrano de Bergerac.

Cyrano, their company, is built on that idea. Their AI analyses people and gives information to you as their client. The goal is to help you make your customers fall in love with you. They will tell you what matters most to your audience so you can better engage and have a more satisfying relationship with them.

Why Analyse Words

Cyrano's AI uses linguistic analysis. Scott believes that words in speech are defining the behaviour of people. If peacocks have feathers and deers have antlers, humans have words. They are simply our most defining quality. The reason that we run the planet is that we can effectively communicate with one another.

He further looks at it from a behaviouristic standpoint: The more you understand the way a person talks, the more you can understand the way a person thinks or approaches anything. And no matter what a person is talking about, they're likely to tell you about themselves and their priorities.

This is why they designed their AI tool to analyse words, which can be spoken or relayed through whatever platform – from Zoom calls to text messages. They think of words as the fingerprint of a person that enables them to deeply know about that person. They then transmit that information to the person on the other side of the conversation (i.e. their customers).

Scott has an academic and medical background in psychology. He's a clinical hypnotherapist and the Chief Executive Officer (CEO) of a mental health clinic. Cyrano's co-founder, on the other hand, is a sociologist and a neuro-linguist.

Cyrano's AI vs Sentimental Analysis

For Scott, sentimental analysis is a fascinating thing and is really about having a fifth-grade reading level. And a lot of multimillion-dollar companies are focusing their efforts on trusting that fifth-grader's advice.

The scenario when using sentimental analysis goes like this: After a call is over, the tool will tag the call as 'not good'. Then, it will make you wonder why it's not good. But when you ask about it, it wouldn't be able to give an answer.

What Cyrano does, on the other hand, is real-time. After the call, they can already put together a report that shows graphs indicating at which point your customer is highly committed, curious, or open-minded. They also highlight the part where the need-versus-want comes in, where they're being irrational, and where they're being logical.

They also have icons to show the priorities of the caller in a ranked order. For example, they can show you if the person is higher focused on facts and data than their ego, or if they're more focused on the relationships of the community.

Then, they give bullet-point sentences on what you should do about the said information. They make it easy and actionable. They can tell you how to collaborate with a certain person; what are the next steps that you should do; how to have a lifetime relationship with them; how to de-escalate conflict; how to mentor someone or negotiate without losing rapport.

Simply put, they come up with specific pieces of advice on what you can do to effectively engage with your audience.

The Need to Build Cyrano

Being the CEO of a mental health clinic, Scott works with at-risk teens and is on the frontlines of watching the teen crisis unfold in America. In the United States, the second leading cause of death among people under the age of 24 is suicide. According to pre-COVID data, there had been 3000 suicide attempts every day among high school students.

If you look at it socioeconomically, it turns out that rich, white kids are killing themselves at historic levels. Scott mentioned this because they are the population that should have access to all the best solutions. However, it's not getting them there. If it's happening in that population, it's happening everywhere.

With this in mind, he saw the need to build a tool that can help people feel listened to and understood – a tool that can create empathy and strategy so that more therapists can do work. There's a need to create tools that can listen to these kids and help them when their problems are still small.

He and his company developed a tool to address that. He was also fortunate enough that he got to speak in Geneva, Switzerland, at the United Nations' AI for Global Good Summit, where he talked about how their work is being done.

Today, tens of thousands of their users are from the sales and commercial side. Ethically, they regard it as a safer place to start. It would allow them to iron out wrinkles because, in a sales environment, there are better data and better apple-to-apple comparisons. When you get it wrong, you can still sleep at night because losing a life is costlier than losing a sale. If kids need their AI tool to work, he has to make sure that their tool really works.

Making Cyrano Sustainable

Scott's idea behind Cyrano is to build it for social good. However, he needed to figure out the economic side of it and make it sustainable. And he didn't want it to have to do with charities or endowments. He wanted it to be something that they can run in their own way.

This gave birth to their sell-one-give-one pricing model. Each time they sell a one-year subscription of their software, that one sale will subsidise another user in the social good space. It can be a volunteer at a teen crisis or suicide hotline centre or a subclinical support group.

They also give their software to college support groups and other similar organisations. This enables these wonderful volunteers who are listening to and communicating with people in crisis to be better at their job. Their tool can help them connect with the other person on the call more effectively. They can also do this at scale.

An API-First Company

Scott said that Cyrano is an application programming interface (API)-first company.

Their Chief Operating Officer (COO) created a tool called Cirrus Insight, which was the no. 1 app in the Salesforce marketplace for almost a year and a Top 10 app for about eight years. Their COO and his programming team plugged their API integration into a more complex stack.

This shows Cyrano's philosophy, which is to scale by empowering existing technology. Today, they're in all email providers and Zoom. They're also building out APIs to plug into specific apps (e.g. crisis support apps).

When people come to them enquiring about having their tool integrated with their API, they also accommodate those. Because, over time, their goal is to be everywhere.

On Getting Noticed as an Entrepreneur: It's All About Community

For a little while, Scott shared that he was very busy patting himself on the back for being smart, coming up with a neat idea, and being awarded a patent for that idea. However, it was this cliched quote – "People don't care how much you know until they know how much you care" – that gave him an aha moment. The key, he realised, is community.

Everything in his life that has gone well has been about community. In high school and college, he played on sports teams. Early in his career, he spent time finding peer networking groups or continued education groups.

He noted that there are communities and groups that you can simply plug into; you don't need to create them. You can find like-minded people there who would want to hear what you're doing.

The real turning point for his company was when they switched from 'Look how smart our stuff is' to 'Hey, how are you?' They started listening to the specific needs and wants of the communities where their tool organically fits in and provides value. According to Scott, this is what got Cyrano noticed. They proved that they're sincere, they care, and they deserve to be trusted. These days, it's also quite easy to do some hype or get thousands of likes on LinkedIn. However, once you reach a certain threshold of quality, the game becomes about consistency and trust within a community.

Cyrano's Vision and Mission

Cyrano shares the same vision with their company's name inspiration. Cyrano de Bergerac is a character who wants to be in the shadows, remain hidden, and whisper the truth from there. When they were just starting, he said to two other officers that if they'll be able to do their business well and everyone will use their tool, no one would have to hear of them. However, the irony is that for that to happen, someone must have heard of them somewhere and passed on the message.

During the interview, Scott also mentioned a guy named Ton Dobbe, who wrote the book, *The Remarkable Effect*. The book gave him the idea of 'Don't be better, be different'. In doing so, you can get people to rally behind your cause. It turns users into advocates.

For their company, their idea is to build something that will really help kids. Their commercial applications are neat that no sane person can hear their mission statement and say that it doesn't matter. Their mission statement? To create a world-class AI therapist and be able to give it to every single kid for free.

They're already making the money on the commercial side and they've already earned the trust. People know that their app is safe and confidential. They're not selling nor mining data – it's simply a sincere, philanthropic thing.

For instance, when Scott talked to a prospect, who's the president of a regional real estate group in California, he reiterated that he needs her to trust their tool first – and show to people that trust, and that their tool is going to help save lives. The president then said that even though she has no idea what Cyrano's technology is, she still believes in it; her response was affirmative.

Going Multilingual

Having a multi-language app is part of Cyrano's roadmap.

They've started with English but they've already done testing in seven languages. In all those languages, the tests yielded results better than they hoped. These languages include Italian, German, French, Spanish, Portuguese, Mandarin. What was surprising for Scott is that their tool did better in Mandarin than Portuguese, even when they haven't put a lot of work into any of them.

They also graphed them all out, and the ratios looked good. Nonetheless, the confidence thresholds were dropping precipitously. So there's still a need for a lot of training. In fact, they recently partnered with a company called HearMe.App. One of the great things about the partnership is that HearMe has a big presence in India, which they can leverage to get a number of training data that they can work with.

PART THREE
CASES

Chapter One

Introduction

It's all good and well to have theory and tools but how are other entrepreneurs doing interesting things to stand out from the competition? In this final section, I have stories from Africa, India, Singapore, China, Korea, and America as examples of how creativity is a simple key to unlock value in a brand.

I've learnt that there isn't a right or wrong to public relations, there is the application of passion to a problem. The solution which arises becomes of interest and so that generates publicity and it becomes a virtuous cycle.

I haven't included media relations case studies because those are simple and easy to find, but included some of the more unnoticed entrepreneurs that you won't have heard of. That's of course not the case with the Rolls Royce story in Asia, but no doubt you will be inspired by the story of the Kidz movie festival of India, one man's mission to explain financial independence from his RV, and the building of a rowing haven on the Kaufe River in Zambia. One take away simply being that there isn't a right or wrong way to get noticed, and that is incredibly liberating for any entrepreneur.

Let's have a peek at who you will be hearing from in the following pages:

Michael Juergens in America builds brands based on stories, including wine from Bhutan.

Mark Thomas shares the vision behind the collaboration between World Rowing and WWF's Kafue River Project in Zambia.

Film maker **Andrew Clark** in Singapore explains the strategy behind Rolls-Royce videos in Asia.

Founder of B1G1, **Masami Sato** in Singapore shares how giving can be a central part of your story.

Mickie Kennedy from Maryland introduces a service which goes beyond press release distribution.

Praveen Nagda was on a mission to help kids during COVID, and is building a story of hope for Children in India through movies and a film festival which reaches over one-third of the world.

Josh Gardner in Shanghai explains how foreign brands can compete with 60 million online merchants in China with Kung Fu Data.

Howard Dekkers illustrates how 'hitting the road' is a great way to engage an audience on his mission to share education on personal finance.

PR Agency owner **Heesang Yoo**, in S. Korea, explains why it is so important to consider the local amplification channels.

Diogène Ntirandekura of Canada used his personal story to launch a podcast for fellow ERP consultants.

Singapore-based Briton **Callum Laing** explains how he communicates between investors and investee companies.

Chapter Two
Shangri-La and Other Stories

Michael Juergens, Founder of Bhutan Wine Company, Trabuco Canyon, California, USA.

How can combining opposites into your brand name help your marketing? That's just one of the insights I have from Michael Juergens, the bestselling author of *Drinking & Knowing Things*. Michael runs the wildly popular Drinking & Knowing Things wine blog, which was adapted into a book that provides 52 specific wine recommendations. He is the founder of the Bhutan Wine Company and is leading the development of the wine industry in the magical Himalayan country.

Courtesy of Michael Juergens

Based in California, Michael Juergens is a Certified Sommelier with the Guild of Master Sommeliers, a Certified Specialist of Wine, and a Master of Wine Candidate with the Institute of Masters of Wine. Michael also owns the award-winning SoCal Rum company, which was recently awarded the highest point score in history for any Silver Rum. Michael Juergens is a professor at the Paul Merage School of Business at the University of CA, Irvine. He lives in SoCal, where he spends his time blind tasting and doing extreme sports.

Telling Stories

In the book *Sapiens* by Yuval Noah Harari, the author talked about how the Sapiens were able to defeat the Neanderthals because they can tell stories. Though they were dumber, smaller, weaker, and bad at everything, they can tell stories.

Michael believes that, somehow, we're neurologically pre-wired around this idea of stories. And we resonate well with them.

This is why one of the things he tries to do in all of his businesses is to tell some sort of a story. It doesn't have to be a long story – but one that people can respond to differently than how they might respond to other mechanisms; one that they can also retell themselves. Just because you have a cool story, you can have these ambassadors for your brand.

The Story Behind the Bhutan Wine Company

The idea behind Michael's Bhutan Wine Company is that there's a hidden Shangri-La in the middle of the Himalayas and they're making wine there.

People who know Bhutan typically think of the place as the happiest place on Earth – they have vistas and stunning landscapes. Then, he thought of putting some wine into that. And with that, he's able to create imagery around it.

Talking about the company's name, he shared that they didn't try to come up with a fancy one. This way, it can spark interest of people about Bhutan having wine. It's a juxtaposition putting two elements that don't seem to be on the same page, because people typically associate wine with France, Italy, Spain, and Australia.

When Michael tells the story about his company, he mentioned that it has to be more precise.

When people think of Bhutan, they don't connect it to wine or they don't even know where it is. In fact, when he first went there, he thought that it was an island in Indonesia. When he scheduled a trip thinking, he was going to Indonesia, his girlfriend said that Bhutan was actually in the Himalayas.

So if people don't know what it is, there's a curiosity that takes over. But if people do know what this is, they can even be more curious. Because they already have a picture of what they thought it is, then you bring up something new. In his case, building a wine industry there.

Different Stories for Different Audiences

This idea of a story and the juxtaposition of the obvious and completely non-obvious can make a kind of intrigue among people. But what do you do with it? Sometimes, entrepreneurs are great with the headline story. But how do you take it out to the people that you need to hear it, knowing that there are different audiences who are not necessarily in the same place?

Michael shared the way he does it is that he has five or six different stories related to Bhutan. And he tells different stories depending on the audience.

One story is how only a few countries in the world can organically grow wine but don't do it. Anywhere in the world that can grow wine has already been doing it for thousands of years. So the idea of getting a whole country to build an industry for whichever product is a fascinating story for an entrepreneur – or an artist. It's sort of: Here's the biggest canvas in the world, you can do whatever you want.

Another story is that in Bhutan, they don't measure economic growth. They measure gross national happiness and that's one of the things that they're known for around the world.

The question then becomes: How does wine fit in with that strategy for that nation? Michael's idea is that wine can bring people together. It's a joyous thing that helps build bridges and communities. When you look at the cultural impact of wine in places like Champagne or Burgundy, it's a very different and telling story.

Then, Michael also has this sort of environmental play. Bhutan is the only carbon-negative country in the world and it's on track to be the only 100% organic country on Earth. So he also has a story of bringing in some additional plant life for biodiversity, sustainability, and agricultural harmony.

Telling different stories about Bhutan depending on the audience is a clever move. And it's really what public relations (PR) agencies ask clients to do – to look at what the readers or the audience are going to be interested in for different media outlets.

The Story Behind SoCal Rum

Michael also has a rum company called SoCal Rum, which stands for Southern California. They received the highest Silver Rum rating from a quality perspective, which is 95 points.

It's a very different story, but it also has the same juxtaposition aspect because rum doesn't typically come from Southern California. The story around this company is more about the Southern California lifestyle, capturing the essence of beach and fun.

People from around the world know Los Angeles. They do their vacations there. They save up money for years to go and visit the place. His company then introduces that he has this product wherein you can experience some of that in a bottle. Their label has sunsets and waves on it, but it also happens to be the best in the world. Rum is sort of the preserve of places like Jamaica; there's an association there with rum and that kind of lifestyle. Through his company, he took that to a different place. Their product can be considered as the Southern California version of the Caribbean and Jamaican lifestyle.

However, it's not just a gimmick. The quality of their product – and their story – is indeed high.

He fuses the SoCal kind of lifestyle and quality of their rum into everything that they do to tell the story of the company. For their marketing efforts, they have a social media person who crafts clever photos and texts to keep reinforcing that message. For instance, one post features a guy surfing and a cocktail, and it sends a message that says, Hey, you can also do this.

On Creating Content

Michael is doing what's called the Master of Wine certification. Around the world, there are about 417 of them; 57 in the United States. It's the highest classification that you can get in this field and he has been pursuing it for a number of years.

It started when his friends were asking him about which wines they should try. They acknowledge him as the wine guy. Though he's not really responsible for figuring such things out, he still gave it a try.

He started a little email, which states his wine recommendations, that he sent to around 10 friends. Then his friends responded by asking for more. They also forwarded that to their friends, and so on. Now, he has thousands of people from around the world on his blog.

Michael never did anything to market it. What he focused on was to create authentic and genuine content for his friends.

Today, there are many bloggers and content creators who measure their success in terms of the number of subscribers or how much volume of content they put out there. He took a very contrarian approach to that.

He wanted to create true content and get it in the hands of people who were looking for that. He'd rather have a thousand super-engaged people than a hundred thousand people who are deleting it every time a piece of content hits their inbox.

For Michael, it's really about visualising content creation as writing for friends – putting his heart as well as his spirit into it.

When you look at the comments on his Amazon page, you'll see how everyone loves the voice that he uses. It's not snobby. There's a lot of f-bombs (which is literally how he talks to his friends). Because the topic is wine, people think it would be written snobby. But he talks about it not in that way. And that authenticity allows people to engage with his content differently than how they would engage with other wine spectator articles.

In a way, it's another juxtaposition. Michael has taken the perception of how wine would be written about and did it differently.

This recurrent theme of juxtaposing two dissimilar things makes his content more accessible and notable. The way he's getting his subscribers is sort of the true definition of going viral; a cascade effect where people share content because they like it and they want other people to read it.

Curating a Book

In *Drinking and Knowing Things*, Michael compiled and curated his articles.

He shared that there was a point when it became very difficult for him to manage his inbox. One of the things that he did was to contract with a company to build him a website where people can self-subscribe. When you go to it, you can simply put in your email – there are no big sign-up forms and credit cards – then you'll be able to get his content.

This allowed people to afford it much more easily: you just have to click on a subscribe button. Whereas before, people would have to email him so he can add them to his list. So removing that obstacle allowed Michael to get a bunch more followers.

The second thing that happened was people started emailing him to ask about past issues. After about 400 requests for all the old articles, he thought of a way to make it easy for people: He then put 52 of his articles together and self-published a book on Amazon so they could just go and grab it.

The book became a bestseller, which was the craziest thing for him because he never set out to make it a bestseller. He only wanted to make his life easy by stopping all those requests for old issues.

When launching a book you have to do the marketing three months in advance. You need to get out to people and do reviews.

For Michael, the secret to him having a bestselling book is that he already has a captive audience – people who really like the content that is coming out and who are asking him for the back issues. When he made his book available, he had already built an audience.

His audience also sends his book to their own friends because they think it's going to be hilarious and entertaining for them. During Christmas time, he also sees his book sales spike dramatically. And he attributes it to people buying the book as a stocking stuffer.

All these aren't part of a strategy. He literally started doing – and he's still doing – wine content creation for fun. The fact that people respond to it is just awesome.

The Moral of the Story

There are entrepreneurs whose goal is to make a billion dollars.

To reach that goal, they need to think about a market niche that they can get into and where they can build a product to fill that niche. Some of them end up making an algorithm that can, for instance, connect printers wirelessly to phones. When they sell it to a company like Google, they make a billion dollars. Nobody in the history of everybody wakes up in the morning already passionate about printing algorithms or whatever.

However, Michael shared that life's success shouldn't be measured by that. Coming from the Bhutan mindset, you should measure your life by how happy you are.

For him, the way he achieves happiness is to do epic things with cool people. So he just focuses on doing that, and if the money comes, then it comes. If it doesn't, it doesn't. Ever since he adopted that mindset, all of his businesses have exploded.

Getting into Bhutan

During the podcast, he recounted how his girlfriend read a book in high school about a woman who moved to Bhutan and married a Bhutanese person. He and his girlfriend have been together for almost 16 years and she's been talking about it all the time.

An opportunity came up to run a marathon in the country (they've been running marathons across the world). So he signed up, thinking back then that Bhutan was in Indonesia. When he heard that her girlfriend was excited to go, he got it for her as a present. This is how they ended up in Bhutan for the first time.

When he was there, he thought how amazing the place was – and how they should have a wine industry there. So he dealt with it.

Taking a Different Perspective

There's a fundamental difference between writing things that other people want to read and writing things that you want to tell them.

In PR, clients often want to tell people what they offer so that they'd buy it. On the contrary, what clients need to do is ask their audience about what they're interested in and then share that with them.

Michael seems to have cracked that code.

When he was first studying wine, he shared that the books that he bought were all very dry and boring. And what he wanted was a story that could capture his attention and teach him about wine but not written in a dry way. However, that book didn't exist. So he wrote one.

He wrote a fictional novel about a secret underground world of high-stakes gambling and wine tasting competition run by the mafia. It's the kind of story that he wanted to read, but it doesn't exist. So he wrote it just for fun, and the book had great success, with the audience asking him to write another one.

He wrote a couple more books containing stories that he wanted to read but didn't exist. Then it sort of led to his friends asking for some wine recommendations. This led to the blog, which led to the book, *Drinking and Knowing Things*.

Michael has this theory that the universe is like whitewater rapids. It's going to take you somewhere, but the question is: How fast can you get there with as little bruising as possible?

If you're in the whitewater rapids, when you just follow the flow, steer and nudge a little bit, you can get to the bottom fast. But if you paddle and try to go sideways, you get banged up and get exhausted because you're fighting the flow.

Ten years ago, this is exactly what he did: He just went with the flow. Every book that he wrote was sort of built on the last one.

Chapter Three
World Rowing and WWF's Kafue River Project in Zambia Aims to Provide Clean Water and Help Hone African Rowers

Mark Thomas, Managing Director of S2M Consulting, Harpenden, England, UK.

According to Mark Thomas, a renowned sports advocate, rowers and the water share a symbiotic relationship: When you're rowing, you're in tune with the water and nature around you.

World Rowing, where Mark serves as a marketing advisor, is an international organisation committed to helping ensure that the water people row on, is fit to row on.

Courtesy of Mark Thomas

Today, however, the world faces different issues related to water – from sanitation and accessibility (over 1.1 billion people don't have access to water) to a decrease in biodiversity. And these are concerns that should be considered as significant as climate change and air pollution.

World Rowing and World Wildlife Fund Team Up

World Rowing is the international federation that governs rowing as a sport around the world. Based in Lausanne, Switzerland, the group is recognised by the International Olympic Committee (IOC) and is responsible for managing all aspects of rowing events. This huge responsibility is shared by a team that, although small in number, is dedicated to ensuring that rowing events and activities are sustainable and environmentally acceptable. As Mark emphasises, it's in the DNA of rowers to be linked to the environment, specifically the water.

In 2011, World Rowing partnered with World Wildlife Fund (WWF) in an effort to be more active in addressing water-related issues. One of their goals is to shine a light on this matter through communications and awareness programmes, and international events.

Also take an active role in making sure that the environments that they row in are clean. In every event that they hold, they implement guidelines and criteria to guarantee that their activities are environmentally safe. They conduct tests and utilise appropriate systems and applications in their venues for long-term sustainability.

World Rowing is the oldest international federation in the world, having been around for almost 150 years now. Rowing is also one of the original sports included in the first Olympics and has been there since. With the innate relationship that rowers and water share, it is natural for the organisation to be involved in this kind of initiative.

Their global partnership with WWF only fostered this responsibility more deeply. Apart from raising awareness, they started taking action – doing things that are more tangible in terms of solving global water issues.

The Kafue River Project

WWF runs freshwater conservation projects in more than 50 countries around the world. World Rowing specifically joined the group's Kafue River initiative. This project endeavours to build the Kafue River and Rowing Centre (Kafue River is one of the tributaries of the Zambezi River in Zambia, Africa).

Part of this undertaking is highlighting water issues that surround Kafue. World Rowing considers Kafue as a reflection of various water problems that the world faces, including access to clean potable water, irrigation issues, and industrial pollution, among others. Through scientific and research projects, experts will have a better understanding of these issues.

The project is also about education. Apart from bringing people – old and young – to enjoy rowing, they also aim to let them see first-hand the issues surrounding the river. The learnings from this initiative can then be applied to and replicated in other water conservation centres around the world, including those in China and South America.

It's a step-by-step process that involves researching and understanding water issues and creating models that can be used in other centres, water crisis areas, and clean water projects that the WWF runs throughout the globe.

Securing Funding

For this project, World Rowing and WWF need to raise a couple of million dollars. Through the goodwill of the global rowing community, the project has already received initial funding. Now, they are in the next stage: to ask for corporate fundings. And they have recently secured one from a Dutch furniture company.

In terms of the project's operation, Mark says that they have already secured the land and title deeds and are now moving forward with the construction proper. Going forward, he acknowledges that securing funding and monitoring cash flow will be more crucial.

World Rowing is fairly open in terms of who they work with or the companies that will give them funding – as long as they share the same values with them.

There are certain organisations that lend themselves to this kind of purpose-driven programme. For instance, beverage companies, which consume a huge amount of water in their manufacturing process, can take part and also acquire learnings as to how they can make their business more sustainable with regard to water consumption.

A Trade-Off

For the Kafue Project, World Rowing and WWF have received support from the local government and from Zambia's national government.

However, Mark notes that in other developing markets, one issue that they encounter is the trade-off between industrial and economic development. When the projects involve the environment and sustainability, a conflictual relationship often arises.

World Rowing sees this as part of their responsibility – a challenge to turn the trade-off into a win-win situation. It's about finding the balance between having a more environmentally sustainable economy without affecting development in terms of industrialisation.

Promoting Rowing in Africa

Historically, Africa is not regarded as the home of great rowers. To encourage more people to engage in this sport, World Rowing has a global development division focused on nurturing rowing in different parts of the globe, including Africa.

Because rowing is traditionally seen as an expensive and elite sport, the organisation helps in building facilities like the Kafue River and Rowing Centre and provides more accessibility to people who are interested to learn.

As not everyone can get into the river, World Rowing also develops other variants of the sport. For instance, they have taken advantage of Africa's vast coast and introduced the so-called coastal rowing. Recently, the group has also held a virtual indoor rowing championship, which saw a good representation from Africa.

The organisation hopes that undertakings like these would serve as a stimulus for more Africans to show interest and take part in rowing.

To learn more about the Kafue Project, visit www.worldrowing.com. And if you're looking for a new sport to try, you should check out rowing, which provides opportunities beyond being a great exercise.

Chapter Four
Rolls-Royce is Driving Their PR With Video in Asia

Andrew Clark, Partner of AsiaWorks Television, Singapore.

Andrew Clark is a partner at AsiaWorks, a creative video agency with offices across the Asia-Pacific region, and is based in Singapore. In his career, he's worked as a journalist, cameraman, and video producer for the likes of the BBC, CNN, and National Geographic among many others. He now works at AsiaWorks, where he creates award-winning video content for his clients in the world of brands, corporate, and marketing.

Courtesy of Andrew Clark

Andrew believes that our attraction to video is primal. Colours, sound, pictures – the moving image – it captures people's attention like nothing else can. And video is everywhere, from the phone in the palm of your hand to huge outdoor advertising screens, ubiquitous in the cities we live in.

He gave three examples of videos, across a range of budgets that he's made, to help bring his clients results, putting into perspective a few formats that you could consider for your own video content, and the unlimited potential of video.

Andy's Best Examples and His Top Tips for Video Creators

His first example is a series of videos that he created for Rolls-Royce Motorcars. Rolls-Royce in Asia is in a position where they're in the business of changing the perception of a Rolls-Royce motorcar as a car for slightly older gentlemen to be driven around in, into a car that you drive yourself, that is more universal, younger, and attractive to an Asian audience.

Over the last few years, he's been working on a campaign with Rolls-Royce to discover real stories. Customer testimonials from Rolls-Royce owners all around the Asia-Pacific region.

They've filmed in Hong Kong, Japan, New Zealand, and Australia, and they've shared first person-told stories about Rolls-Royce owners. This brought great results for Rolls-Royce Motorcars, results they are very proud of.

Although the budget for these videos can sometimes come at a high price – you should never underestimate the power of the video testimonial. In fact, even a quick testimonial filmed on a smartphone, by yourself, for free, can be incredibly valuable. Why? Because the power of a real story can't be beaten. When someone else talks about your product, or brand, or service in a positive and authentic way, you're creating priceless content.

The second example Andrew gave was of a medium budget video where he worked with UNICEF. During COVID, AsiaWorks created a series of social media videos in Indonesia of best practices in the areas of hygiene and communicating UNICEF's important public messages.

Again, this produced great outcomes for UNICEF, but more importantly, Andrew sees this type of work as something that AsiaWorks as a company and UNICEF as a client can be proud of.

It is the type of content that not only informs, but also provides practical and useful actions for people to take. And that's another important consideration in producing video content. Ask yourself the question: Will the video be practical and useful for the audience?

The third example is a project that Andrew produced in 2019 to help a friend of his, entrepreneur Irfan Tayabali, with a passion project, an 'explainer' video for a product he'd invented called the Purpose Planner.

Together, Andrew and Irfan ended up producing a series of videos on a shoestring budget, to help promote the planner on the product website and social media.

Explainer videos are incredibly valuable, because they clearly and simply tell a potential customer what your product is and how to use it. But two key points to bear in mind when making 'explainers':

Copy-writing is key

Audiences get bored by bad and long-winded writing, so ensure that you prepare a script in advance that is compelling, informative, and concise. The best strategy? Invest in a producer who knows how to write for video.

Show don't tell.

Make sure you feature lots of great shots of your product and demonstrate to your audience what it can do.

Irfan's Purpose Planner has been a great success. Not only did the planner itself receive a boost in sales after the videos were posted, Irfan has now developed his product line and the business is growing from strength to strength.

Andrew's examples were great. They were entirely different and incredibly useful if you're developing your own video production strategy. One of the main tips he could offer small entrepreneur-led companies or small medium entreprises (SMEs) that want to make their own videos is to get rid of the assumption that videos must be kept short.

While short videos might work for social platforms like TikTok, Andrew believes that, at the end of the day, once you've won someone's attention, which is key, then the video can basically be as long as you want. Above all, do not to be boring. To find out if your video is boring, find someone you really trust, someone who knows you well, and show them the video. They'll tell you if it's boring or not.

Here are the three top tips for producing good videos according to Andrew:

Keep It Simple, Stupid

Simple messaging. Keep it to two or three messages in the video. Any more, you're overloading the viewer, especially if you're in a sales, product, or customer testimonial situation where you need two to three simple messages to convey, so people take action.

Be authentic and polite: Don't go out to interrupt your viewer. Don't use sales-y style scripts or scriptwriters like you see on TV. Those are old school, and people don't like that, because they don't see it as authentic. Remember, audiences are pretty savvy these days. They know they're being sold to, so instead be polite and be real. Tell real stories and feature real people.

End with a call to action. Make it compelling and ensure there's a specific action the viewer needs to take after they watch your video. This could be a link to your website, or restore. It could simply be 148.

Do's and Don't's in Videomaking

When it comes to filming, one thing Andrew has some specific do's and don't's.

Don't use a green screen or virtual backgrounds when recording your videos if you can avoid it! People obsess too much about using green screens. One thing which has come out of what's been going on with COVID is the buying of a Zoom subscription, a green screen, and a nice microphone off the internet. The green screen, then, becomes a portal to superimpose backgrounds that don't look nice, that break apart, or across your body and face, and that don't necessarily make you look any good or stand out in a positive or pleasing way to your audience. Also, people can get a little bit over the top with green screens and virtual backgrounds, in terms of making them add things that aren't really there. Simply put, from an authenticity point of view, avoid. Rather, he says to work on getting a nice shot in a place that's real.

Do use YouTube as your teacher, and search for videos that teach you about good framing, decent lighting, and what you can do even with a webcam in your home or office, or home office. Work on your writing or scripting for video skills. They are very different to writing for anything else. Watch YouTube tutorial videos about how to develop your video presenting skills. Watch the good presenters and vloggers on YouTube and TV. How do they do it? Bottom line … train yourself to present well on camera.

The good news is there are so many places you can go to outsource your video making at the moment at a whole range of different price points. The bad news is, because there are so many solutions out there, it's hard to get a gauge of things like simple market rates for video production. The simple fact is that if you want to find somebody to shoot something for free for you, you could probably find it. If you want to find someone to put a whole video together for free for you, or for very little cost, you could probably do that as well.

Andrew says that the best way to outsource video making is to find people like yourself, similar businesses, and find out who they're using for video production. Do they use an agency? A videographer, individual freelancer or producer? A video production company? Check your personal and business networks to find any potential partners.

When you find a potential video production partner, look at the past work that they've done to see if you like their work. This is crucial. Check if the work is actually theirs, because sometimes, companies pass others' work as their own. If you're looking for animation, copywriting, or editing services, websites like Fiverr or Upwork can be useful, but again, check the freelancer's credentials and their portfolio.

Why One of the Most Powerful Tools for Video is Your Phone

One of the most powerful tools for video is your smartphone. If there's one piece of technology everyone should have, it's a smartphone with a good camera. Practicing first on a phone camera is a good place to start. Investing in a good tripod is also really important, and so is investing in a good microphone system that works with your phone or computer.

If you're going out to make a video yourself and you don't have any equipment, look into renting a kit, don't waste money on buying expensive video production equipment that inevitably may become obsolete in a matter of months when the next model comes out. There are plenty of places or people online that you can rent camera equipment from, or there will be a local rental house near you as well where you can rent.

The work Andrew does prove that video can play a key role and also that video doesn't have to cost as much as it used to. There are people out there on platforms like Fiverr and Upwork, for instance, that can bring the necessary skill sets. Remember, even the major films are made with basically a consortium of independent production specialists who have come together for a project. Nowadays, equipment can be rented, so you don't even have to buy lots of fixed cost equipment.

Video can and should play a key role in any business strategy, and applications like Zoom have made it easier with its video conferencing and virtual event features. You can livestream Zoom calls directly to Facebook and record and save entire meetings in the cloud to be viewed later, or to be re-edited. All this tech is becoming so much more accessible to business owners and entrepreneurs, and it really is becoming as easy as holding your mobile phone.

Andrew always brings it down to the three top tips when you approach any video project. So remember:

1. Keep It Simple, Stupid.

2. Be authentic and polite.

3. End with a call to action.

Chapter Five
What is the Benefit of Giving Back?

Masami Sato, Founder & CEO of B1G1, Singapore.

Courtesy of Masami Sato

Masami Sato is the founder of B1G1, a Singapore-based social enterprise and a non-profit organisation that stands for 'Buy one, give one'.

Imagine a world full of giving. A world where you can get a cup of coffee and, at the same time, give life-saving water to a child. A world where you can purchase a book and get a tree planted. A world where every time you visit your doctor, someone else receives access to health care. This is what B1G1 strives to make happen by working with businesses around the world and helping them effectively embed giving in what they do.

Since they were founded in 2007, they have worked with close to 3000 businesses. These businesses have already created over 200 million giving impacts – projects that include planting trees, giving meals, and donating books, among others.

What's Missing in the Charity-Giving Space

Looking around, the world isn't actually lacking in giving. There are a lot of opportunities wherein people and companies can donate money to charities.

However, when B1G1 was only starting, they realized that the charity-giving space is missing three important things: impact, habit, and connection.

Impact. When people or companies are donating money, it was always about the amount of money being donated. They weren't necessarily clear or tangible about the impact that they get to create by giving.

Habit. If everything is driven by ad hoc activities – such as a big charity bowl or a natural disaster – donations will only go to a particular cause; it will only happen once then die down. For B1G1, habit is important in making a long-lasting impact.

Connection. Giving can unite people together. It can bring people – businesses, customers, team members – together by allowing them to share the same spirit of caring and giving.

Focusing on these three things, B1G1 helps businesses share what they're doing. For example, for every podcast episode or every download of a specific resource, businesses can contribute to a specific project even for just 1 cent. They can help plant trees in specific regions or help educate children in different countries. When things get tangible, B1G1 provides technologies such as dynamic widgets that can be embedded on businesses' websites. These show the actual impact – rather than merely state the fact that a certain company donated some money to a particular project. This way, the giving becomes more meaningful and impactful.

Connecting Companies and Worthy Causes

B1G1 doesn't target a single industry. Their one-to-one model actually works for all kinds of businesses, including small businesses and startup companies. And they connect companies and causes via referral activities.

In the early days, when there was still no demand and awareness for the social impact of corporate social responsibilities, B1G1 had to get out there, visit, and meet with different businesses. It took a lot of time before they got to know these businesses and had them on board their initiative. However, over the years, awareness has been built. More businesses today now think about how they can do more meaningful work, give, and become more purposeful. With this mindset and through word of mouth, it has become easier for B1G1 to reach more people. Many of the companies that they are working with are the ones that champion this spirit of giving and help spread the word. When they embed the widget on their website or spread the word through different social media channels to empower audiences to share their purpose and make an impact, B1G1 gets to reach more businesses.

Choosing Who They Work with Based on Impact

As B1G1 focuses on the impact, the organisations that they work with are not necessarily famous charity brands. B1G1 chooses based on the specific ways that these organisations bring impact to the world. They may come through recommendations and referrals from other charities and businesses that they are working with. Regardless of how the groups have reached them, B1G1 conducts an assessment, making sure that they meet a certain set of criteria. For instance, the organisation needs to have experience and track record in a specific area. They should have sound financial management as well.

B1G1 works closely with these organisations and breaks down impacts into 'micro impacts' that can cost as little as 1 cent to guarantee tangibility. For instance, every time an email is sent, you can give access to someone in need of something; every time you have a meeting, you can donate a brick and help build a school, plant a tree, or clean up the beach.

Trying to do something big can be overwhelming. When that takes over, there could be a delay in action. On the contrary, if small impacts are done even with a small amount of money, there's actually no need to wait until a business becomes very profitable or super successful. This way, even small businesses can embed giving in the activities that they do. At the same time, they can experience the joy of giving and creating an impact together with the people that they work with.

Currently, B1G1 has more than 500 projects in over 42 countries. These projects are aligned with all of the 17 United Nations Sustainable Development Goals (SDG).

In the early days, businesses tend to support more emotional projects like supporting a child's education or helping people with disabilities. Today, more and more companies are keen to support SDG-aligned environmental causes such as planting trees, cleaning up beaches, saving food waste, and delivering leftover food to people in need. These are creative and innovative projects whose impact can serve two different purposes, instead of just one.

The B1G1 Model

B1G1 works as an intermediary. When there's direct contact between givers and recipients, it often ends up creating a sense of dependency.

What they want is to maximise the effectiveness of the giving that the businesses are doing. Instead of being busy with facilitating contacts between the two parties, it will be better to help them in making an impact instead.

Because they want the giving experience to be more meaningful for the donors, B1G1 also shares all sorts of updates to them, without necessarily offering a direct link to specific beneficiaries. Before the pandemic happened, for instance, they facilitated annual study tours wherein they took small groups of people to visit certain projects and gave them a first-hand understanding of the impact being created by donors. The donors get to learn from the beneficiaries and the beneficiaries get to see the people who will be helping them. This allows the social enterprise to avoid a sense of dependency and, at the same time, establish control.

The B1G1 model is also different from the usual charity model because they never take a percentage from the donations that companies are giving to different degrees. A hundred percent goes to the project. In fact, they even top-up any credit charges that businesses may incur in the process (e.g. 1 cent is lacking to provide water to a beneficiary).

They are able to run their initiative and cover associated costs through their business membership model.

Even a tiny business can contribute to the so-called Movement fund (larger companies may contribute more). B1G1 uses this fund to develop their systems and resource tools for businesses. With this, the resources that are used to build and keep the initiative running and the donations that go to the projects become clearly separated. The giving part goes to registered charities in the States while the membership components go to B1G1 based in Singapore.

Based on experience, there's a lot of value in creating value – but even more in sharing that value with others.

Chapter Six
When is a Newswire Service Good for PR?

Mickie Kennedy, Founder of eReleases.com, Kingsville, Maryland, USA.

Courtesy of Mickie Kennedy

What Does eReleases Offer?

eReleases offers custom national distribution over PR Newswire. They also provide a higher end product wherein they send emails to journalists that they feel would be appropriate for their clients' press releases. The number of recipients varies from 100 to 400.

More than 10 years ago, PR Newswire approached Mickie and offered to send his press release through them. At the time, he was charging $250 while PR Newswire charged about $1000 for a 500- to 600-word press release to go out nationally.

Both built their relationship to be a win-win: Mickie has a client base that comprises small businesses who'd never be able to afford to go directly to the Newswire. Newswire's salespeople, on the other hand, also wouldn't be interested in someone doing only one to three press releases a year.

During his meeting with them, he discovered that they have an overnight editorial team. That's why he said that it wouldn't cost them a thing to work on press releases and set them up for the next day. This enabled him to schedule all of their releases for next-day distribution. They also have other workflow elements that make this easier.

With this, eReleases has allowed small businesses, entrepreneurs, authors, and startups to be able to access the wire nationally. This is great value for just a few hundred dollars.

Pursuing Big Media

With PR Newswire, about 70–80% of their press contact will be unnecessary recipients if the press release that they're sending is for a smaller company.

In eReleases' case, they still go out to the big media. As Mickie pointed out, you'll be surprised at how sometimes, these big media would pick up something and run with it.

Last year, they did a press release for the Dining Bonds Initiative. The campaign aims to help out restaurants that closed down during the pandemic.

Mickie considered it a perfect storm because there was a lot of negative news and theirs was something that was very positive. For the project, they got over 150 articles, including those from the *Wall Street Journal, Washington Post, New York Times* — all of which are major places that they weren't expecting.

This is why, sometimes, it's beneficial to have those big guys on the list even though it feels like they're unlikely to pick up your press release. Apart from getting media coverage, it has generated millions of dollars in revenue that went right back immediately into a lot of restaurants that closed down.

The story proved to be something that people really identified with. It was actionable. It was positive news.

The Importance of Newswire Service

The leverage that you get by going to newswires – which, at times, seems unnecessarily large – can be beneficial.

Newswires act as a distribution platform for press releases.

A lot of people are familiar with newswires such as Reuters, United Press International, The Associated Press, and Dow Jones among others. Their business model is different: They write the content. It's all-original reporting and they're just licensing it to other people. With this, a small newspaper may not need to write breaking news right now because they can simply pull it off of the wire.

Press release newswires work similarly to that in the sense that press releases are transmitted electronically. However, when it goes to the points like The Associated Press and Reuters, it doesn't mean that it automatically runs on there – it's still up for them to consider. And if they do run it, they generally turn it into an article or some content that they themselves have crafted.

It's a wide distribution that's electronic. You could actually go to the website as a journalist and log in and customise your feed. You can see the exact type of content that you want to see. You can include or exclude keywords that can refine what you see.

Boosting Credibility

Mickie sees sending press releases over the wires and sharing it with your own social media as complementary. You get earned media as a result of the press release, and there's no reason you can't share those articles with your own people as well.

He always tells people to document the earned media that they get. Take screenshots, record those, and put them on your website. This gives a huge credibility boost.

If someone visits the website of a company that they never heard of, and they see a series of press releases, then their guard goes down and they'd feel more comfortable that it's not a scam company.

It's also the same with your vendors, suppliers, and partners. You can communicate with them by making newsworthy announcements, issuing press releases, and sharing the earned media that you get as a result of your PR.

As you have leads in your pipeline, you have to share with them when you get earned media.

Take note that earned media are an implied endorsement because a journalist writes about you.

Mickie's customers always tell him that they may not get a huge amount of traffic when they get earned media – but they do attract traffic, convert, and entice people to click. Their audience won't need to open a new window and check if they can get their product cheaper elsewhere. Their customers are willing to do business with them because they've previously read about them. These are customers who are loyal; they're what people are looking for in an optimum audience.

He also has clients who did so well that they sent a pay-per-click track to the article (not to their website) knowing that people can be converted through it. While they can't retarget that traffic, it's still worth it because the people that read the article tend to buy.

When you're doing earned media, it creates the opportunity in which a person who discovers you would want to do business with you.

At the end of the day, if the article does such a great job of introducing an audience to a company and their service or product, and it has the legitimacy of being a third-party piece of content (not a paid sponsorship), it can do really well.

Crafting a Strategic Press Release

Unlike a PR firm, eReleases don't do a follow-up of the traditional press release. Rather, what they try to instil in their customers is to be strategic so that every time they send a message, a press release, or an announcement, they're more likely to get picked up.

For a press release to be considered strategic or newsworthy, Mickie cited one of his clients who got favourable media outcomes during the pandemic.

His client does 30–40 surveys a year and covers a lot of little niches. They're a platform where people can find information about different companies (e.g. who has the best scanning or accounting software).

They do press releases on each of these areas. For instance, if they are to do one about accounting, they'll do a survey of people in that industry including accountants and bookkeepers. Through it, they'll be able to determine what is trending at the moment.

Their press releases then will be very specific and, consequently, will do really well. Usually, they'd get 8–14 earned media articles every time they do a press release on one of their surveys or studies.

Mickie has also coached a local auto repair shop in Pennsylvania that wants to get into industry trade publications. Their website went down (They got their domain name through one of those in Yellow Pages and it went dark). Now, they have a new domain name but still had no links to it. Someone who specialises in search engine optimisation told them that if they can get auto industry publications linking to them, it'll be the quickest and easiest way for their site to start ranking.

Mickie told his client that he's not newsworthy at the time. And what they have to do is to become the news by doing a survey and throwing one or two oddball questions. In their case, the question was: What's the strangest thing a customer left in their car while being repaired? The survey was an open field where respondents can write a sentence or two.

They sent that to other auto repair shops. They reached out to a trade association of independent auto repair centres and 800 of their members responded.

The question that they asked came out of the left field. As it gave no statistical evidence because every response was different, Mickie and his team simply curated the most interesting ones. As a result, 10 auto trade publications picked them up, including their local newspaper.

While he told his client that their customers wouldn't see the content, the goal was to get to those auto trade publications. Within three months, they were able to rank no. 1 under their new domain name. They had all those articles that linked back to them, which helped give them a lot of credibility. Their customers also eventually came in and shared their own stories (e.g. a grandmother leaving an urn for a memorial service).

At the end of the day, it's all about stories. It's about communicating and creating something that an audience would be interested in reading more about.

If you take it to a journalist and gatekeeper and they'd write content about it, you're helping them do their job of passing along some great information to their audience.

Many people are writing about what's important to them. They want to promote a product or a service, making their content self-centric. However, that won't let you come across something that would be captivating or interesting to someone to read or learn more about.

As what I talk about in the SPEAK|PR program, it's not about you or your company. It's about what your customers in the marketplace are doing. You're simply facilitating the conversation.

Advertising eReleases

Being an entrepreneur for 23 years now, Mickie shared that he got his business noticed by doing a lot of pay-per-click advertising among people who are in the buying process of a press release. He and his team also do blogging, communicating, and talking about the subject matter.

Apart from those, he's also doing interviews where he discusses press releases and their value. He also sends articles out there and gets placed in the media as well.

He does anything that can get him and his business out there, including utilising social media. While he feels that it's not a huge driver of his business, he still considers it a necessary piece of the puzzle that supports, links, and helps you interact with all other advertising forms (e.g. email marketing).

He also provides a lot of quick start guides and other giveaways so that people can learn more. Through those, he's able to build a relationship with them.

When it comes to leveraging earned media, he also offers to write an article for an actual publication and make it specific to them. It's a lot more work, but through it, he's able to craft a message that's a lot more relevant for his audience.

In terms of getting it out to some key publications, the majority of where he goes to are business strategy websites and other places that people go for resources. His goal is to be one of the resources on those pages.

How Frequently Should You Issue a Press Release?

Asked about the frequency of issuing a press release, Mickie recommends doing six to eight months. If you're going to test press releases, releasing at that frequency will give you a good understanding of how your PR campaign is faring.

You also have to try different strategic messages for each one. Then, assess if any of those resonated with your audience. Did you get enquiries? Did any of those enquiries come from earned media or actual articles being written about you?

He also said that you have to be strategic with the types of press releases that you're doing. Try to look at it from a journalistic perspective. What can you do that would really help them do their job?

Many people are familiar with newsjacking, wherein you try to align yourself with a hot topic. To elevate the conversation, you have to make your content very specific. Rather than joining on board with everybody else, you have to introduce something new.

For instance, he had a client and there was a big scandal about Target and the hacking of credit card numbers and other personal information. A lot of people are doing press releases for the six months that have succeeded.

They used Target as a case study and introduced themselves as a cyber security outfit that offers the solution.

His client wanted to do the same thing. However, Mickie told him that those people aren't getting a lot of media coverage because there are already many of them out there. He advised him to focus on something very narrow.

One of their client's services is to help small merchants have credit card terminals on their counters. With this in mind, they created a free audit, sharing the 10 things that businesses with credit card terminals should do to determine if they're at risk of getting hacked. By narrowing that down, they were able to get a number of articles written about them.

Rather than simply joining the conversation, Mickie recommended that you should take a slice of it and focus on that. Or, you can say something that goes against what the rest is saying. Either way, it will help you stand a stronger chance of getting noticed.

Chapter Seven
Indian Film Festival for Kidz Reaches the World

Praveen Nagda, Festival Director of KidzCINEMA, Mumbai, Maharashtra, India.

Courtesy of Praveen Nagda

COVID has certainly brought something good and some opportunities to a lot of people. Just like to Praveen Nagda, Founder and CEO of Peregrine PR and Festival Director of KidzCinema, and to the filmmakers who took part in the first two editions of the film festival. From an idea of a project of passion that could also bring some business opportunities, Praveen is one of the people who initiated the KidzCinema 2020 with one-third of the countries worldwide taking part during the first two editions.

How KidzCinema was born

The COVID-19 pandemic presented one good opportunity to Praveen in 2020.

The whole world was locked down, kids were sitting at home, families were living in closed spaces, and people were switching on to online media consumption like they never did before. At the same time, kids were also suffering emotionally because they've always been used to being in playgrounds, being with friends – moving out of their homes.

He has a kid of his own who was then eight years old when COVID hit. He saw him so restricted and feeling claustrophobic at home because his kid would always be out with his friends five to seven hours a day.

This is the same thing that's happening around the world. Many of his friends – whether they're in America, India, or Europe – have the same experience.

That was one angle. The second was, COVID also presented a lot of challenges to the traditional businesses that people were doing. It prompted people to be constantly explore new opportunities and avenues.

Praveen thought about doing something that is an act of passion but can also become a long-term mission for him, personally; at the same time, something that can also bring in some kind of additional business opportunities.

Hence, he and his team planned to create KidzCinema, an online film festival for children.

A Film Fest for Kids

Film festivals are there but there aren't too many kids' film festivals. India has a few, Europe has a lot. But most countries will only have one or two of them.

According to Praveen, kids need a wholesome, healthy form of entertainment wherein they can learn a lot of things and get values education and life lessons. All these things are very important. However, there aren't so many children's films that are made compared to films that are made for the older demographics. There's Hollywood and Bollywood, but for children, we don't have so many films.

The European market is pretty much evolved – there are a lot of film festivals for children that have been running for 30–40 years now – and it is still evolving. India's market is still evolving. They have a few good film festivals for children, but not many of them.

Doing one online is an opportunity wherein one could earn cash. This is why he decided to create one around kids.

Film festivals also give a lot of opportunities to filmmakers to exhibit their work theatrically. But it's a big expense. Many people don't even have the stability, so they reach out to debtors. As exhibiting is a humongous task, festivals provide this chance for them to showcase their work at a very minimal, or even free, cost.

In the case of KidzCinema, he and his team don't charge any entry fees from filmmakers. They let them submit their films. But they only accept films that are recently made, those that were created within one year's time, coinciding with the year of the festival's edition.

An Overwhelming Response

For their first edition, which took place in 2020, they approached UNESCO. They helped them connect with people and reach out to many constituents. They also connected with many embassies in India, which helped extend their outreach.

It's interesting to note that for the first-ever KidzCinema, they received about 1100 films that came from 87 countries. About one-third of the world participated. In 2021, the second edition had more than 1500 films from over 90 countries.

For Praveen, it's overwhelming to see how one-third of the world is actually coming together and joining this cause. There were films that came even from filmmakers living in remote areas such as small countries in Africa and very small islands from different places. There were a number of films from Europe and lots from Iran.

While there were countries that have sanctions and economic conditions that don't allow this kind of culture (but is still there to grow), they still got huge participation.

For the second edition, they also partnered with the International Centre of Films for Children and Young People (CIFEJ), which is one of the largest organisations of filmmakers who are making content for children. It has members from around 45 countries – hundreds of established filmmakers who have made films, documentaries, dramas, and animations for children.

KidzCinema's Film Categories

KidzCinema has categories for live-action and animation films. They also have one unique category for films made by children. Under it are two sub-categories: one for films made by 6–13 years old; another, by 14–21 years old.

The festival got hundreds of people from all over the world participating. And you could see an amazing amount of creativity there – in small and large stories, beautiful animations, and other very interesting creative work from children.

Praveen considers film as a universal medium. It can bind people. It doesn't even require audio. You can see kids watching films without audio and they'll understand what's happening there. It's a really powerful tool of communication; a pretty overwhelming experience for people to really connect the whole world together.

Learnings from the First Edition

KidzCinema's first edition was a lot of learning for Praveen.

It was the beginning of a task that he didn't know how it would unfold. Because when they started the festival, they didn't really know how many entries they would get and how many participants there would be.

They started and finished the first edition within about 52 days. Every day, they'd get 50 entries from different countries. It was overwhelming that they had to constantly add more people at the time of the process of their curation because they had to make sure that they saw each film submitted.

There was a 10-full-member curation team to see each film, evaluate it on certain parameters, and get it for the next process of the selection committee. The committee is composed of well-known and experienced filmmakers.

From there, the next step would be for jury members. Some of the members were from Bollywood and some senior bureaucrats. They have a mix of some judges, who will then award the best films across different categories.

Evolving in the Second Edition

For the second edition, they upgraded a couple of parameters in terms of the whole experience of the festival.

According to Praveen, they had to run the first edition of KidzCinema with much less time to prepare, so they used YouTube and other platforms to showcase the film for the three-day festival. In the succeeding year, they increased the duration of the festival. The main festival activities was increased from three to seven days; and the exhibition, from 3 to 30 days.

If you wanted to see all 40–45 films that are part of the official selection, you could see them very comfortably on the couch, bedroom, dining room, or wherever you want to. You could even watch it in your garden using your mobile phone.

They tied up with a US-based platform called MovieSaints, which delivers films via the internet. You can register, log in, and watch the film just like you'd watch them in the theatre. You can choose the films that you want. There are synopses and trailers of the films available. So, you can actually have a bit of experience first, then watch the whole film. And there's also a bit of revenue generation from there.

Though it's a project of passion, it still requires a certain amount of investment – both in terms of time and money – because there are things that you have to do. The exhibition itself is expensive. How do you show the films? How do you get people from across the world to watch the films?

In festivals, on the one hand, you also support the filmmakers. You give them a platform to express their creativity. There are also other things for kids because it's eventually a kids' event. In the kids' event, Praveen and his team got experts to do a lot of workshops about filmmaking, scriptwriting, and cinematography among others.

One of the interesting workshops was conducted by Ritesh Taksande and he had created a specific course called mobile filmmaking – how you can use your mobile phone to make films. Youngsters loved it because, nowadays, everybody has mobile phones.

There are also nice apps out there and, interestingly, these apps allow you to do good work akin to professional editing. These are tools that allow you to edit films, put overlays, and give special effects without any kind of watermark or any other distraction. You can really put together a nice story.

Last year, they also had one more very interesting concept. Typically, what happens is that adults make films for children and it's also the adults that judge them. This time around, they created a specific child jury of five kids and they asked them to review two short-film categories.

In the live-action category, they have long and short films (the former is full 30- to 90-minute long; the latter is less than 30 minutes). They also have long and short animation films. As mentioned, they also have categories for films made by kids. They got the child jury to judge the short films in the animation and live-action categories. They all discussed and evaluated, and the organisers also had a proper jury meeting with them.

For the second edition, there were child jury awards and professional jury awards. The professional jury judged all the categories. The child jury, which judged the two aforementioned categories, was a good mix comprising a celebrity child artist, a classical dancer, a young author, a poet, and a theatre person. They had creatively inclined children to come together, form a jury, watch content made by adults for children, and give film awards.

It was quite an interesting exercise in terms of involving children and bringing them together. It's a wholesome package that they have created for children.

Promoting the Festival

KidzCinema is a Herculean effort to curate so much content from around the world. But how did they get people to come and watch?

Praveen shared that the primary promotions were done through social media. They have a lot of active social media pages on Instagram and Facebook among others. They also involved the filmmakers to create the buzz within their markets and get people to watch the films.

He pointed out that their promotions were mainly on social media because it's the best way to reach out to people. But you can also put-up billboards and other physical promotional things.

MovieSaints also provided them with a good platform to exhibit anywhere in the world. In terms of the audience figures, though he couldn't disclose the actual numbers, he revealed that they had in hundreds and thousands – good numbers – of audiences who logged in.

Making it Financially Sustainable

From an entrepreneurial perspective, KidzCinema needs to generate enough money to at least fund itself and be sustainable in the future.

Praveen considers the festivals like this are large-scale events that require a huge investment. However, COVID and the online environment gave them an opportunity to create something like this at a very minimal cost in terms of financial expenses on the organisers' side. In their first edition, they got a bank to partner with them (the bank has a product for kids).

As you go ahead producing an event like KidzCinema, you can also scale things up in different ways – one of which is to involve a lot of schools and create certain programmes for them.

In those programmes, you can teach children various aspects of filmmaking and show them other films. You can also have a film director come in and talk about his experience. These kinds of things will mean revenue. Though it's not something that's immediate, good revenues will come in their own time.

What the Future Holds for KidzCinema

Praveen considers KidzCinema as a long-term mission for him, even a lifetime one. He needs to keep building this activity. And as it goes on, he sees KidzCinema being brought to the ground. So, you will see on-ground and online both coming together, with a pretty good audience, at that point in time.

This project of passion started with COVID. In the first year, their theme was 'Togetherness in Distancing Times'. This time, as we're still going through COVID, their theme was 'Stories of Positivity'. When we come out of this pandemic, he plans to create some theme about it – how we survived the pandemic and what lies ahead in the future.

They'll also try to reach out to more partners such as banks and other corporate partners that would want to be a part of the journey. There are brands that want to catch their audiences young and they can possibly be good partners that can be engaged for the more intensive activities.

He also shared that they will always keep KidzCinema global. As he said, the festival has global participation, both in terms of filmmakers and judges. The entire team that's involved also comes from all over the world.

In a couple of years, they also hope to have a firm footing within local markets and could make it a travelling festival. They might do the festival in some other country every year. And this is when they'd require some support from cross-country governments and other related partners.

Praveen believes that all this will happen when the time is right. He's in no hurry. He believes in taking baby steps, then bigger steps, then leaps.

Chapter Eight

How Foreign Brands Can Compete With 60 Million Online Merchants in China?

Josh Gardner, CEO & Co-Founder, Hong Kong SAR, China.

Courtesy of Josh Gardner

Josh Gardner is the Co-Founder and Managing Director of Kung Fu Data, a platform based in China, and he's part of the Entrepreneurs' Organization there. Kung Fu Data has a very simple mission, and that's helping non-Chinese brands thrive online in Chinese marketplaces. Chinese consumers are self-trained experts in everything they buy.

Kung Fu Data revolves around marketplace commerce or what is called the marketplace economy, and these ecosystems in China are gargantuan. To put some context, Alibaba made over $1 trillion in their last fiscal year. This suggests that China's digital ecosystem is far more sophisticated, evolved, and interesting than anywhere else. And so, what Kung Fu Data does is help niche brands find a home in China and drive their commercial success, which they've been doing for seven years. In that time, they have launched more than 50 brands on Tmall, JD, and core marketplaces. They've done hundreds of projects on the market entry side as well helping people fix problems.

Kung Fu Data recently signed a brand that had squatters all over their IP address in China. There were three or four entities sitting on various versions of the brand's name in Chinese and English, and they needed to get back their category. To solve that problem for their client, Josh and his team connected with partners in China that specialise in taking control of IP. Another example is when a competitor of theirs got in a lawsuit with a brand that was trying to cut ties with them. They were refusing to turn over control of the stores and the social accounts to the brand. Even though they were in arbitration, they were still holding it hostage, and so Josh's team served as triage. They were on the phone with different aspects of Alibaba management and different directors of different teams trying to get someone to give them new logins. These situations are somewhat unique to the Chinese marketplace and probably would not be encountered elsewhere, making their SOW quite specific.

Let the Experts Do the Work for You

It's never simple, and it's never just one thing, but the key problem Kung Fu Data solves is sales and amplification. For those wanting to break into the Chinese market, Kung Fu Data is an expert at taking brands from one to 100, however, they can't predict exactly when the company will reach 100. It takes time, but definitely, they are responsible for selling and managing the brand online and handling all the problems related with that. That involves logistics, customer service, returns management, tech integration, IT, data reporting, results, delivery, platform management, events, media, marketing, creative, etc. They do it all as the marketplace partner. In addition to that, they connect people who do things they don't do, which is social media, PR, and seeding. Their focus is more on integrating assets and marketing inside the marketplace ecosystems to be as active on the platform as they can. They aim to drive visible brand equity and push it in through the official channel, which is the flagship store or the authorised dealerships. Their job is to manage the commerce, drive it, grow it, expand it, make the brand as strong as possible, and with the resources that come from it, they are able to create successful brands.

Take note that only one in 20 foreign stores ever hit a million in sales. Most don't, but they're still able to build a good business. There is no doubt that Chinese merchants have the home court advantage, but it doesn't mean that a business owner should give up considering doing business in China. It's not that there's no demand for foreign products. If the demand is outrageous, a business can do really well. The issue is that, internally, foreign businesses are resource-deficient. They are not educated and trained to think the right way about China, and they don't have cultural fluency. Linguistic fluency isn't necessary, but trade culture fluency is.

In terms of the kind of companies Kung Fu Data works with, Josh says these ecosystems are now all-encompassing. They build brands online in the Chinese marketplace, and so their core customers are mostly professional consumer brands or prosumer brands. And because 10 million factories are online and have Tmall and Taobao stores, actual professional trade now happens on retail platforms. WeChat accounts can be used for running the business, communicating with teams, and talking with friends and communities. On Instagram, it's just friends and family. Whereas with WeChat, anything and everything can be done. B2B, B2C, B2B2C, and M2C all happen on the same platform.

Bringing the Business to China

To get into the Chinese market, a business first needs to understand what they're going to be up against, and then they need to act accordingly and plan properly. The amount of competition is insane coupled with the fact that, unfortunately, the business is not unique, so there has to be some kind of unfair advantage or a defendable position in some way. That is the game. Building relationships can help business owners find a position that allows them to build and grow. Otherwise, they're going to be attacked continuously, which is what Josh and his team have learned to avoid after many failed attempts. For those who have had a go in China, the old saying is, the longer you're there, the more you realise you don't know, and that definitely holds true. The market is ever-changing, and so businesses will always have to adapt and learn.

Once a business overtakes their competition, they then need to maintain that level of success, which is tough. Once they're on the other side, it's even harder to stay there because now they're a real target. This is why Josh always tells his clients that they need to come armed to the teeth; in other words, be prepared and have a budget, even for things money isn't usually allocated for, for instance, controlling the IP which is what Josh and his team work out first, because the brand can't launch without it. The next step is controlling the demand routing on anyone's trademark with proper registrations with Alibaba as the brand control unit. Doing this ensures that all the brand's traffic, IP, and visible brand equity are going to the official channels. A more aggressive way to do this would be through introductions Josh makes to a law firm founded by military attorneys which records over a half a million takedowns a year, making them equivalent to the marines of IP protection.

Kung Fu Data works with competent partners, and they always surround themselves with the same kind of talent in different verticals, because it's important to build an infrastructure that secures one's position. Josh emphasises focusing on marketing and PR and not backing off even when the business is already successful. Instead, Josh says to double down. That will get the business to a position where it is unequivocally so far ahead of everyone else, it would require a major disruption to unseat it. After going through all the trials and tribulations and making it into the winner's circle, double down again, because you don't want to give anyone behind you a chance to catch up. Otherwise, they can take you down. The idea is to secure the winnings and to do that, the business needs to invest in the right resources.

Chapter Nine
Travelling Through the US in an RV, This Entrepreneur Will Take You on a Journey to Financial Freedom

Howard Dekkers, CEO of Howard Dekkers School of Success, Boca Raton, Florida, USA.

Courtesy of Howard Dekkers

Howard Dekkers, a Life & Financial Coach and CEO of Howard Dekkers School of Success, has a new life purpose. It is to pay a life-changing system he learned from his dad forward, so that others can benefit from a system that will allow them to one day become financially free, all with a normal job!

Based in sunny Boca Raton, Florida, Howard sold his business with over 150 employees and is now on a mission to help entrepreneurs accomplish their own financial freedom.

A Piece of Financial Advice

Back when he was a teenager, Howard's father never earned more than $35 000 a year working in a factory. His dad's advice to him, at an early age, was that earning for today was great, however, he needed to start building for his future now, so he would not have to work one day in the future. He told Howard that he needed to save and invest 10% of everything he earned, starting with his first paycheck, and put the money in a financial freedom account. This is what his father had been doing since he was 20 years old.

In his youth, all Howard wanted to do was make money. That is what he did. He made a lot of money, working many different jobs. But he never paid attention to his dad's advice.

At a young age, he started building businesses. He had his first business at 28 and began experiencing success. As his success grew, his income grew. In his 30s he found himself earning $300 000 a year and more. However, like most entrepreneurs, and most people in the country, he was spending it all on things. He had the fancy cars, and spent a lot on entertaining. He even bought a house on the intra-coastal waterway in South Florida! His lifestyle with all his stuff made him look rich.

However, his wife, not quite as risk tolerant as he, insisted that they start saving for the future. You see, all the money they were earning was going to buy things and none of it was going towards their future!

His wife got him thinking, he was basing his whole success later in life – on being able to build a business big enough so he could sell it. But then he asked himself: What if we can't sell it? What if the laws change that hurt the company or we have to go bankrupt! We would be in our 60s and broke!!!

This is when he had a light bulb moment: He remembered what his dad told him many years ago. He needed to invest 10% of everything he earned. So, what did he do? He put his dad's advice in action and began investing 10% and more, of everything he earned and began transferring the money into a financial freedom account every month!

Basically, what his dad's programme was all about was taking the first 10–20% out of your checking account and investing it for the future. By taking it out of his checking account, he was basically creating an environment of economic scarcity. Meaning, if the money wasn't in the checking account, it would not be there to spend on things!

After implementation of the programme, even though he was making $300 000 to $400 000 a year, he felt like he was broke because he was forcing himself to save 10–20% of everything he earned. Instead of making this great income and buying stuff, he took it from his checking account and put it into a brokerage account like what his father did. He was about 38 years old when he started this.

As stated, his father never earned more than $35 000 a year. He started at Chrysler Corporation at age 20 and retired at age 55. That 10% over the years that went into his financial freedom account would add up to around $122 000 total money invested. Today, many decades later, his father has not worked since age 55 and his financial freedom plan has grown to $3 000 000 and he earns $85 000 a year from these investments! How did he do this? By simply investing 10% of everything he earned during his income-producing years.

Growing Your Money, the Smart Way

Most people, Howard has found, do not think they can become millionaires. Why? Because they think they have to save a million dollars. Not true says Howard!

What they must do is to save and invest monthly – whether it's $50, $100, or $500 a month. Even if they start out at $50 a month, it's fine because that little amount of money will double many times via compound interest. It is amazing how time and compound interest grow money!

For example, if you were to put $10 000 into an investment vehicle that earns 10% annually and made no further contributions, the $10 000 would grow to $326 000 in 35 years. That same $10 000 in a regular savings account would grow to $10 106!

If you do not have a lump sum and you simply transfer $100 a month for just 30 years into your own financial freedom plan, and it earns 10% annually, you will have invested $42 000 over the years, however compounding would have grown your $42 000 to $227 932. $500 a month into the same plan would be worth $1 139 663 in 30 years and your total invested money was only $180 000, one month at a time!

So, you can see, it is not about saving a million dollars. It's about investing monthly and having a disciplined and consistent plan.

Howard did not wake up and listen to his dad until his late 30s. He saved 10–20% from then on. Today he is a multi-millionaire from this plan alone!

Today, he has decided to pay his dad's teachings forward so others can one day become financially free!

How Entrepreneurs are a Different Breed

Three years ago, Howard sold his company for millions of dollars. He accomplished the dream that he had when he started 20 years prior. He feels he was lucky, however also feels he created his luck by applying a go the extra mile work habit in everything he did. It paid off!

But even if he had not sold his business for millions of dollars, he already had millions of dollars in his financial freedom plan because he had set up the automatic system many years earlier that had been transferring 10–20% of everything he earned into his financial freedom plan.

This concept can be applied by anyone who has a job. Entrepreneurs are lucky because they can put their financial freedom plan on hyperdrive because they have more money coming in than the average person. Whether you have a regular job or you're an entrepreneur, you need to make sure you are not spending all your money on things, and you are not putting all your money back into your business.

Howard shared that he always had a $500 000 line of credit on his home. This is how he built his company. He recalled how he would hate it when his Chief Financial Officer would walk into his office, close the door, and tell him that she could not make payroll! (It's around $500 000 a month). Fortunately, Howard would be pre-paying his line of credit quickly so when he needed it, he could use it again and again and again.

This shows how entrepreneurs are a different breed. They're willing to take risks to get to where they want to go, risks that a normal person isn't willing to take. The online financial freedom course that he built is catering to the person with a normal job. But if you're an entrepreneur, your financial freedom plan can go on hyperdrive.

Building His Programme

After Howard sold his company, he didn't have to work because he had enough money coming in every month from his financial freedom plan. Because his plan grew to a substantial amount, he was able to diversify into real estate and other investments. A year into retirement, he became bored with the lifestyle of the retired and knew he had to come up with something else to do in his life that he could become passionate about.

This is when he put together a PowerPoint presentation to teach his teenage children how to become millionaires. Before he showed it to his 17-year-old daughter and 18-year-old son, he asked them to invite their friends and tell them that their multi-millionaire dad was going to teach them how to be multi-millionaires.

His first presentation was a couple of years ago, on his big-screen TV. He had 10 kids (ages 17–23) sitting in his living room as he presented his PowerPoint on his big-screen TV. It blew them away! What blew him away is that they knew nothing about money. They had no idea how money grew. They knew nothing about compound interest. Nothing on budgeting, or net worth statements. They did not know where to start or how to start. After that, he went to all his sisters' kids, then to more people. He began doing a live six-week course on Zoom once a week with 10–20 students on the screen.

Another light bulb went off! He realized that our schools were not teaching our kids how to accumulate money so that one day they could be financially independent. After investigating further, he discovered that 78% of the people in our country are living just like he was in his 20s and 30s, paycheck to paycheck! He realized that he could be part of the answer. He found his new passion. He realized that this is what he wanted to do with the rest of his life. He wanted to teach people how they could become financially free with a normal job – and if they were business owners, how they could put their financial freedom plan on hyperdrive!

It took 1½ years of work, but after a lot of time and effort, he developed an online course comprising seven modules in video and written format that would teach those that wanted one day to be financially free how to do it. They would not only learn how, but would leave the course with their financial freedom plan setup and running on autopilot. The plan would be set up once, and run in the background of life, building for their future.

Howard's motivation is not to make another million dollars. It is to provide a superior product that he believes anyone with desire can complete and come out knowing enough to one day be financially free. He believes that if the product is good enough, he will make money even though that is not his main objective. He's doing it to help as many people as he can by teaching them his dad's programme and how they too can become financially free.

Just an example how one of Howard's students has changed her life by following his system.

A year and a half ago, one of his students had $40 000 sitting in a regular savings account. She invested it slowly over six months into her new brokerage account that automatically invested it into index funds that pay over 10%. That $40 000 has grown to $64 000 in just a year and a half. That is $24 000 more if she had left it in her savings account. Over 35 years, this $40 000 is expected to grow to over $1 305 000! If she had left it in a savings account it would be worth $40 422 in 35 years.

Rebranding Himself

Howard had previously been successful in publishing and diagnostic medical imaging centres. Now that he's been promoting the new 'Howard', he must rebrand himself as an individual whose domain of expertise is 'financial freedom' with a personal touch.

For this, he said that he's doing everything that he can to get the word out – from Facebook advertising, Instagram, handing out business cards, and being guests on other people's podcasts. While he has been told by others to do his own podcast, he mentioned that he doesn't want a job.

One of the reasons he decided to do a 100% evergreen online course is he had 10–20 people on his screen every week. He was having fun, but his vision had turned into a job, which was not what he wanted at that point in his life. He quickly knew what he had to do. Go evergreen!

Howard's also a big roving vehicle guy. In fact, he just recently came back from a three-month Solo RV road trip.

With just his home office on wheels (his BIG RV), Harley Davidson, his Jeep and his amazing Starbucks coffee maker, he visited six different states and 15 different cities. He'd stay in each city a week and play pickleball every morning, which he considers an amazing social sport. You just show up and play! He'd hand out business cards to almost everyone he met, and he met a lot of people on his last trip. When he goes to a restaurant, he leaves his business card with the paid bill. His card is rather simple. It's just a picture of him, some verbiage about becoming financially free and a QR Code to his webpage. All people need to do is take a picture of the QR code and they will be directed right to his webpage.

It's just a combination of different things.

Does he have the magical answer for growing his business? He said, 'absolutely not'.

He's nowhere near Tony Robbins or Dave Ramsey who's been doing it for 30 years. Howard has only been doing this for 2½ years and he's moderately successful. He has people taking his course. He loves it when he's in his RV and somebody requests a meeting. He built a custom desk with three computer screens so he can do guest podcasts and take care of other businesses he owns.

Once people finish his course, their financial freedom plan is set up and is running on autopilot. Students decide what to start with. $10, $50, $100, $500, or $1000 out of their chequebook every month and put it into a brokerage account under their name. Nobody else can touch it and nobody makes money on it other than the small fees charged to be a part of the Index fund.

In his programme, the monthly investment into the financial freedom plan is being automatically invested into index funds, which are low risk and average 10%. If a student needs a question answered, they schedule a Zoom appointment with him.

He is building a mobile business so he can live the lifestyle of his dreams. With it, he's able to go to people in person (old school), which he loves, but also use technology to grow the business. Even with COVID-19, he's still been able to grow his business.

His Course's Platform

For marketing and the evergreen course, Howard uses ClickFunnels as his platform. It's a lead magnet and works like Thinkific and Udemy for hosting courses.

He recently built a new webpage. His company's name is 'Howard Dekkers School of Success', however, he is branding his name, www. howarddekkers.com. Before his webpage was developed people were directed to ClickFunnels. Now they go to his webpage, which directs them to ClickFunnels.

He's using ClickFunnels because when he was first starting out, he hired a consultant and he paid him a lot of money to build his ClickFunnels account. Howard knew nothing and just did what the consultant advised.

He also reiterated that he's not concentrating on making another million dollars. He doesn't need to earn money because he has millions of dollars working for him, sending him money every month. All he wants to do is to deliver a superior product to his students. If he accomplishes this, he will, in turn, make money. He also uses Calendly to let his students set up an appointment with him so he can answer questions on a one-on-one basis via Zoom.

His Vision

Howard has a background in public speaking. He used to speak before 1000–3000 people, teaching them how to be successful in the multi-level marketing business.

His initial vision of his course: He envisioned that he'd be doing these financial freedom seminars and packing a hotel room. He didn't want to do Zoom, but then he didn't have a choice because of COVID. Then he started loving Zoom and the freedom it gave him, after getting used to it. He loved it except that it became a job. Now, he just does Zoom for support.

Ultimately, an entrepreneur's dream is to make money doing what they're passionate about. It's not even a job to them.

In Howard's case, he isn't really working, and he isn't struggling with cash flow anymore. Whether he is at home in Boca Raton, Florida, or in his RV, he works his programme. The nice thing about the RV is it is set up so he can help people even when he is travelling the country.

It's a lifestyle by design. Though he didn't design it to be exactly like it is today, he opened his mind and took advantage of Covid and decided to go with ClickFunnels, Zoom, Calendly, the RV, Jeep, and his Harley and is continuing to live an amazing life!

With that, people can have $500 000 in 30 years or $800 000 or even $1.5 million or more! It simply depends on their commitment and their goal. But if they continue doing nothing – like what Howard used to do in his 20s and most of his 30s, spending every dollar that comes into the household – they're not going to have anything but a bunch of worthless stuff 30 years from today. With a few changes in their lives, they can be financially free later on in life!

Chapter Ten
Why is There no More Kimchi for Korean Media, Instead it's KakaoTalk and Naver Search?

Heesang Yoo, Managing Consultant of Prism Communications Co. Ltd, Seoul Incheon Metropolitan Area, S. Korea.

Courtesy of Heesang Yoo

Heesang Yoo, the founder of Prism Communications, shared his insights on public relations in South Korea, which is a country located between China and Japan, and it has a population of 50 million. They're not big enough, but not small enough either. Despite that, they're one of the fastest growing economies in the world, and they have a lot of Korean-based multinational companies around the world like Samsung, LG, and Hyundai, to name a few.

Dealing with Korean Media

When it comes to media, Korean media is slightly different than the others. First, they have a lot of media in Korea considering their population. They have around 20 daily media, which is national and divided into general daily, business daily, English daily, IT daily, and more, but it's also more than just the media. It contributes to every aspect of social life, political life, and also business life. The media is constantly changing, yet still somewhat conservative. Many Koreans don't speak English very well, and so Korean remains the most widely spoken language there. It is hard to get into this industry, so Korean journalists hold themselves to a high standard and they are said to have this mindset where they see themselves as above others and that they deserve to be treated better, but this is slowly changing. In Korea, if anyone were to say they were a journalist, they would be treated well by customs and the government. If a Korean journalist were to go to a country like America, they would be asked a lot of questions, so Heesang sometimes tells his journalists not to declare that they are journalists. As a bit of trivia, the birth of Korean media was actually during the Japanese occupation, where they were seen as leading the population in fighting for their emancipation from the Japanese.

Korean media usually has a lot of scouting to do when it comes to media pitches. They used to have more interaction with the PR people, but because of the hardships faced by a lot of publications, they don't have as many journalists as they used to, meaning the journalists have a lot more work on their plate. So, for anyone pitching to the media, present something similar to an elevator pitch. The first and second paragraphs are the most important and should stand out. Otherwise, that will not get the journalist's attention and the media outreach material will go straight to the trash.

When it comes to press briefings with a client, the first thing Heesang asks the client for is translation and then localisation. This way, it will be easier to get the journalists' attention and get coverage faster. In foreign media, one would need to read every single paragraph to get the gist of the story. If that is done in Korea, journalists will not read it, not because they are lazy, but because they have so many other things to do and there's too many other materials that you're competing with. Heesang's advice is to put the most important information in the first and second paragraphs, and then follow up with the less important news. That's definitely a good tip when providing press materials to Korean journalists.

There is a term called 'cash for coverage' in which a company pays for all of a journalist's expenses when travelling to cover a story. In Korea, Heesang says they refer to it as a 'payment tree', but that is no longer being practised due to a bribery law that enacted a couple of years ago. When multinational companies like Samsung or LG would hold press briefings back then, they would provide money even for transportation. Now, every journalist needs to go to an event at their own expense. After that law was passed, most Korean press conferences changed their structure. They used to invite the media for an hour-long press conference after which lunch would be served, but now, they just provide a simple meal or beverage.

While the majority of countries around the world were going on national lockdown, Korea had never been placed on lockdown at all. The government simply enforced social distancing measures and other safety protocols to prevent and track the spread of the coronavirus. They do their press conferences with a hybrid format, where it is done online and broadcasted so that the journalists can listen. As the spread was controlled, they were shifting back to offline, in-person meetings.

KakaoTalk and Naver

For platforms, Zoom is the most popular one in Korea, but Heesang also believes Microsoft Teams is catching up, because there can be some technical issues with Zoom. Next is KakaoTalk which was the first messaging application launched there. It's currently dominating the market, and it is now a platform not just for communication but for finance, shopping, travel, and transportation. Everyone in Korea has KakaoTalk. There is also a Korean app called Line, but this is only secondary to KakaoTalk.

For social media campaigns, Heesang would be using the media relations, KakaoTalk, as well as Kakao Story which is the equivalent of Facebook in Korea. It is also developed by Kakao and is similar but easier to use, and this is great for traditional Koreans who can't speak English or have trouble with English and the older population. When doing media marketing, if the target audience is mostly the younger generation, Heesang says they would use Facebook. If they're targeting older people who can't really understand English, then they would use Kakao Story. In Korea, they do not use Google for search. Instead, they use Naver, which is their number one search engine. They also have Naver Blog, which a lot of Koreans use, and they use these too when doing PR.

Heesang has shared a whole wealth of experience and different challenges for people considering marketing their business in South Korea and working with the media. Always keep in mind localisation and proper communication with the local journalists when going international.

324

Chapter Eleven
Why a Podcast Could Be Part of Your Strategy?

Diogène Ntirandekura, Founder of ERP Happy, Montreal, Quebec, Canada.

Throughout the years of working as a System Applications and Products (SAP) consultant for a big consulting firm, Diogène Ntirandekura felt unnoticed most of the time. Despite the hard work, he never had any promotion – until he became independent four years ago and established ERP Happy. The business offers digital transformation solutions, including enterprise resource planning (ERP), customer relationship management (CRM), and project management tools.

Courtesy of Diogène Ntirandekura

In 2020, he launched his own podcast titled 'Consulting Lifestyle'. He also recently released a French podcast to cater specifically to his Francophone-speaking audience.

What is 'Consulting Lifestyle'

Diogène started listening to podcasts only in 2015, particularly to Pat Flynn's podcast called 'Smart Passive Income'.

When he created his own company back in 2017, he had the idea of having his own podcast because he's inherently fond of listening to and speaking with people. However, he was unsure of what his topic would be.

In 2019, he flew to San Diego and attended an event organised by Pat. Meeting other podcasters who talk about business-related subjects and have a substantial following, he was able to get clarity. He purchased Pat's course and followed his step-by-step guide on how to launch a podcast.

He unveiled his podcast, 'Consulting Lifestyle', for two reasons.

A Platform that Offers Help. The first reason was to have a show offering advice and help to his fellow consultants. Back when he started his career in consulting, Diogène wasn't really aware of what the job entailed and of the work dynamic in a consulting firm. His podcast touches on different topics concerning business-to-business (B2B) consultants – from leadership and personal development to ERP, CRM, and marketing.

An Avenue for Learning. Later on, when he became independent, he realised that there's one dominating business model among consultants: to sell their hours. However, he's aware that other business models also exist. For his second reason, he uses his podcast as a platform to invite talented and unconventional guests, understand these other business models, and apply what he can to his practice.

Now with over 80 episodes, 'Consulting Lifestyle' has become a thriving podcast that offers knowledge, and helps consultants decide which lifestyle they want to have and how they can build a consulting business around it.

Producing 'Consultancy Lifestyle'

'Consulting Lifestyle' is currently hosted via Buzzsprout. The podcast also has a separate website, which contains information about the show, its episodes, and guests.

During his podcast's early stages, Diogène did almost everything – from pre-recording, recording proper, to post-recording – except for the show's graphic materials.

The pre-recording phase includes finding guests on LinkedIn, Facebook groups, and through his network. He reaches out and secures guests through the calendar app called Calendly. This phase also covers researching information to improve the flow of his and his guest's conversation. Though he never sends a questionnaire to ensure that the show is unscripted, he lets his guests understand what sort of conservation they will have.

The recording phase is all about the interviewing proper. He uses Zoom and Squadcast, though he prefers the latter because of the app's better audio and video quality.

The post-recording phase, on the other hand, sees him editing the recording and promoting his content on social media (mainly on LinkedIn, Instagram, and Facebook). As stated, he taps another individual for the graphics.

As he tries to unload some of his tasks, Diogène now has a virtual assistant helping him with audio editing, graphic creation, and show note writing among others. He still handles the recording and takes an active part in social media promotion. Before, producing and promoting the podcast took up around four hours. But now, he tries to cut it down to three hours.

Learning from Others

For Diogène, 'Consulting Lifestyle' has become a significant source of knowledge. He believes that every guest he has on the show has something to share; something valuable to provide. And since he launched his podcast, the learnings he and his audience have acquired have been at different levels.

Business-wise, there have been topics about pricing, marketing, being an entrepreneurial consultant, and collaborating. There are also episodes that share something about personal growth as his array of guests have different backgrounds: There are digital nomads and there are people with kids who still managed to grow their business or passion.

Because of this very nature of his podcast, Diogène does not see 'Consulting Lifestyle' as something that eclipses his consulting business. Instead, he considers these two things as complementary. Through his podcast, he learns strategies and experiences from other people and applies them to his practice.

It also enables him to have the 'Know, Like, Trust' factor. As the podcast allows him to talk about his struggles and milestones, he's able to build trust in his audience. His sharing of valuable information on consulting practices and digital information also helped him gather more listeners who want to know more about these matters.

On Frequency and Duration

One of the hallmarks of successful communications is consistency. For podcasters to be able to be consistent in uploading content, Diogène notes that publishing weekly is recommended. For instance, his 'Consultancy Lifestyle' podcast airs every Monday.

However, the frequency still boils down to the nature of your podcast. If you have long-form podcasts that feature interviews and detailed information that takes time to digest yet provokes a lot of engagement, he suggests opting for a smaller frequency.

For the duration, he limits his podcasts to between 30 and 40 minutes. However, there are exceptions; some episodes can last longer depending on the topic being discussed and the flow of the conversation.

A Podcast for Francophones

Diogène recently launched a new weekly podcast called 'Transformation Numérique'. Airing every Wednesday, it's a show about digital transformation and is specially dedicated to his French-speaking audience. Across the world, different areas speak French, including Quebec, France, Switzerland, Belgium, and some African countries.

One of the reasons behind the new podcast is to cater to the Francophones who send enquiries to his other show, 'Consultancy Lifestyle'.

The other reason is directly linked to his business because he also has French-speaking clients who can't communicate through English.

Why Podcasting?

If you are unnoticed and you want to break out, the first thing you should do is to reach out, expand your network, and connect with people in your niche (LinkedIn, for instance, is a great platform for professionals, especially B2B people). For Diogène, no matter which medium you choose to let your voice be heard, the important thing is to network, exchange ideas, and learn from each other's stories.

When it comes to choosing a medium, it actually depends on you. Whether it's through podcasting, writing emails, or making videos – what matters is opting for a medium that you're comfortable with; a medium that will help you share your message or story most effectively.

Diogène notes that podcasting offers an advantage because doing audio has fewer constraints than doing a video. Audio consumption, in general, is also longer. People tend to watch videos only in seconds. Sometimes, they only read the subtitles. With a podcast, you can get the most attention from people because they can be doing other things at the same time.

Chapter Twelve
Building an Entrepreneur Ecosystem

Callum Laing, Founder & CEO of MBH Corporation PLC, Singapore.

Courtesy of Callum Laing

Even when you're a successful small business, you tend to face a glass ceiling. Uh, you can't, as a small business, you can't win the big contracts because you can't win the big contracts you remain a small business. This is a problem Callum Laing is solving with his company, MBH, a UK-listed company which is a 'global agglomerate of well-established, profitable small businesses', in which privately held companies switch equity for shares in the public company.

The Glass Ceiling Problem

MBH is a solution to a problem that Callum had as a small business owner; that is, even if you're a successful small business, you tend to face a glass ceiling. You can't win big contracts and you remain a small business. It's difficult for you to attract good senior staff. And you don't have the resources of a big company.

What happens is that successful small businesses get sold to bigger players in the industry. The problem with it is that, invariably, you have to go along as part of that deal. Typically, these deals are a three- or five-year earn-out. However, entrepreneurs don't make very good employees. They're not good at being told what to do, especially when it comes to their own business.

When you've been in the industry long enough, you've probably seen scores of entrepreneurs being acquired and spat out by the likes of WPP, Publicis, and Omnicom among others. They quit in disgust or get fired six months later – from their own company. After spending the last 10–20 years creating value for others, that does not seem like a good solution.

The idea behind MBH is that they find good, well-run, and profitable small businesses. These businesses get to swap their private equity for public equity, but the founder keeps full control over their business.

Their brand, their hiring and firing process, and their culture remain. They don't need to run anything past anyone. They could carry on with their business as they always have. But the advantage is that they're now part of an amazing collaborative environment involving other entrepreneurs who now have a vested interest in their success. They will also have stocks so they can go out, give stock incentives to staff, and even do their own acquisitions.

Callum considers himself lucky to get to hang out with cool, successful business owners around the world – and try to share their stories with investors.

Building MBH's Brand

MBH deals with three audiences: the potential companies to buy into, the investors, and the businesses that they've already bought into. To address this, Callum has been working harder on personal branding.

Previously, he (like a lot of people have) had the reticence of not wanting to put himself out front. However, he realised a number of years ago how much time you can save if you're well-known. For example, if you've written a book or an article, or you've been on a podcast, or if you have a meeting with someone who's already heard or read about you, then half of the sales is already considered done. They already know what you're capable of and your values.

This way, you can get straight down to talking about logistics, which is a much more interesting conversation than what you're having back when you're a younger entrepreneur. Back in the day, Callum would spend the first half hour of his coffee meetings trying to convince people that he's worthy of their time.

The worst person to sell yourself to is yourself. But once he embraced the idea, he began investing in things such as putting together a book. His first book is called *Progressive Partnerships,* which came out five years ago.

He's also done numerous other attempts. And he realised that one of the best ways to build his brand is to support other people and help them build their own brand. With that, he built a platform to showcase entrepreneurs who are doing cool things but are not currently featured by the media.

One of the things he discovered about the media is that they all say they want to break new stories and find hidden talent. When in reality, what they do is to wait until somebody else has done it and simply copy what that somebody has done.

If Callum could give somebody their first published interview and put it in his platform called enterprisezone.cc, then it would be easier for them to go and get other media interviews. It gets progressively easier and it kind of snowballs into something bigger. Today, they've already published more than 2000 interviews with great entrepreneurs across the globe.

Systemising His Service

Callum has built a good model in terms of who does the work to get noticed. He recognised that the value he could give to entrepreneurs is platform and distribution.

The workflow that he has first came about when he had reached out to a platform and offered to interview entrepreneurs and business owners in his network. The biggest challenge for that particular platform was that it didn't have enough content. So he proposed to publish an interview once a month. They came back and asked if it could be done once a week. When he jokingly said to do it once a day, the platform said that it would be great.

Callum, however, realised that he didn't have the time to do that. He was running companies and doing other things (he also had a day job). But if he were to do that, he had to get smart about how he'd systemise it.

Originally, he had a lot of virtual assistants (VAs). He would have an automated email setup. People would go into a Google document, fill in their answers to a questionnaire, upload their photos and his VAs would do everything. He wouldn't actually be involved until the interview was published and he'd get to read it.

Those people would also recommend other entrepreneurs who they thought deserve having the same content. Now that there's this so-called no-code movement, there's a lot of automation systems available. And it is through it that they're able to publish these interviews every day.

Last summer, during a sort of lockdown boredom, he launched a micro podcast featuring entrepreneurs answering one question: Tell me about a time that you overcame a challenge in your entrepreneurial journey and what you learned from it.

For this, what he does is to direct them to a webpage, and lets them fill in their details and upload their photos. On the page, they can press a button to record up to four minutes of their content (They can re-record if they didn't like the first take) and hit submit. The file goes to his audio editor before it gets published and broadcast through a network.

At the moment, he's using JotForm (it's similar to Google Forms but has a lot more options). As he pointed out, there are many cool platforms now that you can use. However, the danger is that you can get lost in the technology and spend days exploring it. This is why he tends to find something basic that works and build it from there.

In his case, JotForm allows him to automate email sequences and fire them off to people. The downside, however, is that when you go back to it a year later and something goes wrong, it could be hard to remember the sequencing that you've done (In my case, my VA records with Loom the different processes that we have).

On Investor Relations

Apart from profiling entrepreneurs, Callum has a lot of investor relations (IR) work to do. And he doesn't pretend that he's anywhere nearly as effective with investors as he is with entrepreneurs. IR, for him, entails a very different mindset.

For instance, he first thought that the easy way to build a network of investors is just to replicate what he's done with entrepreneurs. He'd create a platform for profiling investors and ask an investor to recommend someone else (What he does with entrepreneurs is to ask them to recommend three entrepreneurs who deserve more limelight). But as IR needs a different mindset, he's had to change his approach.

One of the advantages that MBH has is that he doesn't run any of the companies. He doesn't have to worry about clients and staff in those individual companies. He's got the time to focus on IR and on the media. He can put together a lot of content and that has given them a huge advantage.

As dealing with investors is a full-time job and CEOs already have full-time jobs, his heart goes out to the CEOs of small companies that go public.

Most people don't have experience in the public market. They tend to get fleeced by advisors who will tell them that they have to engage these very expensive IR people. And a lot of them are just nonsensical and are doing a really poor job.

One of the most high-profile IR companies in the world sent them a proposal and a part of it was to build their social media. They'd publish three articles that MBH has written on LinkedIn for €3000 a month.

In reality, someone somewhere might have already paid that amount for that service. Most people are not aware of it; those who haven't used the platform before can get very easily fleeced by a lot of professionals out there.

On MBH's Investee Companies

MBH's investee companies maintain their independence. These companies are not startups; they are well-established companies with an average age of about 23 years.

Callum has always been puzzled by the fact that an acquiring company would buy a company because it has a great entrepreneurial spirit and brand. Then, they rebrand it and throw away that entrepreneurial spirit.

At MBH, when a company comes in, it is completely autonomous. While they're independent, if they want to collaborate with other companies in the group, they're more than welcome to do so.

If they're pitching and they want to emphasise the fact that they're part of a hundred-million-dollar global public listed company (PLC), they're also more than free to do so. However, if they also want to play the card that they're, for instance, a boutique construction company and the founder will be available to speak with, they can do that as well.

At the market level, they can go out and talk to their market about how they've got record profits and they're growing and they're a great company to invest in. If they're under a brand, it would make it difficult for them to pitch out to clients and try to squeeze suppliers. But because their investee companies are completely independent, they can do just that.

Additionally, they're also kind of protected if another company in the group has a problem or has a PR scandal. Because they're still different from that company, they won't be tarnished by that.

Communications Between Companies in MBH

There's a lot of opportunities for companies to be helpful to one another. But for Callum, it's more about sharing the best practices. If you put a bunch of smart and successful entrepreneurs in a room together, they'd get to share their respective best practices, learn stuff, and apply things accordingly.

At MBH, they use Slack as a platform to communicate. They also do monthly Zoom calls; it became weekly when COVID hit hard in the UK last year as things were changing so rapidly. And with the global financial crisis happening not too long ago, people were sharing what they've done, what they wish they did sooner, how they communicated with their staff, what worked and what did not.

Conclusion ——————————————————————

I am an UnNoticed Entrepreneur, and love the freedom this creates. Since returning to the UK after 25 years in Asia, I have launched the UnNoticed Podcast, this book series, merchandise, and courses, while operating EASTWEST Public Relations with offices in Singapore. I have done these from my studio in Somerset, all using the tools which I research and write about here. Indeed, the very process by which I have been able to publish this book shows the possibilities open to all entrepreneurs. I have interviewed people around the world without leaving my garden, employed a journalist in the Philippines to edit the transcripts and make them into articles for social media and this book, engaged designers in Ukraine and India, and will have a virtual assistant manage the publishing on the Amazon platform making it available to readers around the world with print on demand.

I am a firm believer that being the unnoticed entrepreneur is not a handicap but a starting point, and that the path to recognition and building a company which creates value is within reach of everyone. Done properly the entrepreneur can then sell the brand and the business to investors and then look for another problem to solve. I want to solve your problem of being unnoticed. These 50 articles and those in Volume One, plus the podcast, will give you more options, greater confidence, and a network of people to ask for more support. I am here to help you at any stage of your journey to unlocking the value in your business, so contact me with questions on how to get noticed. In the meantime.

Keep on Communicating!

Jim James

2022

Somerset

https://theunnoticed.cc

337

About the Author

Jim has built businesses from a suitcase on three continents over 25 years, all using public relations. His first brush with #gettingnoticed was at 18 when he jumped out of a plane in return for sponsorship and received expedition equipment in return for media publicity. He hasn't stopped this model of brand+business building ever since.

Having grown up in Europe, Africa, and America, it was perhaps inevitable that Jim would move to Singapore at the age of 28 to start his first company, EASTWEST Public Relations. Since 1995 the B2B agency opened offices in Singapore, China, India, and the UK serving over 500 clients. In China between 2006 and 2019, Jim built the business importing and distributing Morgan Motor Company cars, was interim CEO of Lotus, Vice Chair of the Chamber of Commerce and a number of other profit and not for profit ventures including the founding of the bi-annual British Business Awards in 2008.

Jim returned with his young family to the UK in June 2019 to provide his daughters with a British education, and works with clients to ensure that they are able to get noticed for all that they do. He hosts 'The UnNoticed Show', a podcast for entrepreneurs with tools and tips for public relations.

He can be contacted at: linkedin.com/in/jamesjim

Follow him on Twitter: @jimajames

E-mail: jim@theunnoticed.cc

Guest Directory

(In alphabetical order.)

Adrian Starks, adrian@championup.net,
https://www.linkedin.com/in/adrianstarks/

Akshay Jamwal, akshay@akshayjamwal.com,
https://www.linkedin.com/in/akshaysinghjamwal/

Alastair McDermott, amd@websitedoctor.com,
https://www.linkedin.com/in/alastairmcdermott/

Alex Strathdee, alex@advancedamazonads.com,
https://www.linkedin.com/in/alexander-strathdee/

Andrea Pacini, andrea.pacini@ideasonstage.com,
https://www.linkedin.com/in/apacini/

Andrew Clark, aclark@asiaworks.com,
https://www.linkedin.com/in/andrewlrclark/

Callum Laing, callum@mbhcorporation.com,
https://www.linkedin.com/in/callumlaing/

Chase Palmieri, chase@credder.com,
https://www.linkedin.com/in/chase-palmieri-653337b1/

Colin JG Miles, colinjgmiles@gmail.com,
https://www.linkedin.com/in/colinmiles/

Danny Levinson, danny@dannylevinson.com,
https://www.dannylevinson.com

Diogene Ntirandekura, diogene@erphappy.com,
https://www.linkedin.com/in/diogenentirandekura/

Elaine Powell, elaine@mindspeakacademy.com,
https://www.linkedin.com/in/elainepowelluk/

Erwin Lima, erwin.lima@hotmail.com,
https://www.linkedin.com/in/erwin-lima-90319332/

Fabian Langer, webmaster@ai-writer.com,
https://www.linkedin.com/in/fabian-langer-292b62162/

Frank Buckler, buckler@neusrel.de,
https://www.linkedin.com/in/frankbuckler/

Gina Balarin, gina.balarin@verballistics.com.au,
https://www.linkedin.com/in/ginabalarin/

GJ van Buseck, gj.vanbuseck@gmail.com,
https://www.linkedin.com/in/gertjanvanbuseck/

Heesang Yoo, heesangyoo@prismcomms.com,
https://www.linkedin.com/in/heesangyoo/

Howard Dekkers, howarddekkers@gmail.com,
https://www.linkedin.com/in/howard-dekkers-baa3727/

Jason Weekes, Jason.Weekes@carma.com,
https://www.linkedin.com/in/jasondweekes/

Jarod Spiewak, jarod@cometfuel.com,
https://www.linkedin.com/in/jarodspiewak/

JB Owen, aworldofpink@gmail.com,
https://www.linkedin.com/in/jb-owen/

Jeff Hahn, jhahn@hahnpublic.com,
https://www.linkedin.com/in/jeff-hahn-aa2aa0119/

Joe Schultz, joe.schultz@adplorer.com,
https://www.linkedin.com/in/joakimschultz/

Jonathan Mall, jonathan.mall@neuro-flash.com,
https://www.linkedin.com/in/drjonathanmall/

Josh Gardner, josh@kungfudata.com,
https://www.linkedin.com/in/joshagardner/

Julia Broad, julie@booklaunchers.com,
https://www.linkedin.com/in/juliebroad/

Kate Bradley Chernis, kate@lately.ai,
https://www.linkedin.com/in/katebradley/

Luke Fisher, luke@mo.work,
https://www.linkedin.com/in/lsfisher/

Marcus Ahmad, marcus@marcusahmad.com,
https://www.linkedin.com/in/marcusahmadphotography/

Masami Sato, masami@b1g1.com,
https://www.linkedin.com/in/masamisato/

Mason Harris, mason@thechutzpahguy.com,
https://www.linkedin.com/in/masonharrislistens/

Matthew Stormoen, matthew@mobibi.com,
https://www.linkedin.com/in/mattstormoen/

Michael Hoffman, michael@gathervoices.co,
https://www.linkedin.com/in/michaelhoffman/

Michael Juergens, michael@michaeljuergens.com,
www.linkedin.com/in/michael-juergens-9882212/

Michael Seib, michael@typestudio.co,
https://www.linkedin.com/in/michaelsieb/

Mike Cheng, mike@lumen5.com,
https://www.linkedin.com/in/michaelhsc/

Mickie Kennedy, ereleases2@gmail.com,
https://www.linkedin.com/in/publicity/

Nick Hems, nick@nickhemsstyle.co.uk,
https://www.linkedin.com/in/nickhems/

Nick Vivion, nick@ghost.works,
https://www.linkedin.com/in/nickvivion/

Nir Zavaro, zavaro@streetwise.co.il,
https://www.linkedin.com/in/nirzavaro/

Oscar Trimboli, oscar@oscartrimboli.com,
https://www.linkedin.com/in/oscartrimboli/

Praveen Nagda, praveen@peregrinepr.in,
https://www.linkedin.com/in/praveennagda/

Richard Robinson, richrob@gmail.com,
https://www.linkedin.com/in/richardrobinson/

Robert Da Costa, robert@dacostacoaching.co.uk,
https://www.linkedin.com/in/robdacosta/

Sam Palazzolo, sp@tipofthespearventures.com,
https://www.linkedin.com/in/spalazzolo/

Scott Sandland, scott@cyrano.ai,
https://www.linkedin.com/in/scottsandland/

Sonali Nair, sonali.nair@outlook.com,
https://www.linkedin.com/in/sonalinair/

Bibliography

Podcasts I listen to about PR and business:

7 Figure Small with Brian Clark

https://podcasts.apple.com/gb/podcast/7-figure-small-with-brian-clark/id1017418913

Business of Story with Park Howell

https://podcasts.apple.com/gb/podcast/business-of-story/id1012379862

Buzzcast with Buzzsprout team

https://podcasts.apple.com/gb/podcast/buzzcast/id1446336657

Beyond the Story with Sebastian Rusk

https://podcasts.apple.com/gb/podcast/beyond-the-story-with-sebastian-rusk/id510904010

Content Inc with Joe Pullizi

https://podcasts.apple.com/gb/podcast/content-inc-with-joe-pulizzi/id948387773

Entrepreneurs on Fire with John Lee Dumas

https://podcasts.apple.com/gb/podcast/entrepreneurs-on-fire/id564001633

Genius Network with Joe Polish

https://podcasts.apple.com/gb/podcast/genius-network/id1161195772

Marketing Bound with Laura L Bernhard

https://podcasts.apple.com/gb/podcast/marketing-bound-podcast/id1495717454

Marketing Secrets with Russell Brunson

https://podcasts.apple.com/gb/podcast/the-marketing-secrets-show/id1315130618

PR After Hours with Alex Greenwood

https://podcasts.apple.com/gb/podcast/pr-after-hours/id1496015627

PR Resolution with Stella Bayles

https://podcasts.apple.com/gb/podcast/pr-resolution-podcast/id1423627061

Small Business Radio Show with Barry Moltz

https://podcasts.apple.com/gb/podcast/the-small-business-radio-show/id288125609

Systemize your Success with Dr Steve Day

https://podcasts.apple.com/gb/podcast/systemize-your-success-podcast/id1560955240

The Agency accelerator with Rob Da Costa

https://podcasts.apple.com/gb/podcast/the-agency-accelerator/id1491143609

UnLeashed

https://podcasts.apple.com/gb/podcast/unleashed-how-to-thrive-as-an-independent-professional/id1227297532

The UnNoticed Entrepreneur with Jim James

https://theunnoticed.cc

Books

"Chutzpah Advantage" by Mason Harris. ASIN: B08Z57946T

Publisher: Indie Books International (19 April 2021)

"Sapiens" by Yuval Noah Harari. ASIN: B00K7ED54M.

Publisher: Vintage Digital; 1st edition (4 Sept. 2014)

Index ___

A

action 6, 19, 42, 44, 150, 151, 178, 237, 238, 246, 249, 252, 278, 282, 284, 286, 289, 313

Adrian Starks 3, 41, 340

advice 3, 27, 31, 32, 34, 258, 259, 312–314, 322, 326

agency 3, 28–33, 52, 53, 57, 59, 82, 83, 86, 106, 112, 135, 137, 161, 164, 171, 178, 205, 235, 238, 245–247, 250, 253, 281, 285, 339

AI 78, 111, 169, 172–184, 186, 188–189, 191–199, 207, 208, 241, 251–253, 257–263

Akshay Jamwal 3, 63, 340

Alex Greenwood i, 346

Alex Strathdee 4, 141, 340

Alastair McDermott 3

Amazon 4, 125, 129–131, 141–149, 186, 207, 272, 273, 337

America 3, 32, 157, 180, 194, 216, 259, 266, 301, 322, 339

amplification 42, 183, 206, 212, 227, 309

amplification channels 267

analysis 19, 167, 168, 175, 207, 216, 258–259

Andrea Pacini 4, 95, 340

Andrew Clark 267, 281, 340

anthroponomy 3

API 67, 162, 196, 215, 225, 233, 241, 260, 261

attitude 13–19, 48, 114, 193

audience 3, 4, 20, 23, 36, 42–44, 46–54, 61, 87, 95–100, 102, 105, 115–118, 126, 127, 132–134, 136, 137, 144, 146, 147, 151, 152, 167, 168, 170, 171, 175, 179, 181, 201, 207, 215, 216, 224, 241, 244, 253–255, 257, 259, 267, 270–271, 274, 275, 282–284, 289, 295, 297, 298, 306, 307, 323, 325, 327, 328, 331

Austin 3, 82

Australia 2, 5, 39, 46, 147, 269, 282

author 5, 13, 17, 18, 46, 72–74, 78, 82, 89, 92, 100, 125, 145–149, 170, 172, 226, 253, 268, 305, 339

authority 10, 34–41, 93, 120, 254

awards 12, 304, 305

B

Bali 4, 114, 119

Behind xiii, 13, 22, 40, 110, 116, 147, 216, 260, 262, 266, 267, 269–271, 311, 328, 331

behind Zilliqa 157

being liars 3

Best Seller 4, 73, 77, 80, 126, 273

B1G1, 267, 287–291

Bhutan 266, 268–271, 274, 275

Bibliography 345–346

Bill Gates xiii

bitcoin sponsorship 157

book xi, xii, xiii, 2, 11, 15, 17, 38, 41, 54, 56, 57, 60–62, 74–80, 84, 89, 94, 109, 119, 125–132, 141–149, 253, 257, 262, 268, 273–276, 287, 331, 332, 337, 346